1980

THE CRAFT OF POWER

THE CRAFT OF POWER

R. G. H. SIU

JOHN WILEY & SONS
New York · Chichester
Brisbane · Toronto

Library of Congress Cataloging in Publication Data

Siu, Ralph Gun Hoy, 1917-
    The craft of power.

    Bibliography: p.
    Includes index.
    1. Management. 2. Executive ability. 3. Power
(Social sciences) I. Title.

HD38.S576   658.4   78-23393
ISBN 0-471-04628-0

Printed in the United States of America

10 9 8 7 6 5 4

To
Edwin L. Gustus

PREFACE

This book is directed primarily to executives seeking to expand their personal power. It is not a discourse with managers about the art of leadership but an exposition for aspirants to power about the underlying craft. To be sure, there is much in common between the two groups. But persons of power are driven by ulterior motives completely different from those of conventional executives. The strategies and tactics of the former go far beyond the usual competencies of the latter.

Immediate application for most of what is presented can be found by those who have built at least a moderate base of followers and legitimated authority. A word of caution should be offered, however, for those who have not yet crossed this threshold: "Diligently observe the arts of the masters, so that you will be effectively facile with them should the time come in your future career. Meanwhile, be patiently prudent as you rise in the formal and informal hierarchy through nonthreatening visibility and contributions to the powers-that-be. Do not try to fly higher than fitly fledged. There is nothing more fatal for a fledgling than being swooped upon by an angry hawk. Reminders will be inserted throughout this book in the form of adjustments suitable for your own particular station in the sting and tang of competition." Finally, to readers who have eschewed the path of power and find the contents unsettling, we would nonetheless recommend a clear view of the reality, which they seek to transcend. Empathy always comes easier with understanding, and efforts toward the ideal become more practically productive.

Here, then, are a power posture and operational specifics that have worked from the days of *Genesis* and *I Ching* to *The Prince* and *The New York Times*. An armamentarium for great power. Straight. Unvarnished. To be diluted and painted by the reader as suits his or her own purposes.

R. G. H. SIU

Washington, D. C.
August 1978

CONTENTS

xii *Contents*

THE CRAFT OF POWER

I POWER POSTURE

From all appearances, this brief part is a summary of what is to follow. But its objective is much more important. I would like to invite your closest collaboration. If we are successful, you will be well on your way toward developing the kind of readiness reflex from which durable power springs.

There are two essential facets to this potential. The first is a continuing feel for the relevant totality, so that you always instinctively react in consonance with the enveloping whole, thereby infusing your own actions with its orchestrated resilience and concerted force. The pithy brevity of this part has been

1

adapted to stimulate this sensing of the totality at one glance, as it were. The second is an intuitive facility in sensing the hidden agendas, being aware of what is not said, and quickening to what has not yet happened. Hence, as an introductory exercise, the style of presentation: allusive, epigrammatic.

The following approach has proved worthwhile for many readers. You may wish to try it. Pick up the book on a relaxed occasion, when you can devote forty minutes or so to it. Ignoring the bracketed numbers for the time being, leisurely go over this part as written in one sitting. In the process, let the words enter your eyes freely and fully, without being concerned about what they may mean in particular. Let the thoughts and sensations come as they will. Then lay the book aside for several days or more. Return to it at another relaxing opportunity. Give Part I a "once over quickly" from beginning to end. After that, peruse here and there within it at random: muse, contemplate, think as you please, but do not argue. Now lay the book aside for another week or more. After that, feel free to proceed in whatever way comes naturally to you. You will be appropriately prepared to get the most out of the Operational Specifics—to note the cross-linkages of the various aspects of power, to feel at relative ease with voids and strangeness, to criticize profitably what has been written, to modify and embellish, and to incorporate whatever is valuable into your own repertory.

ENTERING THE ARENA

1 The glare of power[1]* bothers people.

They feel more at ease with the myth of the meek inheriting the land.

They turn aside and pretend.

2 That power poisons

And submission sanctifies.

What opportunities for blessed exploitations!

3 You recognize the essence of democracy[2] beyond the pretenses.

It is the sharing of power.

Most people merely participate in its dance. But you are determined to share.

4 No longer will you be constrained by institutionally assigned niches.

No longer will you rest contented as mere executive.

You will become a person of power,[3] of great power.

5 So you study the books[4]

And decipher the rites in the chamber of deeds:

Power establishes its own legitimacy; not to grow in power is to succumb.

---

*Bracketed numbers refer to Operational Specifics beginning on page 29.

4   *Power posture*

6   You grow in power and grow some more.

A voice within you whispers: What next?

Now, it is your turn to conceal and pretend.[5]

LEARNING THE FUNDAMENTS

7   Embrace the fifteen rules

Or leave the arena before it is too late.

The one who is inept and faint-hearted only gets in the way and messes up the tournament grounds with his splintered lance and sorry carcass.

8   The primary rule is self-discipline—the severe self-discipline of dedication and destiny, of great tyrant and master robber.

If you fail this first test, go no further. Melt into the acquiescent herd. When the heat is not too hot, shadow-box a few rounds. Pontificate from the pulpit and snicker through the editorials. All the while, endure the ghetto deprivations, enjoy the suburban barbecue, dissipate the unearned inheritance.

Great power is not your cup of sassafras.

9   But should you feel that you are indeed of the fiber to stretch your Reach, assert your Will, and proclaim your Consciousness, then pay close attention and learn how to:

Meter the inputs, gauge the activation barriers, inject the impellences, time the catalysts, and channel the outputs.

Be the steely professional,[6] through and through.

10   Power is neither created nor destroyed. It is only transformed or transferred.[7]

Flow does not proceed on its own from higher concentration to lower, from richer reservoir to poorer.

Grab more from those with more. Grab less from those with less. And counter-grab from those who grab from you.[8]

11   The umpire calls the shots. 'Tis true.

But there's a person who made the rules governing him, a person who appointed him, a person who's paying him.

Keep the persons behind the scenes in mind.[9]

12   Conform your appetite to your capacity to digest.[10]

Regroup, consolidate, and reassess after every victory. Delay further forays until refreshed.

Fortify yourself against the likes of you.

13   Crime is here to stay.[11] Professionals of power are well versed in all its variants.[12]

God Himself had expressed discouragement over the sickening sinfulness of the human race.

Expect foul play.

14   Of course, thousands of people will be fired. . . . Of course, millions will be bombed to fleshy scraps. . . .

The remorse can be washed away with the universal absolution: "Too bad, just can't be helped."

Let not the wailing and groaning of the innocent weaken your will to win and keep.[13]

15   Mores constitute the playing field of power.

Stepping out of bounds too often disrupts your game's momentum.

Cater to them.[14]

16   Create a myth[15] sustaining your movement like the deep ocean floating a majestic ship.

Draw an inspiring rationale for your past actions and present position, a ringing call for your continuing expansion, a vigorous condemnation of your formidable oppositions.

Put your best minds to it.

17 Do not confuse exhilaration with power.

Watch the ratios of desired change to total, of necessary resources for planned progress to that expended, of well-executed to all directives issued by you.

Maximize all three efficiencies.[16]

18 Heed the time constraints.[17]

Flutter not in the never-never nebulosities of open-ended possibilities.

Design action increments within the span of personal attention. Adhere to a schedule with a deadline for closure.

19 Pursued attainment is the prime estimate of success.

Applause from the public galleries is vaporous. Gains from unanticipated quarters are peripheral; returns beyond time of interest superfluous. Cruelty is only a tantrum of frustrated power.

Keep meaningful scores.[18]

20 There is a tale about Chinese merchants gambling during the construction of the Great Wall.

They lost first the money in their pockets, then the merchandise on their carts, and finally the clothes off their backs, to freeze to death in the bleak north by the cold winds off the Gobi.

Set a loss limit and stick to it.[19]

21 Power is mortgaged. Repayments are inescapable.

For moderate power: few friends here and there, purity of conscience now and then. For high stakes: uncertain installments of wealth, honor, health, personality, family, life.

Do not fret when it's time to pay.[20]

22   Deserve fully the loyalty of your cadre.

Martyrs must be honored if power is to flourish. Dividends distributed if confidence is to last.

But be very, very, very, very circumspect about the delegation of authority.[21]

23   The constituency must be satisfied.

If you meet its requirements for desired service, it will meet yours for lusty power.

Be beneficent of sorts and reign long.[22]

HONING STRATEGIES
AND TACTICS

24 To overthrow established power is hard enough.

To grasp the loosed power in your own hand is harder still.

The latter is the real name of the game.[23]

25 Effective Offense[24] begins with solid psychological preparation of the home front.

Given legal blessing and a favorable strength ratio, proceed frontally and openly in the name of the law. Without legal blessing but with a favorable strength ratio, inundate with force. With only an equal force ratio, probe surreptitiously for vulnerable spots, at which concentrate an opening wedge, then follow through with thorough mop-up until all pockets of resistance are eliminated. With a highly unfavorable strength ratio, covertly invade the opposition's camp, inflaming loci of necroses against the will to resist. Then slough off infectious cells to other centers and flare internal dissatisfactions into open conflicts.

Attack only with high surety of success.

26 Strategic prudence lies at the core of a strong Defense.[25]

Preservation of large estates? Then assimilate potential opposition. Uncertainty of threats? Then maintain efficient intelligence. Additional insurance desired? Then increase resource ratio. Still more insurance? Then sponsor distracting activities among possible challengers. Vulnerable yourself? Then conceal it. Much weaker enemy? Then provoke an attack. Resisted bait? Then crush with preemptive blow. Much stronger enemy? Then aggravate exasperation.

Conserve and deploy your forces at all times so as to be able to defend yourself anew.

27 For equanimity and longevity, observe the Interstitialist.[26]

Residing within the interstices among the jousting giants, he taxes only a fraction of his capabilities. His freedom is preserved through the facade of uselessness during ordinary times and ineffable disengagement during the occasional defense of his minimal interests.

Include his tactics in your know-how. They are effective for dissembling and essential for recuperating.

28 The Subterranean[27] is the master of power incognito. While the illegal Subterranean may be dangerous, the bureaucratic is irresistible.

The seasoned bureaucrat is adept at servo-bureaucrato viscosity: to every challenge there is an equal and frustrating viscosity. He dwells in the nirvana of historical momentum: reversing a bureaucrat is tantamount to reversing history.

Accommodate to the bureaucrat; he will then ease your life and extend your power. But do you otherwise; he will then drive you out of office and out of mind.

29 The Opportunist[28] profits by astute boresighting on the eventual victor. The front-office watch and hedge betting constitute his trademarks.

Responsive in small favors and fawning on pleasurable occasions, he can barge through the slightest opening with his truckload of sizeable gifts. Sharing in spoils made possible through his timely help is all he asks for. It is true that today the spoils are from your beaten opponent. But tomorrow, they may well be from you. And the Opportunist might just be the one to trip the trap.

Spot him a mile away and keep him there.

30 The Permeator[29] is the ubiquitous stumbling block to persons pursuing absolute power.

Preaching throughout society and pickabacking on everyone else's resources, he demands the faith of *your* followers in *his* self-proclaimed preserves of beauty, goodness, and truth. Because he loudly professes a transcendent disinterest in mundane power, the contentions assume a refined ritual and a sophisticated protocol of a special character all its own.

Be well rehearsed in psychic swordplay as you move among the artistic, the holy, and the intellectual.

31 Coalitions[30] are short-term arrangements among long-term competitors.

Stymie the wily collaborator from profiting at your expense while confronting the common opposition. Ensure the favorable increase in your relative power vis-a-vis each and all on V-day.

Only then have you emerged victorious.

VECTORING RESOURCES

32 People, money, and symbols are the basic resources of power.

Ownership is the old-fashioned, long-haul approach.

Take the modern, shortcut of decision control.[31]

33 People are to be used like fuel in the furnace of power,[32] or cleared away like worn-out gears for more efficient replacements.

So that they burn with the requisite intensity, cleanse them of incombustible allegiances.

Let the cadre prove its selfless commitment and offer up their persons as signed undated blank checks in your strongbox.

34 A power play without money[33] can only be a farce.

Short of funds? Then get some in a hurry. Lots of funds? Then preserve the protective political structure.

And do not alienate the banker in the process.

35 Status and prestige[34] are the sweetest smelling of executive lures.

The Red Hat, the Honorable. A citation on the wall, a gold-plated thermos bottle on the side table. So inexpensive for multiple returns: Your team is motivated; your bandwagon is accelerated; your glory is enhanced.

Fashion an assortment to excite diverse sensibilities. Dispense an abundance to please every nexus.

36 Optimize the mix of instruments against the specific situation.

Should subsequent cooperation of the defeated foe be needed for further exploitation of your conquest, let the pull components dominate the push. But should the defeated lean toward resurgence and revenge, then let the push components dominate the pull.[35]

Nurture the cohesive yet adaptive preconditions within your organization, so that the fitting instruments emerge and recede with locking reflexivity.

37   Violence and nonviolence[36] belong to the same push-pulling series.

Purpose and peace couple in power.

Be sure your responses are chameleonic to the challenge.

38   Insist on cost-effectiveness analysis as part of your decision-making procedure, by all means—but only as an input to inanimate routines.

Power itself is neither measured by numbers nor determined by theory.

Rely more on gut-feeling.[37]

SHAPING COMMUNICATIONS

39 Power reflects the gradient of information.

Distribution of information to subordinates is a decentralization of your power; leakage to the opposition a loss.

Restrict the outward dissemination of critical information by a strict need-to-know.[38]

40 The formal lines of organizational communication govern hierarchical efficiency.

Private networks[39] complying with your own prescriptions amplify your personal power.

Do not be imprisoned by your cordon of courtiers.

41 Only data useful for your purpose constitute information. Right form, right kind, right time, right rate.[40] The rest is noise.

The most disruptive noise belongs to the interesting and intelligible variety, wasting channel capacity and draining staff energy.

Preclude data glut.

42 Reliable and timely intelligence[41] must be embodied in an accurate estimate of the situation.

Do not place undue weight on that course of action promising maximum gain, if successful. Limit the choices to those preventing a fatal blow to yourself, no matter what the opposition may feasibly do.

In the meantime, behave as if the crucial intelligence in your hands is other than what he knows to be the facts.

43 Nothing weakens your apparatus of power more irreversibly than the disintegration of its inner cohesion.

Disband self-serving cliques and cabals. Shift the pleasure tendencies of the individuals toward the utility orientations of the combine. Diffuse a psychological identification with your Cause.

Strengthen the integrative principle[42] through repeated reaffirmations in internal traffic, enriched with morale-boosting overtones.

44 Propaganda is to induce action on your behalf,[43] rather than provide information for intelligent judgment by others. It is to supplant, rather than refute, opposing claims.

Controlling media and adapting messages. Employing sign stimuli. Rallying allies and solidifying biases. Exploiting foibles, pettifogging truths, and spreading innuendos. Remaining silent. The devices are many.[44]

But do not be taken in by them yourself.

ORCHESTRATING CEREMONIES

45   Ceremony without ulterior motive is amateur theater.

Power professionals act for much more than mere show.[45]

Perform to entertain and impress the audience. But always as enhancements of competitive advantage offstage.

46   Things aren't right if they don't look right.

Things that aren't right can be made to look right.[46]

Conduct enabling rites with regularity and devotion.

47   Credibility is the greatest obstacle to many an overture to power.

Repeat your thesis often, for people tend to shun the unfamiliar and embrace the familiar. Use phrases mellifluous to the ear, for people like to identify with the pleasant. Make it sound vital, for people incline to align with the important. Announce your intentions to accomplish something, which is actually well on the way. Promise something that seems difficult but is within ready reach of your unseen reserves.

Then let the people conclude for themselves that you are truly a man of your word.[47]

48   The appearance of reasonableness[48] renders an otherwise unacceptable demand rather palatable.

Pay particular attention to your demeanor as the increments of your ambition increase significantly. Refer often to the suggestions of others and give credit to the value of their contributions. Accept the constituents' preferences in matters of lesser consequence and be overtly generous in miscellaneous items of community interest.

Do not ruin it all by blurting out some accusation or losing your temper even once in public.

49   Power is congealed through pageantry of consensus.[49]

Mass rallies generate waves of local enthusiasms. Publicized tours confer approval upon your person. Favorable polls reassure the multitude of uninformed. Fashionable trends guide the crowds of conformists. Rigged elections spread a sense of partnership among the followers.

Magnetize the masses through rondos of acclamations.

50   People need buttressing in their beliefs by respected specialists.

Quote concurring authorities. Assemble blue-ribbon committees. Carefully weigh their known leanings beforehand; publicize their independent judgment and thorough analysis thereafter.

Introduce your major proposals through the ritual of objective expertise.[50]

51   As long as it appears that the rules are being adhered to, people are disposed to go along.[51]

Puppets are always serviceable, scribes procurable, laws maleable, scapegoats redeeming.

Proclaim an empowering regulation, an approving dogma, an official paper.

52   Fervor is fanned by feigned loftiness.[52]

The more selfish the drive, the more idealistic the label. The more blatant the attack, the more tender the scenario. The more destructive the ravage, the more pious the prayer. Peace, Freedom, Progress, and the People's Good.

Continually emanate an exalted effusion.

53   Words acquire greater impact and directives elicit speedier execution when ascribed to higher echelons.[53]

The more drastic the move contemplated, the more imposing and explicit the ascription should be. The Chief wants it done

. . . The President has taken a personal interest in this . . . God has commanded . . . .

Repeat the refrain with great solemnity, especially on your way up.

54 People bet on winners[54] and sacrifice much for glory re-flected off champions.

Act like one: high official with milling entourage, bishop with sacred robes, general with shining stars. Impart a matter-of-factness to your accomplishments, a verve to your attributes, a grandeur to your forgiveness of some petty assailant.

But never, never, never, never outshine the big boss.

MANEUVERING AND STRIKING

55 The battle for power is simultaneously fought on a wide variety of platforms.

There is an incessant scrambling of esurient men and women, hoisting themselves aboard and heaving others overboard from all heights and angles.

Coil yourself omnidirectionally.[55]

56 There is an optimal time and place to attack or defend, buy or sell, act or be quiescent.[56]

Waiting for the propitious moment without giving oneself away manifests the courage of confidence.

Be observant of the cyclic patterns. Be decisive at the turning points.

57 Meticulously prepare the opening[57]

And promptly seize the opportunity, while thwarting the thwarters.

But note the other antagonists artfully doing likewise.[58]

58 Intensify the hopelessness of the exploited masses to resist.[59]

Mix blame with pain in your punishments.[60]

Tailor the compulsions.

59 For durability in power, preempt the center.

Moving toward one extreme or the other during the indecisive phases of internal disputes may be warranted. But seldom too far and never at the extremities too soon. Someone else will squat astride the fulcrum in your place.

Prevail through adaptive centrality.[61]

60   Let your speed be multifaceted.[62]

Be fast in pursuing and grasping others and extricating self.

Be quick in masking yourself and unmasking others.

61   Remain unpredictable. Preserve surprise.[63]

Ambiguity, inconsistency, evasion, aphonia.

Conceal the cunning through deception of diversion.

62   Nothing is more vital for survival than quick-witted, fleet-footed nimbleness.[64]

Advanced education has equipped the clever man with an awesome arsenal for stabbing from great distances and parrying from unseen quarters.

Sharpen your ju-jitsu of power.

63   No issue in itself can ignite a revolt. Nor is a sound one essential. When discontent is widespread, a phony issue will do. Or none at all.

The prophet of anarchy may serve as the detonator. But the context of people always serves as fulminant.[65]

Let the general social situation rather than specific complaints shape your overall assault upon entrenched power.

64   Let the scholars argue over the authorship of grand principles.

World peace?—yes, but on *whose* terms? Agreements?—yes, but in *whose* records? Progress?—yes, but by *whose* definition? God's word?—yes, but through *whose* book?

Assert the prerogative of interpretation[66] and execution.

65   Temper your drive by the Law of Reversal.[67]

Excess reverses. Continuing exertion beyond the sensitive limit precipitates the loss of prior gains. Victory with exhaustion means defeat without fighting in the engagement to come.

Moderate the demands as you approach the critical threshold. Cease before you reach it.

66 There is an incubation time for every action's maturity. An acquiescence time for every annexation's acceptance. An absolution time for every transgression's forgiveness.[68]

The longer the incubation time available, the more subtle, tolerable, and successful an aggression can be formulated. The shorter the acquiescence and absolution time of the planned action, the more destructive, lawless, and extensive a strike can be perpetrated.

Pry psychologically with the crowbar of time.

67 React to that eerie apprehension of the totality of the instant.[69]

Let every thrust be part and parcel of a continually adjusting envelopment by resilient forces—some loud and clear, others gentle and muted, and still others standing by in silent darkness.

This is the core characteristic of the master of power.

NEGOTIATING AND PRESSING ON

68 Be satisfied with the projected outcome of the ensuing peace before instigating the fight.[70]

Envision the desirable framework for negotiation. Then your ability to bring it about. Finally, the likelihood of the adversary's conviction at that point in time of your continued capacity to damage him to an unacceptable degree and your determination to do so, if necessary.

Only after that, fire the opening salvo.

69 As potential victor, advance enticements for early termination of the ongoing conflict as soon as your minimum objectives have been assured. Avoid the exhausting bog.

As potential loser, recognize the opposition's own desire to disengage for other crises and hang on for terms conducive for rapid recovery. Avoid the castrating surrender.

Much give-and-take exists for either side.

70 Negotiation is a simultaneous exercise in intelligence, bargaining, politics, propaganda, and planning.

Probing the foe's intentions, residual strength, and will . . . wrestling among negotiators for consensually satisfactory terms . . . coordinating positions among allies . . . protecting against domestic competitors finding fault . . . persuading wider community of reasonableness of one's own offers . . . titrating deceptions home and abroad to hasten the desired compact . . . strengthening posture for conflicts to come. . . .

Pay close and innovative attention to all refractions.

71 Don't be dismayed by the initial adamant stand and exhorbitant demands of the opposition. He won't be by yours.

Use the early rounds to bracket your practical expectations. As you nudge the negotiating centroid toward your upper limit, become progressively specific in claims and concessions, provided the other party follows suit.

Be relatively generous with a much weaker opposition, but tightfisted with a stronger. Yield not an inch to one approaching you in strength.

72 It is the ending that counts.

Talk tough, if profitable. Be accommodating, if innocuous. Appear conciliatory, if helpful. Look stupid, if required.

But be smart.[71]

73 Once the minimum objectives are attained, no moves should be made that may jeopardize them.

Once the halfway mark between that and the practical maximum is reached, all moves should be made in concert toward early consummation.[72]

Stop quibbling and split the difference.

74 An inning ends, but the game of power goes on.

The confrontation being seeded overlaps the negotiation being matured.

Do not strike out by breaking the continuum.[73]

REFLECTING ON MORALITY

75 Power churns centripetally in a breeder reactor.

Ends pursued forge new means. Means available fission new ends.

See how the spiral accelerates.[74]

76 With bigness comes increased potential for human happiness.

With bigness, also increased potential for human suffering.

Sense the uneasiness among the people over the actuality.[75]

77 The person of power assumes awesome proportions and de-monic features when licensed with institutional dispensation from personal morality.

The effective leader is expected to protect his own constituency against the evil, guile, and ruthlessness of the external enemy. To fulfill his oath of office, he too must be quite versed with the machinations of evil, guile, and ruthlessness. What if he di-rects his craft inward? Or has he done so already?

Note how apprehensively perceptive people hedge their hopes.[76]

78 Power depersonalizes.

Absolute power absolutely.

Observe the persons converted into modules and the equations of power quantified with impersonalities.[77]

79 The more of the world you crave to dominate, the more imper-sonal your human relations must be. You no longer think of the struggle between good and evil, but of the conflicts between interests and interests.

The less of the world you crave to dominate, the more personal your human relations can be. You then perceive how drippingly wet are human tears, how infectiously delightful the laughter.

Let your actions speak comprehensively.[78]

80   Ethics is a functional component of power; power is a functional expression of ethics.

Duty[79] is dictated by demands of institutions; compassion[80] is awakened by appeals of human beings.

Blend with practical prudence.

81   Luxury among the greedy is distributed through popular power.

Misery among the unfortunate is eased through noble power.[81]

Rule through worthy probity.

II OPERATIONAL SPECIFICS

An elaboration of the more critical considerations and means for acquiring, maintaining, and expanding your personal power is offered in this Part II.

This part is divided into nine sections, covering the spectrum from theory through conflict to morality. The introduction to each section spotlights the more explicit suggestions.

Besides providing realistic counsel on practical techniques, the text seeks to convey a feel of the very roots of power and status.

ENTERING THE ARENA

It is usually preferable to know what we are talking about and in what context before we say too much. This introductory section, therefore, entertains the following questions: What is the definition of power that is being adopted for our purpose? What is the social setting in which this power is wielded? How do we distinguish between the usual effective executive, who does display power of some kind, and the person of power, who happens to be an executive at the same time and about whom we are specially concerned in this book? What are the various explanations that have been given to support the thesis that the pursuit of power is instinctively natural to the human species? And therefore is something to be expected and dealt with on its own terms?

1 **Nature of power** Power is the intentional influence over the beliefs, emotions, and behaviors of people. Potential power is the capacity to do so, but kinetic power is the act of doing so. If you made Jimmy believe, feel, or do what you had wanted him to believe, feel, or do, or prevented him from what he had wanted to believe, feel, or do, you would then have exercised power over him in that particular episode. One person exerts power over another to the degree that he is able to exact compliance as desired. No power is exhibited without an empowering response. The techniques of eliciting empowering responses of the kind and at the time desired from targeted individuals constitute the craft of power.

The state of inequality of power among individuals goes far back to prehuman evolution. Whether it be flocks of starlings, herds of elephants, or packs of wolves, there have always been leaders and the led. Much of the basic patterns being followed today in the human arena of power had been well developed before man arrived on the scene. Desmond Morris described the parallel in the life styles of human and baboon leaders in his book *The Human Zoo*. Like the person of power, the baboon boss adheres to the "ten commandments of dominance" as follows: (1) The head baboon clearly displays the trappings, postures and gestures of dominance as he walks around sleek and beautifully groomed, calm and relaxed, with a deliberate and purposive gait. (2) When rivalry is brewing, he scares the active member with an aggressive and terrorizing charge. (3) If necessary, he is capable of overpowering the challenger. (4) Besides being physically strong, he is also cunning, quick, and intelligent. (5) He suppresses squabbles within the colony, even though these may not threaten his own position, thereby reinforcing his claim as chief. (6) He permits the subdominant baboons, who are helpful to him in warding off external attacks, greater freedom of action and closer proximity to him than weaker males making less contribution. (7) He protects females and infants, who tend to cluster around him, from other baboons, thereby ensuring the survival of the clan. (8) The head baboon determines the programs for the group, which moves to a new location when he moves, rests when he rests, and feeds when he feeds. (9) He continually reassures the members of his concern and love of them as he approaches in the friendly mode of lip smacking. (10) He assumes command at the forefront of battles with external enemies.

Perfect equality in power among people is not only evolutionarily unnatural but also theoretically impossible. Disregarding for the moment such relationships as exist between mother and infant, guru and disciple, and doctor and patient, let us assume a hypothetical situation in which all uneven power of one person over another is suddenly and magically eliminated. For the instant everybody is absolutely equal in power. This state of affairs would immediately create a need for an arrangement to continue the egalitarian status. While the elected guarantor may be able to ensure equality of power among the rest, he can only widen the power distance between himself and the others as he becomes progressively active over time. Out of the ashes of equality rises the phoenix of power. Utopia again reverts to a natural society, divided into the leaders and the led.

We are inclined to conclude from studying the social development of man that the range and intensity of power of one person over others have shrunken over the millenia. The wealthy owner of 100,000 slaves in Rome represents a more fearful concentration of power than the mayor with 75,000 patronage jobs in New York City. The absolutism of the Ottoman emperors and the orthodoxy of the Spanish Inquisition stand in stark contrast to the relative tolerance of today's social democracies and religious ecumenicalism.

Whether the intensity of the competition for whatever power is available has also declined over the years is more difficult to say. It seems that individuals after great power have always contended with everything they can get away with. The most effective approach changes, of course, with the social times. The climb to the peak of power is much more tortuous today in many respects than in former centuries. The way of becoming Czar in the nineteenth century Russia by simply being born into it is a far cry from the involved route of becoming Secretary of the Soviet Communist Party.

Despite our long experience with the fact of power, there is considerable looseness in the use of the term. Many people identify the use of force with the exercise of power. But forcing someone to do something is only a matter of technique. The subject could well have been reasoned, flattered, or bribed into the same performance with far less hostility. Of course, the person who possesses the capacity for brute force, in addition to others, does have an expanded range of potential power. The definition of power per se, however, does not specify the nature of the method employed.

Another confusion equates law with power. This may hold for a law-abiding citizen, who does what the law prescribes. But to a person like "Crow," the law is ineffectually irrelevant. The following is the account by the *Kansas City Star* of his last defiance during August 1961:

"Policemen knew him as 'Crow.' Any friend he had called him 'Pookie.' Last Thursday night, Talmadge Woodson, 25 years old, staggered from the Paseo market with a bullet hole in his stomach and another in his back. He had exchanged shots with [the clerk of] The Paseo . . . after taking about $50 from the cash register and a money bag containing about $150. . . . Less than a half hour later he died at the General Hospital. . . . At the age of 25 Woodson left behind a police file an inch and a half thick that documented years of violence and criminal activity. Since the age of 11, 'Little Crow,' as he was first called, compiled more than 100 arrests."

Even the gods themselves are not omnipotent—so the ancient Greeks taught their children. Events were considered to be matters of contention, the outcome of which are not certain ahead of time. Thus Heraclitus maintained that "We know that war is common to all and strife is justice and all things come into being and pass away through strife." The sun may well decide to deviate from the appointed orbit now and then. To deter the heavenly bodies from disobeying the ordinances of Mount Olympus, the goddess of retribution, Dike, was assigned the task of swift and inescapable punishment. This helped to keep most of the potential violators of the divine laws in line.

The more recent Christians assert that God has given man free will. This is another way of admitting a limitation to God's power. Man can do as he pleases, God's commandments and love to the contrary. But "vengeance is mine," declared the God of the Old Testament, as He rained fire bombs on the men, women, and children of Sodom and

Gomorrah. The Bible further tells us that man had been created after the image of this awesome God. It is no surprise therefore that when men like "Crow" taunt power-jealous society, the public clamors for revenge.

The social sting of crime lies not so much in injuring anyone necessarily but in mocking the power of the presumed authority. A sinner is consigned to everlasting hell-fire for willfully missing a single Sunday service and a young man is thrown into prison for possessing a couple ounces of marihuana. Such acts by themselves do harm to no one. But the Institution has spoken, and the member has disobeyed. The wielders of power have been frustrated and rendered powerless. So they are angry.

When speaking of power, therefore, we should avoid generalizations. No being is almighty in everything and at all times. If we wish to speak meaningfully about the nature of power, we should refer to specific cases and conditions.

Claudius Nero rolled up the right flank of Hasdrubal's army in the Battle of Metaurus and broke the advance of Carthage on Rome. This obviously is power.

The tanner's daughter, Arletta, dangled her pretty feet in the brook at Falaise and seduced Duke Robert the Liberal to beget the most famous bastard in English history, William the Conqueror. Should we not grant this to be power of some kind?

And how about the boss, as he softly mentions the lucrative bonuses that come with increased sales?

2 **Minidemocracies** A government remains government only insofar as it can extract submission from the people. It needs to assure itself of this power on a continuing basis. Bocalini of Loreto had likened the interest of the state to "a hound of Actaeon. It tears out the entrails of its own master. . . . The man of politics gets firmly into his head the principle that everything else must give way before the absolute necessity of asserting and maintaining oneself in the State; he sets his foot on the necks of every other value in heaven and earth. The desire to govern is a demon which even holy water will not drive out."

The Constitution of the United States had originally been framed to mitigate against just such fears by *limiting* the power of the central government over the lives of the individual citizens. Scarcely two centuries later, it has become the very instrument for *extending* that power. In 1975 there were over a hundred Federal regulatory agencies, which exercised formidable control in an incoherent and oftentimes arbitrary manner by bureaucratic barons over a broad range of political spheres, economic activities, and social conveniences. To comply with their overview, Indiana Standard Company submitted 24,000 pages of reports and 225,000 pages of supplementary computer output.

Besides surrendering much of his rights in the ordering of his life and even in the retention of it to the federal government, the individual American has also consented to be governed in elastically delimited areas by a host of minidemocracies. He has transferred much of his freedom for communing with God to the churches, for earning a livelihood to corporations and labor unions, for bringing up his children to the schools, for selecting officials to major political parties, and so on. With each transfer of freedom went yet another parcel of power.

In addition to the maxi- and minidemocracies, which arose through more or less voluntary acquiescence on the part of the citizen, clusters of other minigovernments in the form of special-interest groups have gained ascendancy without the citizen's awareness or concurrence. As James Madison had noted their operations even before the days of the Constitution in the *Federalist,* "A landed interest, a manufacturing interest, a mercantile interest, like many interests grow up of necessity in civilized nations, and divide them into different classes, actuated by different sentiments and views." Many of them are motivated by the "zeal for different opinions concerning religion, concerning government, and many other points, as well as speculation as of practice; an attachment of different leaders ambitiously contending for preeminence and power." Their ancestors go back to antiquity, and their techniques have been refined over centuries.

The checks and balances stipulated in the original draft of the Constitution to preserve the rights of the individual citizen are no longer the determinant factors. The hypothetical mobile involving the executive, the legislative, and the judicial branches of the federal government has long given way to the de facto three-way scramble, involving the constitutional governments, the minigovernments, and the private persons.

After a couple hundred years of devourings by governmental establishments and nibblings by miniestablishments, there is little substantive power left in the hands of the private person any longer in America. Most of it now rests firmly in the grasp of a small select group. We call them executives—but of a special bent. To be more precise, they should be labeled as persons of power.

3 **Executives and persons of power** Anyone with a modicum of energy, concern for others, or a drive to accomplish anything wants to and does exercise power of one kind or another. Parénts, teachers, ministers, policemen, athletes, and managers are familiar examples. These and other individuals may or may not fall into our category of persons of power, depending on the presence of that extra dimension, of which we shall speak.

The average person does not usually demand authority over and beyond that which comes with the social assignment. He or she responds to the needs of the niche and is satisfied with the constraints as prescribed. In contrast, a person of power seeks and exerts influence over people at all times over and beyond that normally associated with his or her institutional and social status.

An effective minister may be satisfied with improving the morality and spirituality of his flock with a moderate flow of converts, but a minister of power would be more fascinated with challenging the church hierarchy on dogmas, converting members of other religious tradition over the objections of their parents, and modifying the secular customs of the land. An effective professor may be satisfied with raising the quality of his or her own teaching and research, but a professor of power would be more fascinated with confronting deans over administrative prerogatives, chasing for outside grants to double the size of his or her floor space every five years, and hustling for votes to become president of professional associations. An effective business executive may be satisfied with maintaining a reasonable return on corporate investments and a steady rate of growth, but a business executive of power would be more fascinated with rising to the very top in the shortest possible time, capturing other organizations for expansion of his empire, and hob-nobbing with politicians in order to affect national policies.

Witness how the Special Counsel to the House ethics committee tried to challenge the State and Justice departments' position in February 1978 that the former South Korean Ambassador Kim Dong Jo was excused by international agreement from giving evidence before his Congressional committee. Leon Jaworski was not content to operate merely as a compliant staff member directing a probe into the bribery scandal among Congressmen. He spoke out as a man of power, reaching out beyond the recognized purview of the House itself into the Executive Branch of government, which is constitutionally responsible for foreign policy.

The executive with the most impressive record of profit and progress for his own operations within the company may not necessarily be a person of power. A junior executive with a less noteworthy history of accomplishments, but sitting on the financial committee of the company, exercising veto over other organizational elements, and serving as an advisor to the United States Secretary of the Treasury may be less successful as a corporate executive but is much more so as a person of power.

To the person of power, the retention of control is of the highest priority. If necessary, the welfare of the organization itself is to be compromised. When the insurgent Democrats in Connecticut, who had supported Eugene McCarthy's bid for the presidential nomination in 1968, put Reverend Joseph P. Duffey across in the primary in 1970, the state party boss convinced former Senator Thomas Dodd to run as an "independent," thereby splitting the ranks of the Democratic voters, ensuring the election of a Republican, and continuing his own domination of the state machinery.

It is true that, in general, at least a satisfactory performance of explicitly assigned duties is necessary as a springboard to power. Over-committed efforts toward an exceptionally high level of achievement in one's formal responsibilities, however, may actually interfere with the acquisition of greater personal power. It might keep one's nose so close to the corporate grindstone that he or she has little energy left for the required probings and exploitations in the more distant alleys.

On the other hand, it frequently happens that an executive of power performs more effectively in a demanding position, even by conventional standards, than an executive not pursuing extra power. The latter, because of his less-aggressive attributes, might have boxed himself into a responsibility without the requisite authority.

When power plays can be kept within tolerable bounds, persons of power are particularly valuable for aggressive institutions, such as labor unions, growing corporations, militant churches, and imperialistic nations. Such institutions tend to encourage power plays so long as they stay within unstated "company rules." The line of demarcation as to just what is permitted varies from situation to situation. To the amateurs of power, it is rather vague. But to the professionals, it is very clear, for they are perfectly able to stay just this side of it, whenever they want to.

In any case, most institutions do require an element of aggressiveness to survive the competitive pressures. A certain presence of persons of power has, therefore, proved essential in the past. From the looks of things, they will continue to be in great demand in the future.

4 **Theories on power** Much has been written on the subject. Leonard Krieger, for example, has presented a lucid survey on the European's concept of the responsibility of political power as it evolved over the centuries.

Plato had advanced the idea that power is a necessary feature of the good. Man will "that which is our good." He was convinced that the principal ingredient of power is knowledge. Power should, therefore, be respected.

Aristotle pointed to a reciprocity between the agent affecting a change in the patient and the patient's capacity to respond. He separated the means from the ends in the process. The primary locus of power was affirmed as "a source of movement or change, which is in another thing moved." He continued to follow the Greek tradition that power can be used to achieve good ends. Political power does not exist as such, but represents merely the political application of an ethical power. Apart from this moral reference political power is impotent. The good ruler is thus always "a good and wise man."

On the other hand, the Romans emphasized a political power, which is independent of ethical purposes. For them power was defined in terms of origin rather than ends. A person is free to choose between the political and the nonpolitical way of life. The public official, however, is circumscribed by certain rights, duties, and laws, which are different from those for the private persons. His power is legitimate public control.

The Greek's ethical form of power, as defined by ends, and the Roman's political form, as defined by origin, were kept separate during much of the Middle Ages. As time went on, they gradually merged into a single theoretical system. Thomas Aquinas argued that since the state is a natural institution and God is the creator of all nature, God must therefore be the ultimate authority for political power. The king should attend to the ruling of people and the priest to the life of virtue. But since the final purpose of life on earth is the blessed life in heaven, the king ought to be subject to the successor of Peter, the Pope on earth. In the thirteenth century the archbishop said to the French kings at their coronation: "Through this crown, you become a sharer in our ministry."

The practical subjugation of earthly to heavenly power broke down as the papal-imperial conflicts embraced progressively larger stakes. Competing theses appeared, such as those in the fourteenth century of William of Occam and Marsiglio of Padua. These denied the political power of the church, refused to rest the authority of the state on God's mandate, and ascribed primacy to the freely chosen ends of the community. Secular rule was derived from the community itself. Accordingly, the priesthood was to become part of the state in the teaching of the divine laws and doctrine, which was necessary for the goodness of human actions both private and civil. Secular authorities began to repeat the words that Lucian had Timon address to Zeus: "Mankind pays you the natural wages of your laziness; if anyone offers you a victim or a garland it is only at Olympia as a perfunctory accompaniment of the games; he does it not because he thinks it is any good, but because he may as well keep up an old custom."

The disagreement gave rise to the two theoretical strands of political power which have plagued Western thinkers down to modern times. We may look on Niccolo Machiavelli as the exponent of one view and Martin Luther as the exponent of the other.

Machiavelli paid scant attention to the nonpolitical legitimacy of state power but expressed the responsibility *to* power. State power looks to internal order and external security as the criteria of success. Yet he did not entirely divorce political power from ethics. There was an implicit assumption of man's depravity underlying many of his suggestions. It would be difficult to see how the ends of state power can be attained without ethical virtues of some kind on the part of the prince and the community.

Luther faced the reverse dilemma, that of the responsiblity *by* power. He had been immersed in a nonpolitical morality of religious calling and only later was required to bring it into some kind of relationship with the behavior of the self-sufficient state. Until his condemnation in 1520 at the Diet of Worms, he had supported the premise of the state being ordained by God to punish evil-doers and protect them that do well. The subsequent persecution of his followers caught him in a bind. If he upheld the primacy of the spiritual rulers, he would not have been able to receive the protective refuge in the political order, which alone could defend his movement to improve the Christian church. As a result, his attempts to harmonize the temporal power with the spiritual remained unconvincing, and the vacillation in his accommodations paralyzed his ultimate position.

As the forgers of the strong nations of the seventeenth century asserted themselves, the theories fell in line. The British constitutionalist government and the Prussian philosopher-king finally merged the utilitarian and the moral versions into workable models. The divine right of kings was replaced by the irrevocable consent of the governed for a given area of political activity. At the same time, freedoms were granted the individual citizens in certain cultural and related matters. The king's function now extended over the gamut of human happiness and the general welfare of his people. The all-encompassing phrase of justification, reasons of state, emerged into prominence.

An analogous evolution in Islamic constitutional doctrine was taking place as the power balance swung from the caliph to the sultan.

During the first two centuries of Mohammedan theology, the caliph was accepted by the Muslims as Allah's agent in preserving the peace and protecting the faith. He was a descendant of the tribe of Quraysh, the one to which Mohamet belonged, and was ordained by Allah. Supposedly, the elected caliph ruled under an agreement with the community. If he did not live up to the stipulations, the people were free to withdraw their allegiance. In practice, however, there was no way for them to do so. Neither the revealed word of Allah, the *Qur'an,* nor the traditions, the *Hadith,* contained any implementing procedures, unless they wanted to stage an all-out revolution. To discourage tendencies in this direction, scholars stressed the importance of obedience to the successors of Mohamet. The words of the Prophet himself were quoted, many of which were, according to H. A. R. Gibb, "forgeries on a vast scale, sometimes by editing and supplementing genuine old traditions, more often by simple inventions."

In the tenth century the caliph of Baghdad became a prisoner of the military chieftan, the sultan. The sultan ruled in actuality, while the caliph restricted himself to religious ceremonies. Again the flexible Islamic jurists made the necessary revisions in the doctrinal books. They now stated that the sultan derived his powers legitimately from Allah through the blessings of the caliph. Palliating formalities were devised.

By the thirteenth century even the pretense of delegated authority was shed by the sultan. A few years after the Mongols had stormed the city of Baghdad and put the caliph to death in 1258, the Egyptian Judge Ibn Jama'ah announced that "The sovereign has the right to govern until another and stronger one shall oust him from power and rule in his State. The latter will rule by the same title and will have to be acknowledged on the same grounds; for a government, however objectionable, is better than none at all; and between the two evils we must choose the former."

Most of the dissertations on power have focused on the political expressions. Perhaps this is as it should be, in view of their magnitude and ubiquity. Yet there are other varieties of power of more immediate relevance to our everyday activities. These include corporation executives gaining control of the board of directors, labor leaders agitating strikes, policemen deterring potential criminals, and panhandlers wheedling quarters from passersby. Power is the universal solvent of human relations.

During the last several decades increasing attention has been directed to the pervasiveness of power in people's lives. What makes one individual tick in contact with another? What is the basis of the drive for personal influence over others? Here again, the opinions are divergent.

One of the human traits that has been singled out for considerable analysis recently is aggressiveness. Some psychoanalysts have associated the desire to subjugate others with male sexuality. The biological significance of this aggressiveness is supposedly found in the need to dominate the sexual object by means other than wooing. It is exhibited as sadism in the extreme form. Other observers, like Robert Ardery and William Golding, have argued that human beings are like all other animals in being innately aggressive. This sentiment has been embodied in many statements, such as that by Konrad Lorenz: "Peking Man, the Prometheus who learned to preserve fire, used it to roast his brothers: beside the first traces of the regular use of fire lie the mutilated and roasted bones of Sinanthropus pekinensis himself." M. F. A. Montagu, on the other hand, rejected the idea. To him, aggression is not intrinsically human, but is learned. The two million years of evolution of the human society showed great reliance on intergroup cooperation. Otherwise, the race would not have survived during those difficult early days of small numbers, before the pastoral community of twelve thousand years ago.

When all is said and done, however, the practitioners of power are not the ones who write theories about it. As Gustave Le Bon remarked some time ago, "At the bidding of Peter the Hermit millions of men hurled themselves against the East; the words of an hallucinated enthusiast as Mohamet created a force capable of triumphing over the Graeco-Roman world; an obscure monk like Luther bathed Europe in blood. The voice of a Galileo or a Newton will never have the least echo among the masses. The inventors of genius hasten the march of civilization. The fanatics and the hallucinated create history."

5 Justifications Rarely has a successful act of power been found wanting in justification. Oppressive labor practices, outright looting, and political shenanigans have been explained away as rugged individualism in building up the industrial strength of a democratic society. Religious strife, persecution, and selling of indulgences have been explained away as tangential incidentals in a divine mission. Decimation of cultures, economic enslavement of peoples, and imperialistic conquest of the weak have been explained away as bringing civilization to the underdeveloped.

The accompanying self-righteousness comes particularly easily in people with tendencies in certain directions. Six of these are sketched below:

The first is presumption. The scholar in the cloisters presumes that wisdom comes only with *his* kind of enlightenment, and therefore all should listen to him above all others. The missionary in foreign lands presumes that *his* message is the only one from God, and therefore, all should heed no other. The political doctrinaire on the platform presumes that *his* way is the only just and practical one, and therefore all should adopt no other.

The second is self-centeredness. Everything is explained in terms of what the person himself values. Plato was a lover of knowledge, so he affirmed that knowledge is power and is good. The Romans were citizens of an expanding empire, so they affirmed that the state is supreme. Thomas Aquinas was a devoted disciple of the Roman Church, so he affirmed that kings are subordinate to popes.

The third is imputing motivations—one's own always being honorable, to be sure, and the opposition's less honorable. This recalls the debates over the Cuban missile crisis in 1962, when the patriotic American housewife declared: "But *our* missiles in Turkey are *defensive* missiles. The *Russian's* in Cuba are *offensive* missiles!"

The fourth is the worship of progress. Faith in progress looks to the attainment of tangible goals, which is assured through power. In that way the faith can be sustained for even greater commitment to progress, which in turn calls for more power and leads to increased faith.

The fifth is sheer animal aggressiveness. Most people rationalize their attacks as offsetting the evil designs of potential opponents and ensuring their own rightful privileges and possessions.

The sixth is the purported high calling of the public good in the present Age of Institutions. This age is characterized by the prevalent belief that the well-being of the individual flows from the progress of institutions. Only insofar as the schools, corporations, unions, banks, churches, and governments prosper can the individual human being look forward to a commensurate allotment of happiness. The individual is no longer the primal consideration, but has become a derivative of the collectivity.

Proceeding along this line of thought, it seems reasonable to believe that institutions are the surest means for attaining the greatest good for the greatest number, that their contributions to social good is a direct function of their efficiency and direction, that it is one's social duty to see to it that they are on the right track, and that therefore one's greatest service toward the greatest good for the greatest number of fellow human beings dictates one's acquisition of a position of strong influence within the institutions.

Power, of course, is what moves the institutions and their emboweled masses. It is the craving for power, then, that generates the good life for aspirants progressing along this path. For them the realizing of more power represents the driving index of success. The pursuit of the maximum constitutes their pursuit of excellence.

The urge for ever greater power has always been and will always be well lubricated with natural and good intentions.

LEARNING THE FUNDAMENTS

All that is needed for defeat in your quest for power is a single chink in a vital area. Your opposition will find it sooner or later—the sooner and the more certainly so as you rise higher in the league. This section covers the fifteen basic ways of ensuring your competitive strength. With respect to yourself: What personal qualities are essential? With respect to others: How do you cultivate the key individuals behind the scenes? Whom should you trust? How about the customs and beliefs of people at large? And their associated suffering? How should you treat your immediate cadre? And your mass constituency? With respect to your actions: How much power should you grab at one time? What kinds of managerial efficiency are required? How about various constraints? What are some of the safer and surer avenues of getting ahead for younger aspirants? And finally, what is the personal price you are expected to pay?

6 **Professionalism** The greater your aspirations in your climb for power, the more deadly professional—not in the know-how of your job but in the know-how of power—must you be. "A man who is weak and vacillating on theoretical questions, who has a narrow outlook, who makes excuses for his own slackness on the ground that the masses are awakening spontaneously, who resemble a trade-union secretary more than a people's tribune, who is unable to conceive a broad and bold plan, who is incapable of inspiring even his enemies with respect for himself, and who is inexperienced and clumsy in his own profession—the art of combating the political police—such a man," said Nikolai Lenin, as he criticised the primitiveness of his fellow rebels, "is not a revolutionist but a hopeless amateur!"

The professional person of power goes about his rounds with calm assurance and confidence. He does not engage in bush-league practices like indiscriminate name-dropping. While he may add his compliments in support of his superiors, he does not join in obsequious flatteries. While he may amplify his praises of members of his team, he does not fabricate them. He does not seek favors but works and fights for what he gets. Yet he magnanimously grants favors, so long as they do not subtract from his position of power. He remains his own man.

Never does he permit himself to be a captive of institutions in which his latitude of movement is overly constrained. Although an executive of intelligence operations might relish a high appointment in institutions like the Central Intelligence Agency, for example, the professional person of power would shun it. Intelligence operations demand that their agents lie, murder, and do other things on command. There is an implicit understanding that their leaders should be prepared to do what they expect of their underlings. The organization would fall apart should the members suspect any weakening of resolve on the part of their chief. It was only true to form that the director of the agency testified under oath before a Senate Subcommittee in 1973 that the CIA was not involved in domestic spying on the antiwar movement, when it was; that it did not try to overthrow the government of Chile, when it tried; and that it had not passed any money to the opponents of Chilean President Salvador Allende, when it did. Being a captive of the agency, the director had to say what he did say. He had risen through the ranks himself.

The professional person of power is imbued with a tremendous tenacity of purpose and keeps the pressure on continuously. This directional self-control refers to not only the unremitting pursuit of the overall objective of ascending power but also unfailing attention to the grimy details. The professional person of power recognizes that the difference between victory and defeat is often just a whisker. In 1967 Edward N. Cole was elected president of General Motors by a one-vote margin over Semon Knudsen after long deliberation by the board of directors.

Because the person of power sees things exactly as they are, he is able to pick his salients unerringly. His perceptive mind's retina reflects the situations as clearly as a deep still lake reflects the sky. His efforts are not sidetracked by passions that ensnare lesser men. He does not permit envy to distract his attention from the actions to be taken to the possessions of the competitor, nor pride from what he needs to do in the next moment to what he has done in the past. Frivolity has no place in his life. He does not even indulge in it during periods of relaxation, for frivolity is the most fatal of poisons to that heroic quality that should always be present in a professional. It is worse than cowardice; it is a faked cowardice, a refusal to expose oneself.

The professional has long known how to accept and learn from mistakes and setbacks. He has acquired the resilience of bouncing back from the darkness of defeat. As the socialist Eugene V. Debs once declared: "Ten thousand times has the labor movement stumbled and fallen and bruised itself and risen again; been seized by the throat and choked into insensibility; enjoined by the courts, assaulted by thugs, charged by the militia, shot down by regulars, frowned upon by public opinion, deceived by politicians, threatened by priests, repudiated by renegades, preyed upon by grafters, infested by spies, deserted by cowards, betrayed by traitors, bled by leeches, and sold out by leaders. But notwithstanding all this, and all these, it is today the most vital and potential power this planet has ever known."

The professional person of power does not pass the buck, except as a calculated move in a power play. He understands that passing the buck is at best a confession of the lack of confidence and at worst a de facto transfer of responsibility, which is first cousin to power. It takes only a few such transfers of the buck to someone else before his days as a person of power are numbered.

His actions reflect the five qualities of Chuang Tzu's master robber: "There is the sage character of thieves by means of which booty is located, the courage to enter first, and the chivalry to come out last. There is the wisdom of calculating success and the kindness in fair division of the spoils. There has never yet lived a great robber who did not possess these five qualities."

7 Skepticism and vigilance Be skeptical of everything and everybody at all times and in every place—to a calibrated degree. There are always extenuating circumstances twisting and shading truth. There is always the ever-present factor of human error. No matter who says it and no matter how supported, nothing in the arena of power is to be taken at face value.

When the American Ambassador to Paris James M. Gavin heard rumors in late 1961 about his being replaced by Charles E. Bohlen, Jr., he anxiously inquired of Washington. The Secretary of State phoned and assured him that nothing of the sort was being considered. The President dispatched a letter in January 1962, saying how pleased he was with Gavin, "the best envoy we have had there since Franklin." Yet it was not many months thereafter that Bohlen did indeed replace him.

The familiar refrain that people aren't what they seem has been repeatedly confirmed again and again throughout history. One of the classical cases is that of the Flemish woman, Marthe Cnockaert, during World War I. She worked indefatigably and most effectively as a nurse tending the sick and wounded in the German hospitals. For her great service she was awarded the German Iron Cross. All the while, however, she was a British intelligence agent, reporting German troop movements, blowing up German ammunition dumps, and directing British air strikes responsible for many of the very casualties she was so devotedly caring for the following morning.

Look around you and observe how easily others have been duped. Think not that you are sharper than they. Even the greatest man of power in his time, Otto von Bismarck, had been outwitted. During the siege of Paris in the autumn of 1870, Bismarck took up residence at Versailles, awaiting entry into the city. A military aide introduced an impressive caller to the Prussian Iron Chancellor. His passport read: "M. Angel de Valleyo, Vice-President of the Spanish Finance Commission in Paris, attaché to the Spanish Embassy." The orders of the Star of Isabella and the Cross of St. John of Jerusalem showed prominently on his chest. Bismarck was impressed by the Spanish grandee's rank and title and invited him for supper that lasted three hours. It was only after the visitor had left for some time that the Chancellor had the guest investigated. The latter turned out to be Angel de Miranda of the Paris *Gaulois*. The story of the hoodwinking of the great Bismarck spread throughout the French capital, to no end of laughter.

How often have you read a newspaper, book, or magazine, discovered many errors and distortions in subjects of which you were expert, yet kept on believing the rest of the contents of which you were unfamiliar? The fact is, of course, that the latter is no more accurate than the former. Even if everything were factually reported, the accounts are still only partial; what was omitted might have provided an entirely different perspective. At the least they are suspect as partial truths.

How often have you heard a professor-consultant deliver a learned proposition, only to find another equally respected professor-consultant advising a diametrically opposite course of action? One of them must be wrong. There is a good chance that both are, at least in degree. The same holds true for judgments by old-time chiefs, economists of Nobel laureate fame, and the rest of the population with less impressive credentials.

Remember that loyalty is fickle. A person who appears loyal as a subordinate may not be so as an associate or a superior. He may not even be loyal as a subordinate, so finely practiced are some people in simulation.

Remember also that reformers are no less selfish than special-interest groups and that their data are no less biased. Reformers constitute merely another interest group. Even if their intentions may be commendable, their judgments as to feasibility and fairness may be somewhat questionable. The more so, the more they absolutize their position.

Do not swallow too much from a defector or an informer. Some of his revelations are probably true. But a considerable fraction consists of intentional exaggerations to please your ears, unintentional falsifications out of subconscious revenge, and unrepresentative sampling of data. Neither should you count too much on concessions obtained from someone under duress. When the moment of truth arrives, such persons more often than not fall back on the accepted custom that promises exacted by force need not be kept. Do not plow through what appears to be a gaping opening in the opposition's defense without prior double checking. It might well be a trap.

Be always skeptical, therefore, but never cynical. The latter would mean that you have tossed perspective to the winds. You have lost your nerve. You are planting trees to hide behind, trees with sour fruit, which curdles your judgment. Retain a healthy balance, tinted with just that trace of paranoia that provides the tingling alertness, so critical for vigilance.

8 **The big game** "No man lives without jostling and being jostled," said Thomas Carlyle, "in all ways he has to elbow himself through the world, giving and receiving offence."

The complex social mechanisms of modern times, the widely distributed competences, and the deeply inculcated ambitions have greatly enlarged the number of seizers of power. Democracy has widened their eligibility; technology has provided them additional tools; graduated income tax and state regulation of wealth have reduced the guarantees of inheritance to descendants of the once entrenched. Each successor to established power must struggle to retain it. As William Somerset Maugham describes the state of affairs in his biography, *Summing Up,* "So long as some are strong and some are weak, the weak will be driven to the wall. So long as men are cursed with the sense of possession, and that I presume is as long as they exist, they will wrest what they can from the powerless to hold it. So long as they have the instinct of self-assertion, they will exercise it at the expense of the other's happiness."

So it is that there is no such reality as a power vacuum, into which a person can simply waltz in and take over. The so-called power vacuum is merely a pretext for insatiate persons to barge into an area where power is more or less evenly distributed among relatively weak people. Avaricious men of power can never pass up a lucrative opportunity, whereupon they call this condition of equality a power vacuum and assert their right to fill it with "leadership." All the while they remain steeped in the traditional orientation of power. In the words of Richard Tawney, "The conviction that advantages which are shared are not advantages at all is, in England, deeply ingrained."

In general, the primary objective is not the creation of new power so much as the redistribution of available power, which usually remains the same in toto for a given set of circumstances. This is seen most clearly in the yes-no sessions of collective bargaining. The economic gains sought by the union represent economic losses to management. Operational decisions passing into the hands of the union represent power lost by management. Equally straightforward arithmetic balances hold for proxy fights and court judgments. In these instances the governing procedures are fairly well established.

Complications arise in cases in which the issues are not clean-cut, the purposes not fixed, and the options not well-defined. For example, the exact boundaries of the invasion of management rights by labor unions in many arguments cannot be determined on the basis of strict legalism, as distinct from the endeavors of the respective groups to accommodate to changing conditions.

There are various avenues for reaching out in power within the work environment and outside of it. Although some may seem independent of the others, they are actually mutually synergistic. Success in one area more often than not stimulates success in the rest.

Two principal outlets exist within the work setting. When perched at a relatively low echelon, the most promising route is to reach upward by getting promoted into a higher status, thereby coming into control of a greater number of people.

In this regard, no matter how much talent you may have, how great your fame, or how impressive your potential power, do not wait too long for the powers-that-be to beckon. After a discreetly short wait, you must push yourself forward with determination, although not without the grace appropriate to the circumstances. If there is a vacancy for which you qualify, let the proper people know. If there are no foreseeable vacancies on the books for some time, move out to create situations that will result in one. Even if you do not get the nod on the first go-round, you will gain increased exposure and recognition, which will stand you in better stead on your next try.

The number of possible promotions at the junior executive level is much less than at the lower rungs of the ladder. You should then consider another avenue for your accretion of power. This is increasing your responsibilities and/or functional scope in the present job. Chester

Burger gave an actual example of how to get ahead along this path. It concerned a sales manager who had been intrigued with the sales potential of a product that had never been clearly assigned to any particular individual but left informally in the hands of several executives, who paid only routine attention to the product. He felt he could develop its volume of sales significantly but intuitively realized that if he asked for the authority to do so, he would be turned down. So he went about it gradually, quietly, and elliptically. Finding $125 from an unexpended budget item, he obtained approval from his supervisor for running a little advertisement in a trade journal. The supervisor did not question the request, in view of the small amount of money involved. After the exercise proved moderately profitable, he did the same with $500 worth of uncommitted funds with equally satisfactory returns. When the amount reached several thousand dollars, the supervisor casually inquired about the nonbudgeted expenditures. The sales manager showed him the data on net profit, whereupon no further questions were asked. By the end of the first year, $100,000 of unbudgeted monies had been spent and the product continued to perform well. When the picture was presented at the annual budget review, top management decided to formalize his complete authority over the product and set up the accompanying budget line item.

As far as reaching outside the work setting for increased influence on people is concerned, two main patterns have been exhibited. The first is available to individuals at all echelons. This is to serve in personal or semi-official capacities on advisory and voluntary bodies to outside institutions, such as governments, community drives, and trade associations. This is the more commonly followed approach. In 1975 the National Petroleum Council, advising the Secretary of the Interior on national energy policies, had 155 members, of whom 140 worked directly or indirectly for petroleum companies. There were 1500 committees in the federal government alone. Thousands of others exist in state, municipal, academic, church, and other institutions. Besides direct influence on others, these connections provide entrees to much wider spheres of power. The elites in a community are usually interconnected through such anastomoses.

The second practice is usually restricted to those at or near the top of an institution. This is the capturing of other institutions. It is accomplished on a low-profile basis by serving on boards of directors. It is implemented on an overt basis through the acquisition of subsidiaries, such as Radio Corporation of America's buying out Hertz Rental Car Company in the mid-1960s, or annexation, such as Russia taking over part of Sakhalin from Japan after World War II.

Other things being equal, the chief executive officer of a conglomerate like Textron, which corrals subsidiaries regardless of similarity in product lines or services, can be regarded as being more a person of power than an executive. In contrast, the chief executive officer of a corporation like Dupont, which expands along technically allied lines, can be regarded as being more an executive than a person of power.

Capturing institutions provides the fastest rate of growth. From the standpoint of power, it does not matter much what the organization stands for or what it produces at the moment. The important thing is to bring it under your umbrella, as long as it is relatively sound or potentially so. If necessary, endorse its practices and policies to expedite the acquisition. Once it is under your control, it can then be brought around in harmony with your own long-term bearings and redirected for your immediate purposes.

Francis of Assisi, for example, was one of the most gentle, humane, and compassionate of saintly men that ever lived. Not only other human beings but all God's creatures were his brothers. He founded the Franciscan order in the early thirteenth century to spread his brand of devotion to God through personal poverty and love. But within less than a decade after his death, the Franciscans became recruiting agents for sergeants in the bloody wars of the Guelfs and Ghibellines and, in a number of countries, the chief executive arm of the Inquisition. It even burned its own members, the Spiritualists, who insisted on strict adherence to the saint's teaching on poverty, for heresy.

Those who wish to remain unbloodied or unsoiled in the free-for-all gulpings of institutions are invariably left on the sidelines, possibly to be swallowed several gulps away. This was the dilemma facing Woodrow Wilson in 1914–1915. While proclaiming American neutrality and determination to stay out of the war, he was concerned about the division of spoils afterward. In the words of Walter Karp, "As soon as war broke out in Europe, Woodrow Wilson was fired by a truly grandiose ambition: to preside over the ultimate peace settlement and establish through a league of nations the foundation of 'permanent peace.' As Wilson's friend Colonel House said to the president in November 1914, what lay before him was 'the noblest part that has ever come to a son of man.' That ambition some may deem sublime and others vainglorious, but such was the president's ambition, and there was no way to achieve it except by entering the war. As Wilson himself told Jane Addams on the eve of our entry, he would have no influence at the peace conference if America remained neutral. At best, the belligerents would let him 'call through a crack in the door.'"

Persons of power do not relish the role of kibitzers. More than anything else, they want to be in the thick of the big game.

9 **Kingmakers** If you wish to be king, the obvious first step is to find out who the kingmakers are and bow to them. Unless they nod in your direction instead of others, your rise to power will be diffusively slow. But bow with grace and dignity. They ignore aspirants who cannot.

Although your immediate boss may not be a kingmaker himself, he can upset the applecart. A few words about relationships with the boss may be in order for readers who are just beginning on the road to power. Although a number of successful persons of power have ridden roughshod over their bosses as they sped to the top, it is much easier to have the boss on your side. Being loyal to superiors should not be construed as detrimental to your standing as a leader. On the contrary, repeated studies have shown that the great leaders have also been, as a rule, great followers in their day.

From an overall standpoint, your conduct vis-a-vis your immediate boss should be continually shaped to maximize the following on his part: (1) feeling of the essentiality of your contributions to his personal advancement and his unit's progress, (2) appreciation of your talents as primarily complementary to his deficiencies rather than supplementary to his strengths, (3) confidence that you are no threat to him personally, (4) willingness to grant latitude and time for your extracurricular as well as curricular activities, (5) reluctance to hurt your feelings, and (6) respect. Do not jeopardize them by haggling over office perquisites, stock options, and salaries while you are still trying to build a beginner's base of power. These will come in due time.

Do not pick quarrels with the boss. If you disagree with his ideas, say it clearly, logically, and matter-of-factly, but only once, and do not pursue the matter further. Let him come back to you, if he cares to. If at all possible, let such disagreements be voiced in private. In any case, if no great harm can be done by first trying out the boss's plan, then do so. If might turn out to be better than yours.

Should you find yourself under a boss who is relatively weak—and most bosses are more-or-less weak for their positions—do not "come on too strong" as a subordinate. If the organizational climate favors decision making by committees, then curb your lone-ranger inclinations. There is nothing more disrupting of your plans to ascendancy than to have an insecure boss determined to "cut you down to size."

Some bosses are so insecure that they would interpret even a spectacular accomplishment on the part of a subordinate as detracting from his own status. Should you find yourself working for such a personality, take steps to transfer elsewhere. In the meantime, always render unto him palliative credit for suggesting the idea, approving the program, guiding the project, or something—you can always find something good to say in this regard, as well as spread generous acknowledgment of the collaboration of your associates and modestly dilute your own role. This will ease his apprehensions considerably.

As far as the kingmakers are concerned, it is a fallacy to identify the individual enthroned in the legally supreme position as the chief among them. Many a eunuch, major domo, or confidant dominated the emperors of old; many a banker, insider, or relative guides the officials of today. Not only are they important in the decisions involving appointments to high positions, they also play an active part in discovering young talent and grooming them along.

Before someone can select you out of the many as worthy of special patronage, he or she will have to come to know you, your achievements, and your potential. This means that by chance or design you will have to become exposed to them in a proper light. Professional and social networks assume special significance in this regard. Join the right groups and people will think you right and fit; join nobodies and people will think you a nobody. Should your current position not offer any visibility of the right kind in the near future, you should consider moving laterally, or even a step downward, to another, more conducive setting.

One of the most rewarding avenues for favorable exposure for younger persons is a willingness to carry out the many low-level chores of corporate committees as a member or staff assistant. As long as such persons proceed relatively anonymously and do not seek to stand out from the rest, they will actually wield a disproportionately large share of the corporation-wide authority invested in the committee. At the same time they are enhancing their own stature through approving exposures in the many contacts they must necessarily make. The opportunities are widespread in our committee-encrusted culture. They should not be passed over lightly.

At times, the young person may have a choice in steering his or her own career pattern. Careful planning may be very important in plotting the most direct route to power. Of the various departments in an industrial corporation, for example, sales is usually acknowledged as the most influential. Not only does it exert authority over its own activities, like any other department, it often sets the movement of the corporation as a whole. Next come finance and production. R and D generally lags far behind. The young person should, therefore, not spend much time in R and D, technical service, or administration, but should move out from these departments as soon as feasible. Sales would offer the greatest opportunity for top management influence. On the other hand, production controls the largest number of workers and hence offers the greatest immediate power over internal personnel for midmanagement. Although finance throws considerable weight within the top executive suite, it controls far less employees and therefore provides much less practice for apprentices interested in refining their art of leadership and power. For a technical person interested in a life of growing power, one promising channel would be a few years in R and D, moving over to production through midmanagement, and ending up in sales.

Be circumspect, however, about the way you go about trying to impress people. There is nothing more counterproductive than a sycophantic demeaning of yourself. Kingmakers see through such phony characters without a second look. Unless you are running for political office, do not try to impress everybody. It is not the number of people sponsoring you that counts, but who. Nor should you resort to attention-drawing gimmicks adopted by celebrities of the arts and let-ters, such as beards, clothes, and mannerisms. Conform to the conven-tions of the arena, be trusted by the institution, and fashion differences from your peers and competitors only in the direction that would cause the kingmakers to prefer you over the others.

Early on, you should be aware of the preferences of the kingmakers regarding the qualities expected of their organizational leaders. Lewis Austin tells us in his book, *Saints and Samurai,* that sincerity and warmth are most prized among leaders by the Japanese, whereas hon-esty and knowledge are by the Americans. On the other hand, the "bad" leader among the Japanese is one of timidity, inconsistency, irresoluteness, and vacillation. Among the Americans, he is one of deficiency in understanding, communication with subordinates, and delegation of authority.

In all your encounters with superiors, never for a moment think that you understand fully what is really going on in their minds. Hedge your behavior accordingly. The advice given by Han Fei Tzu of the third century B. C. as to how courtiers should approach the em-peror is worth pondering: Suppose that the monarch you are addres-sing really desires a good name and you appeal to him only on the basis of material gain, he will look down upon you as of low principles, treat you without respect, and banish you from his future councils. Suppose, on, the other hand, that the monarch really desires material gain and you appeal to him only on the basis of a good name, he will look down upon you as impractical, sneer at your lack of common sense, and make no further use of you. Again, suppose that the monarch really desires material gain but professes to care only for a good name and you appeal to him on the basis of a good name, he will pretend to be pleased with you but keep you at a distance; but should you appeal to him on the basis of material gain, he will secretly follow your advice but outwardly disown you.

Relating profitably to kingmakers calls for a higher order of skills than identifying them. It requires a keen insight into human nature in general and individual motivation in particular. Never cease refining it.

10 **Capacity limitations** Ambition and passion constitute poor premises for setting realistic objectives. So are ideals and dedication. Bear Shiki's famous haiku in mind:

> All through the night in the cold
> The monkey squats scheming
> How to capture the moon.

William Foster failed to do so in 1919, when he believed that "the steel trust can be beaten" with 200,000 workers in his union. In undertaking the strike against United States Steel, he had not accurately calculated the enormous retaliatory strength of the industrial combine. The newspapers accused the work stoppage of imperiling the safety of the country. Governor William Sproul of Pennsylvania blasted the striking "foreigners of the community, who have neither sympathy for our policies nor interest in our institutions. Tradition means nothing to them, and lawlessness and disorder are 'music' to their 'ears.'" Martial law was declared in Gary, Indiana after a minor skirmish between strikers and "scabs." After fifteen weeks of depressing difficulties the strike had to be called off, and the 100,000 workers out of the mills had to fend for themselves.

The same overestimation of one's own competitive muscle was repeated in the 1969 bid of the Leasco Data Processing Equipment Corporation, with assets of $400 million, to merge with the Chemical Bank, with assets of $9 billion. When the New York bank's chairman William S. Renchard heard about the move, he vowed: "We intend to resist this with all the means at our command, and these might turn out to be considerable." *Fortune* summarized the outcome in these words: "Just how considerable Steinberg [Leasco's chairman] learned as the banking establishment linked arms to thwart him. Leasco's two investment bankers, White, Weld and Co. and Lehman Brothers, are said to have told Steinberg that they would not support a hostile Leasco bid. Even some of Leasco's own clients, friendly to the bankers, made noises about taking their business elsewhere. And his credit lines to banks were reported threatened for a time. Large blocks of Leasco stock, presumably held by institutions, were dumped. Finally, Steinberg retreated."

In recent decades American presidents have also lapsed into over-extending themselves. After being twice set back in Korea and in Vietnam by second-rate and fifth-rate military powers, America moved out in an attempt to impress its own moral concepts of human rights on the rest of the world within the first few months of a newly elected President in 1977. The Soviet Union stalled the pending disarmament talks in protest over his intrusion into her internal affairs involving dissidents; the fingered Brazil and other allies bristled. Before long, he was forced to be more selective in his salients.

Making big promises and fanning great hopes are especially dangerous in democratic societies operated by elected officials. You should heed the admonition of Machiavelli, as he said in his *Discourses*: "there is no easier way to ruin a republic, where the people have power, than to involve them in daring enterprises; for where the people have influence they will always be ready to engage in them, and no contrary opinion will prevent them. But if such enterprises cause the ruin of states they will more frequently cause the ruin of the particular citizens who are placed at the head to conduct them. For when defeat comes, instead of successes which the people expected, they charge it neither upon the ill fortune or incompetence of their leaders, but upon their wickedness and ignorance; and generally either kill, imprison, or exile them, as happened to many Carthaginian and Athenian generals. Their previous victories are of no advantage to them, for they are all cancelled by present defeat."

It is easy to understand how it is that most persons of power eventually overreach themselves. They are flushed with gigantic egos and extraordinary self-confidence. This is only a short step to the magical transformation of what they are into what they are reaching for.

The nugget of practical wisdom had long ago been recorded by Kuo Hsiang in the third century. "If a person loves fame and craves supremacy and remains dissatisfied even when he has broken his back in the pursuit," he wrote, "it is because human knowledge arises from our losing our balance and will be prevented by intuitively realizing one's peak capacity. . . . Thus it is that even if a person may be carrying ten-thousand pounds, he will remain oblivious of the weight upon his body if it is within his capacity. Likewise, even if he may be carrying ten-thousand matters in his mind, he will remain oblivious of their being upon him if it is within his capacity."

It is not the weight you carry but the overweight over time that crushes. Be guided by the back-breaking threshold of weight times time.

11   Illicit means   History has left us with a long string of people getting rewarded for breaking the law: Agrippina poisoning her emperor-husband to ensure the throne for her son, Nero; the Venetians plundering Moslems and fellow Christians alike during the Middle Ages in maximizing their profits; Bolivia undergoing an average of more than one *coup d'état* attempt per year in her century and a half of existence.

Machiavellianism was not original with the Italian princes. The techniques had been polished to high artistry by the Hindus a thousand years earlier in their doctrine of *Kautilya*. The basic premise was described by Karl Jaspers as follows: "On principle, it says right is whatever succeeds. All moral qualms are discarded; the total lie is good politics if only it succeeds in its deception. It is good politics to refrain from direct action until the opponent has been sufficiently weakened by cunning and trickery and so confused with apparent friendship that the last act of subjection can take place without the risk of combat—as wild beasts are lured into a trap. He who calculates correctly, who does not allow the slightest moral scruple to bother and inhibit him, follows the rule that is valid in politics and inexorable in this entire sphere."

Coming closer to home, we find lawbreaking widespread in America. The parade of petty infractions go on and on: In 1966 the Claims Bureau of the American Insurance Association identified three-fourths of the claims as exaggerated. In 1974 an investigation by the Westchester District Attorney's Fraud Bureau revealed that one out of five butchers substituted a cheaper grade of meat when asked by a customer to grind up a top-quality piece. At about the same time, a medical scientist in one of America's most respected research institutions was exposed as having falsified his experimental results, which had been internationally acclaimed for their potential benefit for cancer treatment and transplant surgery. The New York State Council of Arts refused to endorse a grant to a leading ballet organization because of suspected financial discrepancies in the application, stemming from a statement of its president, who had been reported as having said that he had manipulated the figures. Not long thereafter, a group of nuns operating a nursing home was publicly singled out by federal inspectors for using Medicaid funds paid by the government for the care of the poor to purchase a birthday present for their bishop.

But these are little crimes by lesser people. What the person of power should be more concerned with is the criminal inclinations among his peers in the higher strata of society. A relevant generalization was advanced by Pitirim A. Sorokin and Walter A. Lunden as a conclusion of their studies reported in *Power and Morality*. "The moral behavior of ruling groups," said they, "tends to be more criminal and sub-moral than those of the ruled strata of society." It seems that we need not strain our eyes for empirical support.

In the 1960s organized crime was active in eighty percent of the cities with a population above a million and in twenty to fifty percent of those of at least a hundred thousand. A variety of offenses is perpetrated in business and the professions under the name of white-collar crimes.

The assistant comptroller of an aircraft manufacturing subsidiary during the 1950s was charged in sworn testimony with having ordered his accountants to falsify data to the United States Air Force to show only a ten percent profit, which was the limit set in the contract. At the same time he allegedly also ordered the accountants to falsify entries in reports to the parent organization to show a high profit. After litigation and an independent audit by an outside CPA firm, the parent company agreed to refund the overcharge of $43.4 million to the Air Force.

The continuing practice of bribery and variations need only be represented by two examples drawn from the files of the 1970s. One involves the score of companies and executives convicted of illegal political contributions, including such giants as American Airlines, Goodyear Tire and Rubber, Lockheed, Minnesota Mining and Manufacturing, and United Brands. The other involves government undercover agents discovering numerous payoffs of up to $50,000 each to members of the International Longshoremen's Association in all parts of the country.

As far as the highest councils of the government are concerned, we may simply refer to the forced resignation of the Vice President of the United States in October 1973, after a lengthy investigation of his evasion of income taxes and acceptance of bribes from contractors while he was Baltimore County executive, and to that of the President himself in August 1974, after the House Judiciary Committee voted articles of impeachment involving the obstruction of justice through such acts as directing his subordinates to commit perjury to conceal illegal acts by his office and his misuse of power to violate the constitutional rights of the American people. In the process four cabinet officials and practically all his senior aides were compelled to plead guilty to various charges of conspiracy, perjury, obstruction of justice, and/or bribery; were indicted; or were sentenced before the year drew to a close. Barely were we able to heave a sigh of forgiving relief when we began to learn that scores of the very Congressmen who were to sit in judgment of the President were themselves engaging in white-collar crimes at the same time, such as accepting "gifts" of up to $100,000 from representatives of foreign governments for legislative favors, facilitating illegal contracts for American businessmen for a fee, and soliciting prostitutes for important constituents.

Illicit means, it seems, cannot be eliminated from human transactions. In a survey during the 1960s of 1020 males and 678 females, mostly from New York State, nine-tenths admitted having committed at least one offense for which they could have been given a prison sentence had they been caught. In another sampling of 9945 boys born in Philadelphia in 1945, one out of every three had been arrested at least once before they had reached the age of eighteen.

There appear to be so many sinners all over the world that apparently even God Himself, at least on one occasion, was on the verge of giving up. "When Yahweh saw how great was the wickedness of man upon the earth, and all the desires of his heart were bent only upon evil all day long," so it has been stated in *Genesis*, "Yahweh regretted that he had ever made man on earth, and he was grieved to the heart."

12 **Legal porosity and elasticity**   There are three ways, two of which are quite socially acceptable, for escaping the pincers of the law.

One is blindfolding the law. This is usually achieved through incurring an indebtedness on the part of its agents. The association of crime and politics in America goes back to its earliest days. A French trader known as the "Mole" conducted a thriving business of selling illegal rum in 1670 to the Potawatamie Indians from a stand on the spit of land at the junction of the Chicago River and Lake Michigan. Jacques Marquette protested repeatedly to the Governor of New France, Count Louis de Frontenac, but in vain. The Mole, Pierre Moreau, was too close a friend of the governor.

Modern practitioners call it the "fix." The fix takes the form not only of buying off policemen and other law enforcement officials, but also of contributing to political organizations and charitable activities and collaborating with reputable businessmen and attorneys. One of the men arrested at the meeting of leaders of organized crime at Apalachin in New York in 1957, for example, had been voted the "man of the year" in Buffalo for his civic contributions just the year before.

As a rule, the underworld remains nonpartisan on the political front, offering men and money to any likely successful candidate who susceptibly fits into its plans. Manpower is furnished by the organization leaders through the hustling of the mob and its families, as well as their extensive connections throughout the community. Money is contributed generously. One of the more powerful personalities of the 1940s was Frank Costello, who was syndicate boss in New York. The Senate Kefauver Committee showed how a New York judge, following his nomination, phoned "Francesco" to express "undying gratitude." A Manhattan borough president, after his election, went to the Costello home to pay respects.

The second way is placating the law. This is usually achieved by stroking its varying idiosyncracies in the right manner. During the 1960s, for example, the more astute attorneys would not file a civil rights suit in certain courts because the ensuing proceedings would have been an uphill fight all the way. The attitude of the judge is often pivotal not only in civil rights suits but also in all kinds of close decisions. Judges react quite differently in such things as the selection of facts to be considered germane to the case at hand.

The interpretation of a given rule in a court of law often varies not only within a given premise but also among the very premises themselves. One basis for judgment is the so-called true meaning of words, the understanding being that each word can have but one true meaning. Another basis is the intention of the author of the rule. A third is the intention of the author if confronted with the specific case at hand. A fourth is the anticipated outcome of an appeal involving the construction of the law. A fifth is the common-sense interpretation of the layman.

At times a recognized rule is even reformulated to justify some judicial decision. Karl Llewellyn illustrated how a New York court went about it in one instance. The preexisting rule was: "Technically speaking there is a marked distinction between issuing a draft, or traveller's check and receiving money for transmission." The court's revision for governing the case at hand was: "Technically speaking there is a marked distinction between issuing a draft, or traveller's check or transferring money by cable and receiving money for actual transmission." The two rules differ in at least one important aspect. The new rule can no longer be, in the words of Gordon Gottlieb, "an inference guidance device for the decision of *that* case. *It is a rule of justification rather than a rule of guidance.*"

The third way is out-dancing the law. This is achieved by constantly being half-a-step elsewhere by the time the laws are made to apply where you once were. The chief executive officers of multinational corporations are most agile in these complex maneuvers. They move capital around to avoid income taxes. They set up dummy corporations to divert profits through artificially set prices. They overprice imports and underprice exports through such practices as "transfer pricings," when it is advantageous to do so. It is extremely difficult for a small local competitor to withstand the inroads of such power.

Taking advantage of the porosity and elasticity of the law is much smarter than trying to buck it.

13 **Associated sufferings** When Liverpool was enjoying great prosperity in the late 1700s, a hundred slave-trading ships were busy full time at the Merseyside port. Thousands of African slaves were wrenched from their homes and shipped out from there.

When Henry Ford had to raise money in 1920 to pay off bank notes that were becoming due, he demanded cash payment from the car dealers and canceled all orders from supply firms. By so doing he won the financial battle with the banks and retained complete control of the company. But many long-time dealers and suppliers were forced out of business.

When the Allies won World War II and the United States emerged unscathed as the most powerful nation in the history of the world, over ten million Europeans had lost their lives, countless millions of homes had been destroyed, and a third of the territory had been ravaged.

Robert Southey had explained the scene after the Battle of Blenheim centuries earlier in these words:

> They say it was a shocking sight
>   After the field was won;
> For many thousand bodies here
>   Lay rotting in the sun;
> But things like that, you know, must be
>   After a famous victory.

One man's gain so often rests on another man's pain.

14 **Custom** Disapproval by custom is as trenchant as sanction by law. To question it invites even greater hostility. When the bulk of the population accepts a body of notions, it becomes consecrated. The less educated and the poorer the community, the stronger is the hold of custom in setting the fashions and norms of the times.

During the Middle Ages the powerful German Emperor Frederick II attempted to strengthen the civic institutions vis-a-vis the ecclesiastical. To his disappointment, the very people he was trying to elevate in status rose against him. He had not paid adequate attention to the deep-seated mores of the period. It was a matter of common acceptance that all European states were Christian, and a Christian state naturally did as the Pope said. According to the popular way of thinking, to make an institution independent of the Pope was just not the thing to do.

Accommodate your actions to community traditions and company rules. If as a dean you are thinking about becoming the president of a university, then say nothing adverse about faculty tenure and search committees. If as a small-time labor organizer you are thinking about becoming a big-time labor leader, then say nothing complimentary about the fine things any corporation is doing for its employees. If as a Catholic bishop you are thinking about becoming a cardinal, then say nothing justifiable in the use of contraceptives.

When trying to move people to action, it is preferable to be doctrinally slightly behind than too far ahead of your time. Even if many of them are inwardly disenchanted with the popular cliches, be not the first to mouth the doubt in public.

Should a strongly imbedded tradition constitute a major barrier to a prime objective of yours, it would be prudent to seek ways other than a head-on confrontation. One of the more effective approaches is to wean the people indirectly through a gradual, though persistent, adaptation of the rituals and routines of daily living, until the old beliefs no longer fit the new habits. As the former obstructions wither away, new variations abetting your own purposes can then be substituted. Doctrines that mesh with the new learning, mannerisms, and conventions will become the prevailing guidance for the masses. It is to be noted that witchcraft was not abandoned as a result of brilliant defense attorneys at the Salem trials. It disappeared when the advancing knowledge in the population at large made it look ridiculous.

You should be sensitive not only to the traditional beliefs, but also to the customary behavioral patterns obtaining in your particular institution. Banks prefer conservative, careful, and cautious deliberations in their quiet handling of money transactions with a civil and courteous demeanor. Food manufacturers lean toward the quick-witted, aggressive, and competitive activity necessary to get their products onto the limited supermarket shelves. Giant utility corporations foster community-related, committee-oriented, and team-playing operations. These behavioral differences do not mean that the power plays going on under the more judicious appearance of bankers are any less intense than those under the more agitated manners of food manufacturers. They only mean that the tactics and styles that succeed in one theater may not necessarily be those that succeed in the other.

No greater sensitivity to mores has been exhibited within the context of power in recent decades than the first message drafted by Ho Chih Minh, following the declaration of independence of Vietnam in the Autumn of 1945. It was addressed not to the loyal supporters, the militant communists, the soldiers, nor even to the people at large in this moment of national triumph. It was addressed to the children and in so doing to the family, which holds a central place in the Vietnamese culture. His letter to "My dear children," as translated by Jean Lacoutre and Peter Wiles, read in part as follows:

"Today is the mid-autumn festival. . . . You are rejoicing and your uncle Ho rejoices with you. Guess why? First, because I love you very much. Second, because last year, at this same mid-autumn festival, our country was still living under oppression and you, my children, were still little slaves, whereas this year Vietnam has won back its freedom and you have become the young masters of an independent nation. . . . Next mid-autumn festival, we shall organize parties both for the children and for the old. What do you think of that?"

15 **Myth** Myth is the favorite song of the Sirens. But what song do the Sirens sing? "They sang of all that is above fulfillment and beyond clear vision; of the innumerable, the uncontained, the half-imagined; of that which is touched but never held, implored but unpossessed," replied W. Compton Leith. "They sang of the vileness of all who live contented on alms, and are at ease in bond, the slaves whose servitude is made sweet by habit."

No power of major proportions can effectively be exercised over a prolonged period of time without an array of myths to sustain it. Regulations and laws themselves are largely the practical outcroppings of accepted myths. As long as the myths obtain, the prevailing regulations and laws will be obeyed, and their spokesmen will retain their dominance. But once there is widespread disaffection from the supporting beliefs, a reinterpretation of the regulations and laws will ensue, which might well lead to a collapse of the prevailing power establishment.

To be most effective the myths must be ingeniously framed, implanted, nurtured over long periods, and revered as elements of obvious truths. They must be adapted to the disposition of the followers, to the state of their maturity and their passions, hopes, and fears. They should directly provide moral justification for the extension of your power. There are many prototypes in the library. The Aztec rulers, for example, perpetrated the faith that the only two certain ways to paradise were dying in battle or having one's heart cut out while still alive in sacrifice on the altar of the gods by the priests.

The most important myth in sustaining the power of the propertied class in the West against the attacks of communistic ideologies is the sacred right of private property, divinely conferred. This concept has been championed by most proponents of natural law from Hugo Grotius to Immanuel Kant. Yet, as noted by Hans Kelsen, anthropological studies indicate that although the laws of primitive men accepted the superiority of magicoreligious forces to man's, the prohibition of homicide except in conventionally justified cases, the relative exclusiveness of marital rights, and the private possession of some goods, they rarely held land as an object of legal property. The Holy Scriptures had recorded God's gift to mankind in common but did not mention individuals as private owners. Nevertheless, the scholarly arguments on behalf of the principle of private property have been extensive and varied.

John Locke asserted that it is beyond the state power to take away a man's property without his consent. In his view the end of government itself is the preservation of property. In some instances the right of property supersedes even the right of life. The point is starkly clear in the context of military discipline. In this instance an absolute obedience to superior officers is required for the preservation of the army and the defense of the commonwealth. Therefore, "it is justly death to disobey or dispute the most dangerous or unreasonable of them; but yet we see that neither the sergeant, that could command a soldier to march up the mouth of a cannon or stand in a breach where he is almost sure to perish, can command that soldier to give him one penny of his money; nor the general, that can condemn him to death for deserting his post, or for disobeying the most desperate orders, can yet, with all his absolute power of life and death, dispose of one farthing of that soldier's estate or seize one jot of his goods, whom yet he can command anything, and hang for the least disobedience."

Should you hold great legitimate power in the West today, there is no more essential myth for you and your kind to keep reverently alive than just this sacred right of private property.

Much of the difficulty experienced by the American labor movement during its early days can be traced to its failure to modify this mythical foundation of the capitalistic way. The concept of private property and the tight control over it by the owners and managers had been a cornerstone of the free enterprise system. The employer's claim that labor's demand for a voice in the distribution of resources constituted an infringement of the basic rights of all Americans aroused substantial public sympathy, and the labor organizers were raked over as anarchists and communists. The necessary change in ideology had to be recognized formally before the tactical gains of the unions could be consolidated into a strategic victory. This was finally achieved through the enactment of the National Labor Relations Act of 1935, which guaranteed the right of collective bargaining. The act not only gave legal authority to the unions but considerably weakened the hold of the former myth of private ownership. It led to the inevitable erosion of the power of the propertied class and its transfer to the workers.

In a comparable analysis Harold Cruse concluded that the failure of the black power movement in the United States during the 1960s to gain mass support among the blacks themselves stemmed from its inability to tie its related actions to black culture. Attempts had been made to fill the void. Black consciousness and black history were advanced as part of the necessary beginnings of a black mythology. Even Christian theology was to be changed into black theology, the object of which was, in the words of James H. Cone, "to analyze the black . . . condition in the light of God's revelation in Jesus Christ with the sole purpose of creating a new understanding of black dignity among black people, and providing the necessary soul in that people to destroy white racism." The white man's myth in the New Testament was to be reinterpreted to serve the advancement of the black people. So far, these spasmodic sparks have lit no mythical fire.

Once you have hit on a very convincing myth for your purpose, you should stick with it for considerable time. Do not substitute a seemingly more appealing one to alleviate a temporary anxiety. Just because the opposition comes out with a new slogan does not mean that you should follow suit automatically. A radical modification may be considered if you are planning to move into a new line of activity. In that case, the transition should be as gradual as circumstances permit. You may begin with a stretching of the definition of terms in the old myth, then with an extending of the interpretation of its spirit, and finally with a modernizing to fit the prevailing social conditions.

In this connections Roser Reeves showed that the same advertising copy served most effectively for decades in the case of dental creams, despite great onslaughts from competitors. The same held for soaps, candies, cigarettes, drugs, and other products in his long experience in advertising. The expert concluded that (1) "Changing a story has the same effect as stopping the money, as far as penetration is concerned." (2) "Thus, if you run a brilliant campaign every year, but change it every year, your competitors can pass you with a campaign that is less brilliant—providing he does not change his copy." (3) "Unless a product becomes out-moded, a great campaign will not wear itself out."

At the same time, you should not hesitate to exploit the opposition's established myths if they should happen to fall in line with your plans. The rapidity with which Hernando Cortes conquered the Aztec world was due in part to the coincidence with a religious event, which had been ingrained in the Aztec mind long before his arrival. The major deity of the Aztec Indians living in the valley of Mexico at that time was Quetzalcoatl, the "plumed serpent." It was their article of faith that eons ago, when Quetzalcoatl left the earth by disappearing over the western horizon, he had promised to return by way of the east. The Spaniards had already psychologically conquered Emperor Montezuma, when they stepped ashore at Vera Cruz in 1519. There was no doubt in Montezuma's mind that Quetzalcoatl was back to reassume authority over his Toltec kingdom.

"There is always a ruling minority, but such minorities never stop at the brute fact of holding power," stated Gaetano Mosca in his political theory. "They justify their rule by theories or principles which are in turn based on beliefs of ethical systems which are accepted by those who are ruled. These 'political formulas' contain very little that could be described as 'truth,' but they should not be regarded as deliberate deceptions or mystifications on the part of scheming rulers. They express, rather, a deep need in human nature whereby the human being more readily defers to abstract universal principles than to the will of individual human beings."

These foundations of power are the practical fruits of flourishing myths.

16 **Efficiency**   Economy of effort results from optimizing various efficiencies. Pay close attention to three in particular.

The first is change efficiency, which is the ratio of the kinds and magnitudes of total change to those essential to your objectives. The forces at your command should not be allowed to get out of hand and

bring about more changes than planned, especially of the unanticipated varieties. At best, these entail a waste of resources. At worst,
they sow the seeds for damaging countermovements.

It is only rank amateurs who exhilarate with the noise and churn-
ing in the game of power; it is only the rank amateurs who get carried
away with their own obscenities and shocking nonconformities. Gaining control of an institution without perturbation is far more desirable
than leaving a trail of harsh feelings and divided management; carrying out a smooth *coup d'etat* is far more desirable than a bloody revolution.

The second kind of efficiency is resource efficiency, which is the
ratio of resources actually expended to that needed. Conserving resources is facilitated through more precise definition of objectives, better intelligence, more fitting strategy and tactics, fewer emotional ex-
peditions into ancillary paths of irrelevant glory, and, it goes without
saying, greater managerial skill. Typical of the cunning abracadab-
ras of persons of power for acquiring major gains from uninvested
resources is bouncing inferences off people's ambition and greed. A
presidential candidate thinks out loudly and the fund-raisers whisper
the confidential inside information into the potential contributor's ear
that he is being seriously considered for a top political post or that his
son-in-law is high on the list for a coveted judicial post. The target
individual then snaps at every call for assistance. The same message is
being whispered into the flapping ears of a dozen others at the same
time.

The third kind of efficiency is command efficiency, which reflects
the responsiveness of your subordinates to your directions. Command
responsiveness is quickened, among other things, by the appearance of
feasibility in the opinion of the action officer. You should not degrade it
by giving so many directives that your followers find them exhausting
or impossible of fulfillment.

Chester Barnard offered a fine piece of advice along this line.
"When it appears necessary to issue orders which are initially or apparently unacceptable," he suggested, "either careful preliminary education, or persuasive efforts, or the prior offering of effective inducements will be made so that the issue will not be raised, the denial of
authority will not occur, and orders will be obeyed. It is generally
recognized that those who least understand this fact—newly appointed
minor or 'first line' executives—are often guilty of 'disorganizing' their
groups for this reason, as do experienced executives who lose self-
control or become unbalanced by a delusion of power or for some other
reason."

In efforts to raise the overall efficiency of your workings, you should bear the duplex nature of your goal-set in mind at all times. One pole is your best performance as a member of the institution; the other is your best performance as a person of power. By and large most of the actions are identical for most of the time. But the dichotomy is very sharp under certain circumstances, and you should be very clear at such junctures. While a manager in an institution would not object too strongly against the abolishment of his unit, shown to be no longer necessary, for example, a manager of power will vigorously resist the proposal, insisting on alternatives, such as transferring responsibilities from other groups to his and consolidating his unit with another, with him in charge of both. While the former will volunteer cuts in his personnel strength on appeal from top management, the latter will not be as ready in giving up personnel, even those in excess of what is needed for his specifically assigned functions. These extra individuals constitute his active instruments for the acquisition of new territory and responsibilities through reconnaissance, emergency assistance to faltering programs in other jurisdictions, and beachheads in ill-defined areas.

The delicate balance between these two at-times conflicting interests should be maintained with such discretion that its existence is not overtly manifested. If you do not drain off sufficient resources from your institutional responsibilities for your growth in personal power, the latter will remain stagnant and fall behind that of your competitors as a consequence. If you drain off too much, then your operation itself will suffer, thereby endangering the very platform of your power. A continuing fine tuning is required throughout the duet of the executive and power tympani.

17 **Time constraints**   Be sure to crank four temporal factors into your projected course of action.

The first is the lapse of time required for the total transformation under consideration. Do not permit objectives that require decades and centuries to bring about to sap a significant portion of your emotions and energies. Should you be the head of a large cultural or political institution, such as churches and states, you should, of course, align your actions generally in the direction of its long-term values. But those parameters should not override your specific zigzagging after the immediate targets of personal power.

About 1000 years passed before monarchy and church domination in Russia was brought to an end. A hundred years were required for the completion of the last step, involving the rapid decline of the Romanovs from their peak in 1814 under Alexander I, when Russia was the greatest power in Europe, to the demise of Nicolas II at the hands of the Revolution in 1917.

The decentralization of power from the king to the barons in England took about 150 years from William the Conqueror in 1066 to the Magna Carta in 1215. The reverse process of centralization of power from the citizenry and the state governments to the federal government in the United States took the same order of time.

The first president of the American Federation of Labor showed an astute appreciation of the time required under various strategies to bear fruit. During the early days of the American labor movement there was considerable discussion among the leaders and socialists regarding the formation of a Labor Party to push for favorable labor legislation. This was rejected in 1906 by Samuel Gompers as being unprofitable. Under such a strategy, benefits would be delayed "until labor elects a majority of the legislature and a governor and then a President of the United States, who shall appoint the justices of the Supreme Court. I am afraid we're going to wait a long time! Trade unionists don't propose to wait so long to secure material improvement in their conditions." So said the father of the AFL, as he led labor down the political path of tipping the scales in favor of candidates and legislation matching its own interests, regardless of party.

The second time factor to be considered relates to the nature of the particular game itself. Is it to be played within a specified period, as in an election campaign? Or is it to be completed when a resolution is reached, as in a proxy fight for corporation control? In the former case, you should be ready to participate at a certain time, distribute your forces vis-a-vis the opposition, and implement your strategy to come out ahead at the final moment. In the latter case you should start the game when you are good and ready, your probability of success highest, and your opposition at his own greatest disadvantage. You should also be prepared to guard your own domain against incursions by the opposition at unpredictable times of his own choosing.

The third factor is the natural tendency of people to lose enthusiasm with time. If your power play lasts much beyond eighteen months, there is a sharply increased likelihood that your mass supporters will begin to falter, their values vacillate, and the overall momentum decline.

Of necessity, programs for organizations encompass much longer durations than those for an individual. The buildup of family fortunes, corporations, political parties, churches, and nations take many multiples of eighteen months for attainment. In your capacity as head of such organizations, you should divide the general programs into realizable increments of less than eighteen months each, so as to maintain synchronized focusing of the different contributions. Each of these, in turn, should be subdivided into tactical segments with recognizable beginnings and endings. At each milestone the coordinated posture of your team needs to be checked and the imbalances redressed. The complexities are to be sorted out, the misunderstandings untangled, and the plans for the next drive sharpened. You should be careful, however, that the momentum is not lost in the process by pausing longer than necessary. Your opposition should not be given any respite until he has given in. Yet you must also take pains not to exhaust your own men in so doing, so as to render them ineffective at the decisive closure.

The fourth factor is the moment of termination. It is important to develop an accurate sense of the appropriateness of a flexible or a rigid deadline for a given situation. A rigid deadline may not be appropriate for most confrontations, yet it often produces a striking effect on the resolve of a well-practiced team to meet it.

Sigmund Freud reported an account of a related experience with a rich, young Russian in a state of complete psychiatric helplessness. After several years of treatment, the patient regained much of his interest in life and social adjustment. "But then we came to a full stop. We made no progress in clearing up the childhood's neurosis, which was the basis of his later illness, and it was obvious that the patient found his present situation quite comfortable and did not take any step which would bring him any nearer to the end of his treatment. . . . In this predicament I resorted to the heroic remedy of fixing a date for the conclusion of the analysis." Freud then told his patient one day that the sessions would end precisely in a year. The patient recovered fully in a hurry.

Given an intuitive grasp of such temporal factors, events will not appear as puzzling and discouraging to you as they often do to others. You will have assimilated the essence of timely patience.

18 **Indices of progress** Keeping track of even relatively simple kinds of progress requires an array of measures. Business enterprises are typical.

The executive committee of one of the largest chemical companies, for example, maintained 350 management charts, which were reviewed several times a year. These were divided into twenty series.

Each department of the company was evaluated no less frequently than once every three months. The current year's performance was compared against the ten preceding years and the forecast of expectation for the succeeding twelve months. The central point of reference was return on investment. Next in importance was earnings as a percentage of sales, which indicated the efficiency of the operation. Third came the turnover, which indicated the intensity with which the capital was being worked.

No single index therefore should be adopted as the criterion of your progress. In many cases, the prime measure can be reduced to the number of conversions in the relevant population into your way of thinking and doing. If you are a politician it may be the number of voters supporting your slates; a businessman, the number of clients subscribing to your services; a scholar, the number of peers referencing your publications. Such attempts, however, may constitute reasonable measures of only your institutional performance and not your progress in personal power. A differentiating qualification is to be introduced to assess the latter. This is the number of people influenced in ways beyond the specific confines of your assigned functions, whether it be in technical scope or level of authority. The call of the American president in August 1977 to George F. Meany of the AFL-CIO labor federation for help in pushing Senate ratification of the Panama Canal Treaty is a high-level acknowledgment that Meany is not just a competent labor leader but a leading person of power. Furthermore, his ensuing actions in throwing all of the lobbying and other strengths of the unions into an extra-union battle is a clear statement that he indeed relishes being such a national figure.

Technical speaking, a decisive majority represents dominance. But this is reliable only insofar as it is not opposed by an organized, sizable, and militant minority. Qualitative factors of personal loyalty and confrontational spirit on the part of your followers, therefore, need to be taken into account as an equally important factor. It was this lack of a strong commitment, among other things, that doomed the continuity of the revolution of 1848 in Germany. The uprising went swiftly, bloodlessly, and successfully. But the liberals of the emergent Frankfurt Parliament simply did not have the dedicated perseverance that was necessary to modify the basic economic structure and policies of the Central European society.

The formulation of meaningful indices is fraught with conflicting difficulties and pitfalls. In the case of churches, for example, a direct estimate of the kind of moral and spiritual progress, which is what religion is presumably all about, would be the increase in goodness on the part of the communities in which they are influential. An index of goodness the man in the street would understand is the inverse of the relative number of crimes, of wars participated in, and of people denied the minimum biological necessities of life. But the leader of an aggressive religious institution of power would straightway recognize that the ensuing statistics might not demonstrate the superiority of his own church in influencing people to the good. Such a finding would be disastrously self-defeating. It would not be prudent for a churchman of power to broadcast this kind of unnecessary risks. If power is one of his main pursuits, then the prime public index of progress can only be the additional numbers of communicants. The increase in morality and spirituality can then be defined as membership in that body and adherence to its philosophy, rules, and values. In this way the theoretical construct can be made internally self-consistent. A continually positive slope of the membership curve as percentage of the world population would confirm his ascendancy in the struggle for power.

No matter how crudely fashioned, however, some system of continuing assessment should be maintained. The following four rules of thumb may be a starting indicator for your own qualitative appraisal from time to time: (1) If your peers and seniors are regularly seeking your advice and assistance within the confines of your institutional responsibilities, then you are doing well as a manager. (2) If they and other people are regularly seeking your advice and assistance involving the practical influence of human events beyond these confines, you are then doing well as a person of power. (3) If both (1) and (2) obtain, you are doing well in both. (4) If neither, then in neither.

19 **Levelheadedness**   As you progressively move into the big leagues of power, you should simultaneously sharpen your sense of the differences among turning panicky, remaining calm, and acting foolishly. The subtlety involved can be discerned in a passage from the letter sent from Portugal by the Duke of Wellington. The British government had written him about its apprehension over the safety of the army, as it watched the French building up a mighty attack from Spain. Whereupon Wellington confirmed his estimate of the situation in these words in 1810: "I understand that if there exists a military necessity for me to evacuate the country; which means that I am not to be frightened away by a show of force which I do not consider superior to my own. This means that I have to bring matters to desperation but not to extremities." When he was asked years later as to what constitutes the best test of a general, he replied, "To know when to retreat and how to do it."

Knowing when to quit is especially important for persons of relatively inferior talent and character who had suddenly been favored with circumstances of good fortune. If they have gauged the temper of the times well, they may enjoy a great reputation and even begin a distinguished lineage of powerful men and women. It often happens that in the ups and downs of organizations, a period of decline and deterioration occurs. Turmoil ensues. Inferior persons gain ascendancy. Superior persons retire from the scene. This is the time for the inferior talent's star to rise, by jumping into the opportunity with gusto. The sole objective should be short-gain gain. He or she should store away the maximum wealth, honors, and indebtedness attainable during the shortest period possible and retire before the resurgence of the deposed good men. In this way, such persons are able to present their children and grandchildren, who no longer have to worry about the origin of their springboard to power, an extremely advantageous start on the competitive stage, if they are so inclined. He or she can then glory in their legitimate career in power in his or her own old age.

Should you be a person of superior talent and character, you may wish to remember a common vulnerability in people of this kind. It is the fear of and disoriented reaction to being called a coward. They may stand impassive and collected in the face of vicious criticisms and vile abuses, hurled by fierce opponents and disgruntled constituents. But were they called cowards in public, their feathers would ruffle stiffened. This, of course, is exactly what the taunting competitors would like to see. They are much easier to pluck that way.

Do not therefore indulge in foolish bravados. One of the prevalent forms of misdirected courage is the chicken confrontation. The name is derived from the American slang "chicken," meaning coward. The game of chicken was popular during the 1950s and 1960s among some teenagers, crowded into an automobile speeding down a highway. At a certain point, the driver presses the accelerator to the floor and lets go of the steering wheel. The individual who is the first to lose his nerve and grab the steering wheel is called "chicken." The rest would then sit back, greatly pleased over their own proven bravery. Adults do not seem to have outgrown this trait, as we keep witnessing daily variations of the theme: I-bet-I'm-less-scared-than-you-are or I-bet-I-can-take-more-punishment-than-you-can.

Another variant of imprudence is unnecessarily taking on all challengers at all times. Unless there is no way out, you should avoid a direct all-or-none engagement with martyrs. People of the martyrdom complex act with the same degree of intensity, regardless of the worth of the objective under apparent contention. To the martyr, the issues involved are often only pretexts. The real goal is martyrdom. The martyr invites all the force the other party can apply, takes it, incites more, takes it all the more, incites still more, until the other party exhausts himself. There is also the possibility that a person who will sacrifice his own life for a cause will just as soon sacrifice yours. Try to rely on some other means for handling a martyr, if at all feasible, such as shunting him off on somebody else or diverting his attention to some side issue, which you can well afford to lose with dignity.

A more common temptation during the heat of argument with superiors is the threat to resign. There are times when matters of personal principle call for your resignation. In these cases you should by all means resign. But the threat to resign as an instrument of power is often nothing but blustering foolishness. The boss may very well accept your resignation, for he might have wanted to promote a protege of his own for some time. You might then lose your platform for power when you are least prepared. If he could not afford to do without your services for the time being, you can rest assured that he is beginning to plot your removal at an occasion of his own choosing in the very near future.

In general, you would do well to heed the words of Karl von Clausewitz: "As the expenditure of force becomes so great that the political object is no longer equal in value, this object must be given up." In any event, regardless whether you are winning, losing, or stalemating, you should disengage as expeditiously as you can, even at a reasonable loss, when you are bogged down to such an extent that you are compelled to repeatedly forego far more remunerative opportunities or when the cohesion and morale of your cadre are approaching the point of being sapped beyond recovery. Beware of blindly driving toward a premature victory under extreme stress by pouring everything you have into a gigantic final push. If you succeed, it may very well be your last.

20 Mortgage payments It ill suits persons of power to lose their poise when payments are due. For those with a charmed life, power comes free, like the emperors of old. For the rest, power comes with little price tags. If you lose, the payment may be high—in the game for less power, getting fired; for greater power, losing reputation; for greatest power, being assassinated. If you win, the payment may be relatively low—but never absent.

In battling for power, sooner or later you will meet up with opponents who are willing to forego honor to gain their objectives. In the words of one of William Shakespeare's players, "Honor pricks me on.

Yes, but how if honor pricks me off when I come on—how then? Can honor set to a leg? no: or an arm? no: what is honor? a word. What is in that word honor? sir. A trim reckoning! What hath it? he that died o' Wednesday. Doth he feel it? no. Doth he hear it? no. It is insensible, then? yes, to the dead. But will it not live with the living? no. Why? detraction will not suffer it. Therefore I'll none of it. Honor is mere scutchum. And so ends my catechism."

The minimum fee you should be willing to pay for entry into any major tournament of power, therefore, is personal integrity. It is easy, of course, to justify the compromises as being a sacrifice for the general good. But be that as it may, pay with inner honor you must if you are to get to the very top. Frederick the Great explained his views on the matter simply: "One sees oneself continuously in danger of being betrayed by one's allies, forsaken by one's friends, brought low by envy and jealousy; and ultimately one finds oneself obliged to choose between the terrible alternative of sacrificing one's people or one's word of honor." In this case, one's word of honor is to be given up, as he later stated the inviolable law of state power: "Rulers must always be guided by the interests of the state. They are slaves of their resources, the interest of the state is their law, and this law may not be infringed."

At the end of a long and hard strife, even the victors sometimes wonder whether the payments have been worth the anguish. A not too rare episode is exemplified by the proxy fight for Lowe's Incorporated, which produced Metro-Goldwyn-Mayer movies. The move to depose the Hollywood magnate, Louis B. Mayer, was a vicious affair. At the stormy meeting of the board of directors, Mayer was given control. The hard-driving opposition carried the clash into the courts. Just a few days before the stockholders' meeting, the judges voided the Mayer election. The path was clear to dump him. At this point the grand old man of the movies died.

Louis Niser, the legal counsel for the opposition, reflected in his memoirs about Mayer's death shortly after the jarring court decision. "Where his desire for revenge had been so neurotically intense, where his exuberance at victory, which he thought was certain, was touched with ecstasy, where the subsequent legal decisions struck him down as a director, throwing him out a second time from his company, and where these violent swings from complete triumph to despair had humiliated him and etched bitterness in his heart as if with acid, who can say what mysterious endocrinal effects his body suffered?" He then went on to relate how the new chief executive officer sent a resolution of profound sadness and sympathy of the board of directors to the widow and added: "At Lowe's, the bitterness of contest had given way to the reflection of the futility of the struggle and the finality of death."

The escalating payments for insatiable power brings to mind Honoré de Balzac's story of the young man with the magic skin. Any wish of his was fulfilled. However, with the granting of each, his skin shrank a little. He tried to stop the shrinking, but without success. Yet he could not resist satisfying one passion after another, until the fatal finale ended it all.

Every player hopes, of course, that the time of extremity never comes in his or her case. But should it ever come in yours, you should strive at least to match the homespun dignity of the old-time frontier horse thief. The following account of the swan song of George Shears in Montana Territory was given in 1866 by a newspaper editor, Thomas J. Dimsdale: When the vigilante caught up to him, he gave up without any argument. He then nonchalantly escorted his captors to the corral and identified the stolen horses. "When informed of his doom, he appeared perfectly satisfied. On being taken into the barn, where a rope was thrown over a beam, he was asked to walk up a ladder, to save trouble about procuring a drop. He at once complied, addressing his captors in the following unique phraseology, 'Gentlemen, I am not used to this business, never having been hung before. Shall I jump off or slide off?' Being told to jump off, he said, 'Allright; good by,' and leaped into the air with as much sang froid as if bathing. . . . George's parting question was, for a long time, a byword among the vigilantes."

21   **Treatment of cadre**   The talents essential within the members of your cadre to push you into greater power and keep you there are also the ones that can push others into your place. As to which direction they will turn from month to month depends on your ongoing relationship with them. It should maximize their contributions to your person, yet minimize their threat to your power.

Since people are more likely to help those from whom prior help had been received, you should make it a point to provide unsolicited assistance to individuals within your cadre on a regular basis. Maintain a reserve of funds and personnel vacancies which you can parcel out to someone struggling with some difficult task, failure in which would prove personally embarassing to him. Or suggest another member of your cadre to go over and offer help. This would also increase the spontaneous reciprocal interactions within your unit, thereby strengthening its teamwork immeasurably.

To derive the greatest value from the distribution of incentives and rewards, reference should always be made to performance and results.

The story of the Turk humorist of the fourteenth century, Nasreddin Hoca, is instructive in this respect.

During a visit to a strange village where he was unknown, Nasreddin Hoca went into a public bath. Observing that he was poorly dressed, the attendants paid him scant attention. He was issued a sleazy, torn, and dirty rag and given no help at all. As he left the place, Nasreddin Hoca gave a gold piece to each of the astonished attendants, who had been completely deceived by his humble attire.

The following week Nasreddin Hoca went to the same bath. But this time the attendants brought him new towels, fresh soap, and perfume. They scrubbed, washed, and massaged him, and carefully helped him dress—their palms tingling with anticipation of another gold coin. But on leaving this time, Nasreddin Hoca gave only a penny to each of them—much to their consternation and protest. To which he replied: "The gold pieces I gave you last week were for the manner you treated me today. The pennies I gave you today are for the manner you treated me last week."

Consideration should also be given to the effects of promptness in the recognition of contributions. The fastest learning in animal experiments occurs with rewards given immediately on the successful completion of a test. The longer the time delay in reinforcing a response, the slower will the animal learn. Of equal practical significance is the development of much greater persistence in the behavior of animals subjected to a variable schedule of partial rewards than of those subjected to a fixed schedule of full rewards of the same total amount and kind.

Of the various personalities, particular attention should be paid to those unique individuals who extend their spiritual selfs, as it were, through their leader. They deserve special treatment. In G. E. G. Catlin's words, "The devoted follower in the train of his leader, the affectionate friend, the weaker brethren, the submissive subjects, attain their purposes and are satisfied in the success of their hero; his glory is theirs, and through his will they prevail and become more fully persons."

Suitable accommodations should also be made for the zealot. Invariably he will be exceeding the bounds of good judgment and even the law on behalf of the leader and their cause. Should this happen in your organization, especially when he sacrifices himself in so doing, do not add to his misery. As leader, you should implicitly express your appreciation by assisting him in his troubles.

A good illustration arose during the United Automobile Workers' strike against the Kohler Company in 1954. Some of the strikers were arrested for violence, tried, convicted, and sentenced to jail. The union provided their legal defense and even continued their pay while serving out the prison terms. When questioned by a Congressional committee over the propriety of this subsidy to a lawbreaker who had broken a nonstriker's ribs and punctured his lungs, the president of the union replied: "I for not one second will defend what he did, because I think he was wrong. He was punished [by being jailed]. He should have been punished. Things that we did [were] to help his family. His family didn't make the mistake. I did not think they should have been punished." In one stroke, the chief managed to appear respectful of the law; human-hearted toward women, children, and dependents; appreciative of the support of his members; and reassuring to the rest that they, too, would not be abandoned should they ever get into trouble fighting for him.

These manifestations of loyalty and devotion to the welfare of your cadre will foster loyalty and devotion from them in return. But do not expect permanent loyalty and devotion from all of them. Within any group of talented individuals there are always persons of power panting to grow in power. Some of your most capable lieutenants probably fall into this category. They are important contributors to your machine. You should recognize them and promote them within your unit and, when the time comes, to higher positions elsewhere, where they can pose no threat to you and might even continue to be allies of yours.

The power distance between you and your subordinates should be kept distinctly evident, so that a kind of respectful fear of you is ever present. As a reinforcing reminder to the rest of your cadre, do not hesitate to abruptly dismiss someone who has attempted to close the power distance too much or to destroy the principles on which your power rests. This does not mean that you should go around, as many an insecure executive does, with a glowering mien hurling expletives at cowering aides. Be always courteous and even considerate. But do not socialize with your subordinates on too frequent a basis. Socialize with your peers and outsiders. Think twice about employing close friends and relatives as your direct subordinates; if they need jobs, help them get one in some other organization. The best way to make use of social and intimate friends is not as subordinates but as confidants on selected matters.

The injection of fear for ensuring the unity of an organization goes back to antiquity. Augustine himself advocated coercion and fear in preserving the unity of the church in persecuting the Donatists in the fifth century. Fear of punishment by the church was seen as the only effective means of countering the fear of the faithful of the fanatically heretical Donatists. They "have usurped the sacraments of the Church outside the Church and in hostility to the Church, and have fought against us in a kind of civil war." In their free choice of "a pernicious error," the Donatists were themselves the authors of their own suffering—so explained the learned saint. Not only was Augustine successful in his campaign of fear and persecution in eliminating the Donatists, he felt fully exhonerated.

The intensity of fear among your immediate cadre, however, should never be so great that it interferes with the performance of duties. It should be particularized against intentionally interfering with your own rise in power. An effective chief of state, for example, does not punish his field commanders for losing battles because of ill fortune or incompetence. The incompetent are transferred to make way for commanders who can win the next engagements, but the incompetent are not punished. Should the word of such treatment spread throughout the army, his commanders will be so distracted for fear of possible defeats that they will not be able to devote full attention to the immediate matter of fighting.

Letting a subordinate get away with currying favor with your opponent or even your peer at your expense, however, is suicidal in the game of power. The act should be viewed with much greater severity than a direct challenge. Wittingly or otherwise, he is forming a coalition against you. He must not only be dismissed, but dismissed in such a fashion as to discourage others from entertaining the notion. Even if he is forced back into your organization through legal means, he must be treated thereafter as an enemy within your midst, an anathema. He will soon leave on his own accord, because a humiliated person of power cannot bear being reminded of it.

An illustration of this kind is an industrial engineer in the United States Air Force in 1968. As a deputy for management systems at headquarters, he testified before the Congressional Joint Economic Committee's Sub-committee on Priorities and Economy in Government that inefficiency in the production of the giant C-5A transport aircraft had incurred a $2 billion overrun. He was applauded by the chairman of the subcommittee and the press for his honesty and courage. But he was immediately fired by the secretary of the Air Force. No similar incident occurred within the Air Force for at least a decade. The secretary himself was not hurt in any way. He was elected president of the National Academy of Engineering and was nominated by the United States President and confirmed by the Senate to head the newly created Energy Research and Development Administration.

The delegation of authority calls for considerations over and above the urgings in conventional textbooks on management. It is true that the more constraints you place on your subordinates, the less initiatives will they take. The less initiatives they take on their own, the more overladen will you be, the greater the chances of your landing in the hospital from overwork, and the sooner your failure to produce in the eyes of your own boss. No sizable organization can function well without considerable decentralization of both responsibilities and authority. Yet this can be carried too far.

"Never ennoble anyone in such a way that he may molest you," cautioned Han Tzu. "Never trust anybody so exclusively that you lose the capitol and the state to him."

Since you are concerned both with your organization's progress and your growth in personal power, you should pay close heed to matters that do not usually cross the minds of those who are only pursuing the former objective. The differences are often a matter of degree rather than qualitative distinctions. But the shadings can be critical. The following represent four situational examples.

The first involves the necessity to make sure that the recipients of your transferred power are susceptible to your continued overall influence and are compatible to your natural skill and pattern of operation. Failure to take appropriate cognizance of this safeguard led to the resignation of Giovanni Giolitti as prime minister of Italy in 1913, at what appeared to be the peak of his political strength. He had been undisputed leader for over a decade, pushing through an impressive liberal program of improving working conditions for the laboring class, abolishing child labor, establishing sickness and retirement insurance, and reducing taxes on the poor. He was able to do this largely because of his great ability in the manipulation of personalities rather than political parties, the backstage deals of promised favors for the votes of the deputies. Giolitti used the *trasformismo* with great finesse; against strong opposition, he pushed the capstone of his liberal program—the extension of suffrage to the working people. His secure grip on Italian politics was never more impressively demonstrated. But when the 1913 elections were held with the participation of millions of new voters, Giolitti's methods of controlling notables no longer worked for the masses. Radical deputies were elected, who refused to play the game of *trasformismo* in the chamber. Protests against his secret manipulations rose. Seeing he could no longer command the votes, Giolitti had to step aside.

The second involves the managerial application of the golden section. There often arises a time when you are forced to decentralize authority to an ambitious subordinate of power in order to get a job done. The dilemma at hand is to make sure that he is given sufficient authority to accomplish what you desire, yet not too free-wheeling an authority for overflowing his boundaries. A workable guide to judicious counterbalancing is the golden section. The golden section is that point on a line which divides it, so that the smaller section is to the larger section as the larger section is to the whole line. This turns out to be 0.38 to 0.62. When weight is distributed in accordance with this golden section, the minority exerts a significant input to the joint decision. At the same time, the majority retains sufficient weight to assume leadership but without being able to squelch the opposition. If the cunning, vigor, and technical ability of the project leader is much superior than those of the junior collaborator, you should then divide the decentralized authority between them closer to the ratio of 0.43 to 0.57. If they are much weaker, you might change it in the opposite direction like 0.33 to 0.67. In general, the ratio should not fall below 0.25 to 0.75 nor above 0.45 to 0.55.

The third involves the transformation of an individual struggle for power into a class struggle. In dealing with subordinates challenging your decision, you should be aware when the basis of the game is being changed and adjust your reactions accordingly. A clever subordinate does not hesitate to take advantage of transforming the battle for power from the corporate arena of person-to-person contests, should he or she be losing, to the societal arena of class-to-class conflicts, or still better, of class-to-person indictments. This is in part what is happening when wily and otherwise incompetent and lazy subordinates accuse you of racism, sexism, or religious bigotry. They are calling on the class of race, sex, or religion to stamp you out as an individual enemy. You are no longer fighting the person as an employee, with your corporate top management as judge. You are fighting such persons as representatives of a class, with the rest of the class as judges. Other things being equal, a single individual has little chance bucking a class of people. Those days are long gone. If you yourself had been duly chosen as representative of a class, you might then ride forth to combat the class enemy. But since you have not been so appointed, you have only two alternatives. One is to always so conduct yourself in your corporate life so that when accused, the relevant class will repudiate one of its own members and proclaim its confidence in you. If, however, the situation is such that every move on your part for strengthening your power ends up as a class struggle against you as an individual, you should continue your growth in power in another setting.

The fourth involves your immediate deputy. A clearly designated second-in-command always carries a germ of danger to your continued power. If personally ambitious, the deputy might well make a move against you. Even if not so inclined, such persons might be used by your opponents, who might rally around him or her. This is one of the reasons why the Manchu emperors of earlier centuries never named a crown prince until on their deathbed. There are two practical avenues toward minimizing this potential threat. One is to arrange your immediate team that your authority is decentralized more or less equally to an echelon of at least six individuals. Do not leave an impression that any one of them is "more equal" than the rest. The other protective device is to maintain a base of support independent of this group. This can be done either by your ability to vault over them for personal appeal to their followers or through a completely separate channel. The latter avenue was followed triumphantly by Juan Peron in 1945. As a colonel in the military government, he was given the lowly post of minister of labor. When his fellow officers became apprehensive of his growing power, they had him arrested and thrown into prison. In the meantime, Peron had nurtured a close personal alliance with the *descamisados*, the "shirtless ones" of the laboring masses. They rose in defense of Peron. The junta had to back down for fear of civil war and released him. He became the undisputed strong man of Argentina after that.

22 **Constituency**   In order that your constituency will stand firm in their support of you, three requirements must be met. First, that they feel you are one of them; at the very least, your heart is with them. Second, that they remain satisfied with your services to them. Third, that no more than a scattered few among them harbor any hatred toward you.

The first condition begins with an admission into the community by some concrete act of identity, a continuing symbol that you remain its kind and endures through constant touch with its changing thinking. One of the initial things a revolutionary trying to organize the poor must do to gain acceptance, for example, is to be labeled a threat by the establishment. A model of an effective continuing symbol of solidarity between the leadership and its constituency is found in the Electrical, Radio and Machine Workers of America. The head of the powerful union, which forced General Electric Company to capitulate after a 101-day strike in the winter of 1969–1970, receives no more pay than the highest weekly salary earned by top electricians.

A vigorous proponent of the second approach was the former head of the International Ladies Garment Workers, David Dubinsky. He not only delivered consistently improved wages, fringe benefits, and working conditions to the union members, but also built cooperative housing, health centers, and vacation resorts.

Ward politicians are particularly attentive to their charges when it comes to personal services. D. H. Kurtzman quotes a Philadelphia political boss as follows: "In every precinct of the city there are two representatives of the Organization, elected directly at the Republican primaries and who are known as committeemen. They maintain contacts with the voters and are at their beck and call for 24 hours of each day of the year. In time of stress the poor or other unfortunates always turn to these Organization representatives to assist them. It is they who see that the sick are cared for and that the poor are provided for, and that even in death aid may be rendered. The Philadelphia Organization gives a real social service and one without red tape, and without class, religious, or color distinction."

No matter how firmly entrenched a person may think he or she is, there is no escape from this requirement of minimum satisfaction to the constituents. This was dramatically shown in the sudden switch of national leadership in Poland just before Christmas in 1970. Joseph Cyrankiewicz, the premier since 1947, and Wladyslaw Gomulka, the long-time Communist Party boss, were abruptly dumped following only a week of relatively small street riots in a few towns over increases in food prices and generally unsatisfactory economic conditions.

You must therefore be willing to be held accountable in the rendering of services. This does not mean that you have relinquished your power. But it does mean a recognition on your part that unless you pass that basic hurdle, your tenure in power will become progressively more difficult. A labor leader must be accountable to the rank and file in terms of actual dollars and cents in wages; given such accountability, one can deal in strong-arm tactics with relative impunity. A business leader must be accountable to the stockholders in certified financial records of profits; given such accountability, one can pay oneself a million dollars in stock options and salaries and dabble in international politics with relative impunity. A church leader must be accountable to the communicants in effective consolation on occasions of guilt and sorrow and enlargement of their numbers; given such accountability, one can intrigue with rulers with relative impunity. A president of a democracy must be accountable to the voters in the fairly high level of social benefits and security from military threats; given such accountability, one can appoint one's cronies to high positions and send a million citizens to war with relative impunity.

Even if you are accepted as one of their kind by the majority of your constituents and even if they are quite satisfied with the services, your conduct must be such as never to incur excessive hatred. There will always be a certain amount of misunderstandings, disagreements, and disordered personality traits that will engender some animosity toward you. But you should not inflame this necrosis of hatred to a menacing virulence, wilfully or otherwise. Do not get into the bad habit of poison-dripping and picadillo-throwing. Under the guise of telling a truth, but in effect jabbing a barb into someone's reputation; under the guise of telling a joke, but in effect taking a dig at someone's expense—these are the ill humors of small men. Do not stand unconcernedly by as some constituent of yours is being unjustifiably stripped of his possessions. Even the loss of loved ones is more readily forgotten by most people than the loss of their property. Never blatantly wrong your people. The tyrant of Syracuse, Dionysius the Elder, was emphatic on this point of not incurring hatred, as he instructed his son in the art of kingship. He admonished the young man severely one day for running off with a citizen's wife. When the son argued that he was born the son of a king, Dionysius replied sharply that unless he changed his ways forthwith, *"your* sons will never be born kings."

HONING STRATEGIES
AND TACTICS

Having surveyed the general requirements for a promising career of power, we now proceed into the specific techniques which are to be refined. The most important overall strategies and tactics are surveyed in this section and are given more explicit treatment in subsequent sections. What moves are common to all power struggles? What adaptations are called for in trying to seize power from others? in trying to hang on to what you have? How do you deal with those slipping into the ranks and eroding your power from within? those buried in the formal woodwork on whom you must nonetheless depend to get the work done? those current supporters of yours who would just as soon switch over to the opposition? And your present allies? What can you learn from those whom you cannot dominate?

23 **The eight axioms** In shaping your strategies and tactics, do not confuse the platform for power with the levers. Platforms are broad and strategic; levers are pointed and tactical. Each platform is the springboard for many options; each lever is the commitment to a specific act. Many people spend much energy building up the platform, such as social status, financial base, and entrees into high places, but do not know how to exploit an opportunity when it does arise or bring about a profitable closure. In contrast, many others keep poking lever after lever into the competitive stone wall without first gaining the necessary fulcrum of a suitable platform. Both types always end up exhausted losers.

The following eight axioms constitute a reasonably sound framework for the formulation of overall strategies and tactics: (1) Adjust the objective to the resources, expending neither more for an intermediary target than it is worth in its contribution to the ultimate objective nor less than is needed to gain it. (2) Keep the objective always in sight, ensuring a clear line of attack without ending in a cul de sac. (3) Shape the operations so as to allow alternative tactical targets, thereby placing the opposition on the horns of a dilemma. (4)

Exploit the line of least resistance, always pointing in the direction of final objectives. (5) Pursue the course of least expectation on the part of the opposition, deceiving and beguiling to widen his miscalculations. (6) Maintain a flexible posture, responding to exigencies of the unexpected. (7) Refrain from repeating a line of attack that has just failed, recognizing that the opposition had in all probability reinforced themselves in the interim. (8) Dislocate the opposition—upsetting their strategic balance and disjointing their psychological reserve with goading lures and traps—before striking the decisive blow.

These eight axioms had been found operative in all of the victorious encounters in warfare by B. H. Liddell Hart, based on his analyses of the battles and wars over the last 2500 years. The same general stratagems of power apply over a broad spectrum of contests far beyond the battlefield. An illustration of the applicability of the same eight axioms and others in the commercial theater is the carefully planned and well-executed takeover of the United Fruit Company in 1969 by the AMK Corporation. As pieced together by Stanley H. Brown, the sequence of events is presented below, to which are added the approximately applicable combat axioms in parentheses.

In 1968 the banana empire of United Fruit, with $100 million cash, no funded debt, borrowing potential of $300 million, and annual sales of $500 million, looked highly attractive to the AMK Corporation. Quietly AMK went about formulating the strategy and carrying it out. Its goal was clear—the acquisition of United Fruit (Axiom 2).

Having recently taken over the asset-rich John Morrell and Company, grossing $800 million annually, AMK had the financial muscle to undertake the campaign (Axiom 1). It engaged the services of Donaldson, Lufkin and Jenrette, the stock exchange firm, which, among other things, knew where the stocks of United Fruit were held (Intelligence). With a $35 million loan from Morgan Guaranty Trust Company and the brokerage services of Donaldson, AMK was able to purchase about 10 percent of the United Fruit shares at $4 above the market price at $52 per share. This was done before anyone suspected what was happening (Speed). By restricting its block to less than 10 percent, AMK was not required to report its trade as an insider to the Securities and Exchange Commission (Secrecy). Furthermore, AMK could take short-term profits in the event it chooses not to go through with the merger. The chief executive officer, Eli M. Black, estimated the situation as follows: "We felt that the purchase had to be sound in its own right. If nothing more happened this has to make sense. We felt it did. The stock purchased was thirteen times earnings, and the company balance sheet was extremely conservative. So our risk on the downside was very limited. Even if nothing further happened, we would probably end up by selling it at a substantial profit." (Axioms 3 and 6).

Before long, AMK's strategic posture stood thusly: With about 10 percent of the shares in its hands and another 10 percent from Donaldson sources being fairly assured, AMK could enter tender competition having to obtain only 30 percent more shares as compared to the opposition's having to obtain 50 percent (Estimate of the situation).

Black sprung his lure and trap with the chief executive officer of United Fruit caught unawares and in a way he least expected (Axiom 5). John M. Fox of United Fruit was telephoned by William Donaldson, and later by officials of Morgan Guaranty and Goldman Sachs, who told him that they would like him to meet a new stockholder, a nice fellow, but refused to mention the gentleman's name. He was kept in suspense, not knowing what was coming up next. Finally, Black phoned, introduced himself, and invited Fox to dinner that evening. At dinner Black stated that he saw much to gain from a merger of the two companies, but he would not want to make a move without Fox's agreement (Psychological predisposition).

Fox said, "No, thanks," and went about trying to find his own partners to fight off the attack. After several attempts, Fox was unable to regain his strategic balance. Black had dislocated his holdings (Axiom 8). One by one—Dillingham Corporation, Textron, Zapata Norness Incorporated—fell by the wayside. Finally, Fox admitted that the Black strategy had been so well planned that he had to capitulate: "Black had been saying right along that others would drop out, and he was right. I finally came around to his view that our companies could do well together." With psychological advantage from the outset, Black had not only exploited the line of least resistance (Axiom 4) but of certain success (Axiom 7 not needed). The two firms merged, with Fox as vice chairman of the board. Stockholders tendering stock to AMK exchanged shares earning $1.40 during the previous year for debentures paying $2.09 (Rapid return to normalcy).

24   **Offense**   Although the general principles for a powerful offensive are the same over a wide range of activities, the tactics vary greatly from situation to situation. Do not mount a grab for new responsibilities, authority, or territory without a clear picture of the specific tactics required for the expressed context of your operations.

Competing within a corporation at midmanagement entails a different repertory from that between corporations, in turn between churches, and again between nations. You can win or lose, depending on tactical mistakes as well as strategic blunders. The greater the power at stake, the more important are strategic considerations over the tactical. But neither can be slighted at any time.

Three representative offensive operations are discussed below. These are: (1) junior executive in a corporation, (2) head of an ideological movement, and (3) an insurgent leader.

If you are a junior executive contemplating an expansion of your scope of activities within a corporation, you should first consider whether you have a legitimate claim to the function currently under the jurisdiction of someone else, which you are eying. If it can be interpreted as being covered by your own job sheet and not by his, you have a legitimate claim. Before you move frontally by asking the boss to transfer the area to your cognizance, however, you should first gauge your competitive strength specifically pertinent to the issue at stake. If your own performance over the past year or two has been excellent and his rather poor, you might consider forging ahead with your claim. However, if the reverse is true, then the first order of the day is for you to improve your own record and wait until he falters.

On the other hand, if the area coveted by you does not fall within your job description, but lies at the periphery just outside of it, do not initiate activities duplicating or directly pointing at it. This would raise the issue at a time when the cards are in his favor. You will lose in a show-down, which will foreclose future chances of your taking it over. Instead, you should be satisfied at the beginning with a presence, exerting a loose influence in the area, as a collaborator on a project within his responsibility.

Do not be stingy about assigning your personnel as junior partners to his team in the area. It is important that you develop skills within your subordinates that can contribute significantly to projects within other jurisdictions. If these experts are essential within both your own sphere and others', they will serve as extensions of your influence within the corporation. Since they belong to you and not to the other parties, you are exercising a reconnoitering and presence in their domain and not vice versa. In this way, you can come to identify certain gaps in no-man's land. You can then assign your own men to start work along some of these ill-assigned and ill-defined functions, as phase one of enveloping the area to be under contention.

Once you have performed well in these isolated tasks in the eyes of your common boss, you should then begin phase two. This is the linking of the islands into a coherent project, which is tied directly to the core of your own job description. By so doing, you have essentially enveloped the area. At the appropriate time, you might move forward to close the pincers and consolidate your acquisition by asking for a formal transfer.

As you consolidate your acquisitions and determine your future plans for growth within the corporation, you should distinguish between the magnitude and the territory of your responsibilities. The former simply represents the total collection of various functions assigned to you. Some functions, such as ancillary services, may not be naturally related to each other, or even to the corporation's long-term interest. Therefore, the magnitude of your assigned functions or personnel is not a reliable measure of your potential power. To consolidate real corporate power, you should think of a territory of responsibility. Territories have boundaries, through which others cannot penetrate without being tagged as an invader. What should command top priority in your plans and operations is to connect your disconnected functions into a territory, formalize your assigned authority over that territory, and intensify your control within it. At the same time, as has been discussed in Section 9, you should select territories that are part and parcel of the central operations of the corporation, such as sales in a perfume company and loans in a bank. Rather be promoted to a line manager of a profit center than a higher-paid staff officer in charge of administration.

While skirmishing within the corporation, do not damage your competitor or his job security, if at all possible. Do not let the contention degenerate to a personal level. This is a diversion of your attention and energy. Keep your intentions to yourself, favoring the more flexible envelopment over the readily blunted thrust. Do not move for official blessing too early. It is better to leave some things unsettled than to lose them definitely. And let patience be ever on your side.

If you are the head of an alien ideological institution intent on dominating a country of people, you must place great emphasis on attacking and modifying the basic tradition on which they have been brought up.

A Catholic hierarchy in an America, which started with the Protestant notion of a clean separation of church and state, for example, must break it down by first suggesting a cooperation between church and state and then occasionally injecting, with progressively greater insistence, that states are subordinate to God. As the Jesuit John C. Murray puts it, the "first article of the American political faith is that the political community, as a form of free and ordered human life, looks to the sovereignty of God as the first principle of its organization." This God is not that of the Hindus with their spokesmen, of course, nor that of Islam with still other spokesmen, nor that of the thousand and one others, but only that of the Jesuits represented solely by their Pope. The former essentially white Protestant culture indigenously matured is to be transformed into an essentially aracial Catholic culture styled by the Vatican.

Conversely, a Communist Party moving into an Italy, which had been living as a Catholic-dominated culture for 1000 years, must snap this linkage by first suggesting that the relation between God and an individual is strictly a private affair and that God is omniscient enough to speak to each person directly without a middleman, who is no different from the millions of other middlemen throughout history who have exploited others through false pretense. Furthermore, the God of everybody is good and wants the workers and the poor to live well, not just members of the church hierarchy and wealthy laymen. The Communist Party would then insidiously, without explicitly mentioning it, fan the thought among the Italian people that in standing up for the poor man's right and happiness, the party in real fact and not the church and her supporters is implementing the living God's desires on earth. The traditional Catholic culture long shaped by Italian popes and curias is to be transformed into a non-Catholic one with non-Italian Marx-Lenin stripes.

But should your ideological movement not have the financial and other encouragement from a powerful center, like Rome and Moscow, you would then have to proceed much less noticeably. One example is the way in which W. D. Farad Muhammed began his religious sect in Detroit in 1930. As related by a convert, "He came first to our home selling raincoats, and afterwards silks. In this way he could get into people's houses. . . . If we asked him to eat with us, he would eat whatever we had on the table, but after the meal he began to talk."

It was through these sessions that Muhammed initially spread the doctrine that the white man had tricked the black man about the true god, who is actually Allah and not the Christian God, who is a devil. The devil was created by the mad scientist Yakub on the Island of Patmos. Allah had allowed the devil to rule for a set period of time, which has now elapsed. The black man should rise up to assume his rightful place. Muhammed indoctrinated his followers well in the quiet of their intimate conversations. This is how the Black Muslims apparently got started in America.

If you are an insurgent trying to throw out the entrenched authorities, do not commit the common tactical mistake of rebels. Their overeagerness for action dooms their efforts from the very beginning in many instances. They are too wild-eyed to persist through the prolonged effort needed to spread the necessary degree of uncertainty and incipient paralysis of the will to resist on the part of the established power. Unless you have managed to lay the revolutionary groundwork, win the relevant constituents over to your side, and jockey the opposition into an untenable position, do not even think of openly throwing your main body into an offensive shock action. If you do, you will certainly be defeated. Instead, pay close attention to the advice of Ignatius of Loyola, who instructed his disciples to act like "good fishers of souls passing over many things in silence as though these had not been observed, until the time came when the will was gained, and the character could be directed as they thought best."

Once the opposition has been deposed, you must take safeguards not to give him a chance to return to power. Roman history provides many examples. The most striking is that of Marcus Brutus. After he had restored liberty to Rome through the assassination of Julius Caesar, he took drastic actions to eliminate all obstructions to the new order. He not only sat in judgment at the trial of his own son and condemned him, but also watched the execution.

A more recent example of thorough large-scale political mopping up is that conducted by the Communists in China against the former landlords and capitalists. "If they talk and act wildly their [action] will be prohibited and punished immediately. The democratic system is to be carried out within the ranks of the people [working class, peasant class, petty bourgeoisie, and national bourgeoisie], giving them freedom of speech, assembly, and association. The right to vote is given only to the people and not to the reactionaries. These two aspects, namely, democracy among the people and dictatorship over the reactionaries, combine to form the people's democratic dictatorship." Thus instructed Mao Tse-tung on the eve of his revolutionary conquest of mainland China in 1949.

25 **Defense** In a defensive role, you cannot pick the time and place of engagement. Even if you wish to avoid a confrontation, you cannot succeed if your opponent is intent on it. You must therefore be prepared at all times for the worst, like the Oriental King Mithridates. His precautionary stance has been poetically described by A. E.

Housman in *A Shropshire Lad*. He gathered all kinds of poisons and took them in increasing amounts until he became immune.

> They poured strychnine in his cup
> And shook to see him drink it up;
> They shook, they stared, as white's their shirt:
> Them it was their poison hurt.
> —I tell the tale that I heard told.
> Mithridates, he died old.

To guard against the creation of vulnerable openings in the defense of sizable power, the following measures are minimal: (1) know the overall context of your power and the ensuing strategic consideration in its basic and interrelated facets, (2) establish a system of deterrence embedded in the tailored laws and rules, (3) manifest a system of deterrence backed by the power to punish, (4) continue the process of assimilating incipient oppositions, and (5) defuse trouble spots and attack when necessary. A brief discussion of these points follows in order.

Persons at the higher rungs of institutions recognize that free people are much more difficult to dominate than dependent people. If you belong to the ruling body, your greatest strategic defense against deterioration of your continued power over people is to maintain their dependence on you and the institutions you control. The crux of the battle for power is just this issue: on whom are the constituents or masses to be dependent?

To maximize their dominance, members of the ruling industrial and banking elite must, wittingly or unwittingly, prevent the people's relative level of wealth from ever enabling them to attain all their desires, without further parceling from them. This can be done by maintaining welfare payments to nonworkers and minimum wages to workers at the barest minimum to keep body and soul together. They must keep the working class aways reaching for a style of living that makes the prevailing level of income grossly inadequate. This can be done by an educational system that reinforces the more expensive tastes and accoutrements of social status and an advertising campaign that extols luxuries. They should discourage the concepts of contentment and simple living from taking hold in the general population. As a large segment begins to accumulate financial reserves so as to reduce their dependency on them, they should welcome compensatory happenstances, such as inflation rising at, say, 8 to 10 percent per annum with an official interest on their savings limited to a maximum of 5 to 8 percent, accompanied by a 40 percent tax for the upper middle class. This will gradually shrink their savings at a rate they will tolerate, yet keep them in financial dependence on those from whom their continued income flows.

To maximize their dominance, members of the ruling religious elite throughout the world must, wittingly or unwittingly, inculcate the firm belief that unless the people follow their guidance, the chances of getting to heaven is rather low. Furthermore, they should strengthen a set of relationships in which they are progressively essential to the people's spiritual well-being at birth, wedding, guilt-laden moments, sorrow, death, and other critical periods. The greatest enemy against whom they must guard is not the atheist or even a competing church, but the sincere believer who speaks directly to God without need of any church. They should not let this heresy, more than any other, spread at a faster rate than their own rate of expansion. An almost equally cancerous enemy is the voluble agnostic in these days of widespread college education. To neutralize infiltration by the likes of him, disputants should be maintained as skillful in the use of modern logic, as in the appeals to the old-fashioned faith.

To maximize their dominance, members of the ruling labor elite must create conditions so that significant numbers of workers can get major raises or jobs only through their direct intervention within their area of concern. Furthermore, they must maintain lively communications to make sure that even the most ignorant among their constituents know it. Even if they do believe in individual freedom, they should not be so carried away as to make the slightest accommodation if they can help it to the open-shop or freedom-to-work principles that are being mouthed by the opposition from time to time.

As far as a supportive system of enforceable laws, rules, and/or regulations are concerned, continuing adaptations are required to keep them up to date with the tenor of the times. The prescriptions are not only elaborations and justifications for the dominating sector to which you belong, but also accredited norms and reconciling mechanisms binding on future parties in conflict. A special kind of respect is to be inculcated for your set of institutional regulations.

The strongest institutional discipline, according to Robert Merton, occurs when the sentiments are transferred "from the *aims* of the organization onto the particular details of behavior required by the rules. Adherence to the rules, originally conceived as a means, becomes transformed into an end-in-itself; there occurs the familiar process of *displacement* whereby 'an instrumental value becomes a terminal value.' Discipline, readily interpreted as conformance with regulations, whatever the situation, is seen not as a measure designed for specific purposes but becomes an immediate value in the life-organization of the bureaucrat." Individuals so indoctrinated can be relied on as the innumerable little gears of a smoothly operating power machinery. Their face-to-face association and cooperation form the spirit of the organization. Their identities are fused into a "we." Each member finds his or her own will and wishes in that feeling of "our" will and wishes.

Yet do not place too much reliance on laws and cleverness to protect your position. In *The Mind and Society*, Vilfredo Pareto cautioned that the overreliance of constitutional governments on diplomatic skills and cunning to the detriment of strong military forces often resulted in upsetting the balance of power, thereby precipitating wars and revolutions. You should always retain your capacity to inflict harm, which is obvious to both subordinates and potential oppositions.

A consistency should be maintained in the level of coerciveness over members of your cadre in particular. It has been observed that when the level of political coerciveness on the citizenry of a country fluctuates, the amount of political violence usually increases.

There often comes a time when the only alternative to complete breakdown is to share a small portion of your power with a disgruntled minority. This should be accompanied with a delicate but effective program of assimilation. To ensure that you are not letting the camel's nose into the tent, you should first neutralize or isolate the most militant, who are trying to foment mass action, then bring the more moderate leaders, one after an assimilated one, into your higher councils, while incorporating his followers into your own constituency at large. If the allegiance of their former constituencies is not transferred, however, the invited leaders will continue to be autonomous of your control with their own power base, resulting in the increased danger of potentially challenging you on your own turf.

This achievement is not easy, and partial success is often the best that can be expected. Any experienced person of power can see through the scheme. A Communist leader joining an Italian coalition government in the late twentieth century, for example, will certainly not transfer his personal following to anyone else. In his book *Fascism,* Renzo De Felice described such a miscalculation on the part of the Italian ruling classes when they took in Benito Mussolini in 1922 and constitutionalized fascism. But the political followers supporting Mussolini were not assimilated into the policies and attitudes of the ruling classes. Within ten years, his party had taken over all power in Italy except that of the crown, the army, and the judiciary.

Yet sharing power, followed by assimilation and/or cooptation, has frequently worked. An example of assimilation is the decision of Charles the Simple of France during the tenth century. The invincible Viking bands were marauding the coastal areas without letup. So Charles made one of the most powerful of them, Hrolfr, the first Duke of Normandy, to rule over the Northmen, who actually held the area anyway. The Norwegian-Dane chieftan defended the king thereafter from further attacks by other Vikings.

A modern case of cooptation is the Soviet government in the twentieth century. In the years immediately following the revolution, the scientific and other specialized experts were kept outside the ruling bodies. When it dawned on the Soviet political leaders that the latter, whose high achievements were essential for catching up with the industrialized West, would not be satisfied in a subservient role, they decided to share power through cooptation. The specialized elites were taken directly into their mid- and top-management. By 1952 they were accorded 26 percent of the representation in the Central Committee and in 1961, 44 percent. After 1960 the scientific and intellectual insiders were very prominent in replying to criticisms of dissidents against the Soviet government.

Because of the implications of such a strategy, the assimilation of the black race into the American hybrid would constitute a disconcertingly nebulous problem for a black leader in the United States today. Should the goal of black power advocates be a separate state with preservation of the American strain of the black race as a Lost-Found Nation of Islam? Should it be the status of full integration and identity with all Americans, in effect, dissolving the issue of black power by the disappearance of blackness? Or should it be a wait-and-see stance, as been voiced by John Killens, when he said: "Integration comes after liberation. A slave cannot integrate with his master. In the whole history of revolts and revolutions, integration has never been the main slogan of the revolution. The oppressed fights to free himself from his oppressor, not to integrate with him. Integration is the step after freedom when the freedman makes up his mind as to whether he wishes to integrate with his former master."

When viewed strictly from the standpoint of long-term national power, however, continued segregation would be disastrous. The longer the delay, the greater will be the difficulty of assimilating a genetically dominant black minority which is increasing at a faster rate in population than the average. Were the blacks to acquiesce to segregation, they would naturally begin to congregate and, unless liberty is suspended entirely for everyone, would migrate into those cities and states with greater tolerance and economic generosity. The 1970 census showed that of the cities over 200,000 in population, Washington, Atlanta, and Newark consisted of over 50 percent black. Those with a third to a half included Chicago, Philadelphia, Detroit, Baltimore, Cleveland, New Orleans, and St. Louis. If the present differential segregation and differential rates of population increases continue, United States will be confronted with a de facto internal split into two citizenries within several generations.

Regardless on what party platform the president of the United States runs for office and regardless of his personal ethical standards, the considerations of national power alone will drive him to push integration as rapidly as his political supporters will permit. He must ensure that the rate of integration will not fall below that necessary to prevent the formation of a stable and expanding solid black community with its own distinctly black leaders in the country. Quite apart from constitutional guarantees, private feelings of many of the white segregationalists and black nationalists, and considerations of humanitarian values, he as a president of power will instinctively bow to the inescapable realistic demands of unity and national survival. The Civil Rights movement of the minority blacks of the 1960s for greater opportunities is now becoming a movement of the majority whites of the 1990s for the preservation of their union.

Should you belong to an established power with large reserves, you should recognize that the most dangerous opposition comes not from the lowest but from middle-class leaders. A certain number are always out to take on the establishment. You can never eliminate their defiance. Not all these protests are of the same order of danger, however, despite the sound and fury of their outcries. Some of them might even be advantageous to you. You should not attempt to suppress all antimovements willy-nilly.

The environmental and consumer interest movements, for example, for the large part, are not without benefit to the maintenance of the establishment. These are basically movements on behalf of the upper- and middle-class interests. Only those who have enough to eat and sleep can afford to think about the quality of the environment. Only those who have money to consume care about consumer protection. Such demands do not attack the fundamental basis of its power. The fact that they have diverted attention from the more rebellious agitations of the jobless, as well as prevented the fusion of capable middle-class leaders from arousing the more dangerous assaults from the poor, should not be overlooked in your irritation. Losing a series of rounds to the environmentalists and consumer protectionists often mean no more than raising the price of your commodities. But it will not endanger the basic framework of your power. In contrast, a violent loss to the ably led lower class of society might seriously alter the basic structure of your world, so that your children might well live in a social setting with a completely different alignment of power.

Diversions for the masses in general should be continuously fostered by those in power. There is no better way for defusing potential threats. For this reason alone it is important to maximize the number and kinds of life interests available to the public. Given a large variety, there is an abundant opportunity for everyone to engage in attractive pastimes. It also provides opportunities to a large fraction of the people to excel in one thing or another and thereby share the trappings of prestige. That is one reason why the amusements, arts, sports, and hobbies should always constitute well-supported elements of an ordered society. That is also why self-centered orthodoxy which draws attention to only one all-consuming life interest is always a sea of malcontent in today's ambitiously educated society. Nobody else has a chance to shine except members of the exclusive set, who knight their friends, consecrate their own, and reward their kind in the restricted number of pedestals of eminence. The opening up of professional sports in the United States to blacks has probably contributed as much as any other single move to foster relative racial tranquility in America in the mid-twentieth century.

Should the challenger appear to be mounting an actual offensive against you, while you are still superior in force and resources, then deliver a preemptive strike. This is particularly effective in arenas, such as the international scene, where a superseding code of enforceable laws does not exist. A hundred years ago, Charles de Montesquieu repeated the thesis that the right to national defense requires a country to attack, should it be in danger of being destroyed by another which has prospered. Such was the case with the Israelis who sent their devastating armed forces against the Arabs in 1967.

In defending against an offensive by a stronger party, you should not lose sight of the critical element of initiative. Even if your overall posture is one of defense, you must maintain the tactical initiative. This is necessary to fashion the situations and shape the events such that they gravitate to the context and timing of your own preference for the decisive engagement. A classical specimen of its successful employment in military maneuvers is Scipio Africanus drawing Hannibal out of Italy into Spain, back to Carthage to protect his base of supplies, finally up the valley where the food was grown. Zama was Scipio's choice for the main battle, and Hannibal was brought around to it through a complex series of moves. The destruction of Hannibal at Zama saved Rome from Carthage.

The same tactical principles hold on a much smaller scale in office politics. When someone suddenly makes a strong inroad into your responsibilities, do not rush forward to meet him directly in contact with his spearhead. His momentum might crumble your makeshift defenses. Instead, let him capture some of your tasks and even projects. Fall back to a position that is well integrated into your main sphere of functions, which in turn is tied to a core interest of the parent institution itself. Draw him in, all the while activating your own tasks and projects enveloping him on all sides. When his own activities appear pretty well extended beyond his main functions, then close the trap and make your claim to the common boss for a transfer of all of his tasks, projects, personnel, and resources in the enveloped area to your jurisdiction and a rewrite of your mission statement to preclude any future misunderstanding of the disputed territory.

When the force of the opposition's offensive is overwhelmingly superior to yours, you may have to resort to the tactical ruse of the unwitting artillery. In this case you will have to inveigle a third party of even much greater strength than your opposition's to lash out at the attacker in a momentary fit of anger, so to speak. It is important to determine ahead of time, however, that this third party is in fact not interested in the things of prime value to you. It would be a neat stunt, of course, if he did not even realize what is happening. The federal government has often been drawn in as the unwitting artillery in many a domestic argument. The artistry of such techniques has been portrayed in the Eastern folk tale in the *Panchatantra* of how the crow-hen killed the cobra.

Once upon a time there was a crow and his wife who had built a nest in a banyan tree. A big snake crawled into the hollow trunk and ate up the chicks as they were hatched. The crow did not want to move, since he loved the tree dearly. So he went to his friend the jackal for advice. A plan of action was devised. The crow and his wife flew about in implementation.

As the wife approached a pond, she saw the women of the king's court bathing, with pearls, necklaces, gems, garments, and a golden chain laying on the shore. The crow-hen seized the golden chain in her beak and flew toward the banyan tree with the eunuchs in pursuit. When she reached the tree, she dropped the chain into the hole. As the kings' men climbed the tree for the chain, they saw the swelling hood of the cobra. So they killed the snake with their clubs, retrieved the golden chain, and went back to the pond.

And the crow and his wife lived happily ever after.

26 **Interstitialist** The Interstitialist feels with Yang Chu, who asked over 2000 years ago: "What is life for? . . . Is it for the sake of being driven into frenzied activity by the lure of reward or fame? We waste our lives in a mad scramble, trying to catch the ephemeral praise of the moment, hoping that somehow some of it will last after we have passed from the scene. We go through the world in this narrow track, preoccupied with the petty things that we see and hear, moping over our prejudices, and ignoring the joys of life without even knowing it. Never for a moment do we taste the heady wine of freedom."

Yang Chu was the most popular philosopher of his day. But he was such an Interstitialist in letting the world go by that Mencius accused him of being so selfish that he would not pluck a single hair off his head, even if the whole world would benefit by it.

The Interstitialist is primarily interested in the qualitative excellence of his own self-shaped way of life and the welfare of those immediately within his restricted sphere of personal responsibility. Not being concerned with power over others, his mode of thought and behavior reflects a desire for avoidance of external recognitions and commitments. He seldom assumes an active role in the many confrontations that excite others. For him, refraining is not a matter of moralistic, but of practical wisdom. Should the Offense seek to "improve" the status quo, the gains in the area of his basic interests would be in excess of his threshold of contentment anyway. Should the Offense seek to "destroy" the status quo, the changes would probably not dip below it. From his philosophical vantage point, there is little cause for him to be either greedy or alarmed and jump into the fray.

Only when there is a high probability that the Offense would degrade the status quo below his requirements for contentment, which rarely happens, might the Interstitialist join the Defense to resolve the temporary crisis. Of course, if the established power permits the status quo to degenerate below the threshold of contentment, then the Interstitialist would cast his lot with the Offense for the rectification. It is during these times of conflict that the Interstitialist's special technique of ineffable disengagement comes into play. This is retirement from the fracas without being noticed or missed by either side, as soon as success is assured. This ensures his not being ensnared in continuous strife or recruited for future escalations.

To be effective during these occasional protections against encroachment into his essential minimum, the Interstitialist maintains some modicum of reserve resources. His assets are principally of the expertise variety rather than of the physical. The magnitude of his physical resources is bracketed by two limits. The lower limit is that which is necessary for maintaining him and his family at a reasonable standard of living. The upper limit is that, which would interfere with free movement within the zone of inattention on the part of the contending powers.

A crude estimate can be made of the theoretical level of resources that would not be considered as constituting a potential threat by the competing persons of power. In a normal sampling, a value twice the standard deviation from the mean would be regarded as indicating a significantly different population. If the Interstitialist maintains a size of resources much more than two standard deviations below the mean of the contending parties, he would probably be overlooked by them as not belonging to the same league. Given appropriate self-effacement on his part, he would have a good chance of being left alone. This value represents the maximum below which he intuitively remains without attracting any threatening attention from the jousting giants.

For long-term survival and serenity, the Interstitialist relies primarily on the facade of uselessness. Because of this appearance, no one envies him. No one imposes upon him. This wisdom has been summarized in two old adages: "People cage only the beautiful birds," and "the useful jackass carries the load."

27 **Subterranean**   There are two classes of Subterraneans—the illegal and the legal. Both are largely guided by Omar Khayyam's quatrain in his Rubaiyat, in Edward FitzGerald's version:

> Some for the Glories of This World; and some
> Sigh for the Prophet's Paradise to come;
>   Ah, take the Cash, and let the Credit go,
> Nor heed the rumble of a distant Drum!

The most widely publicized of the illegal Subterraneans during the first half of the twentieth century in America was the Mafia. After decades of steady infiltration beneath the law, the members had attained a considerable power, especially in Sicily and New York City. By 1945 its hold in Sicily was reaching into every field of activity. The organization not only bought the farmer's produce cheaply and carried it in Mafia trucks, but it was delivered only to those markets "guaranteed" by the Mafia at prices approved by it. The organization then worked its way across the economy, including sulphur mines, rock salt, building trades, cemetery plots, fishing fleets, and little shops. In New York City much of its income was derived from a multitude of small assessments. It might be a 50-cent bet, a 25-cent juke box selection, a

3-dollar monthly private garbage collection charge. The most lucrative source of revenue was gambling, off-track betting on horse races, casinos, and dice games.

Illegal combines of this kind have lost much ground during the last decades as the law enforcement agencies grew in effectiveness and the state itself began to operate gambling, lottery, and horse-betting on a legal basis with well-advertised and much higher grand prizes than could be offered by the smaller-scale syndicates of the underground.

Much more potent among the subterranean congregations of power, although more amorphous, is the legally constituted bureaucrats of the modern governments. Operating in the wings and backstage of the political drama and generally hidden from public view, the senior career civil servant and military officers exercise considerable power on their own with far greater security, comfort, and flexibility than the prominent political leaders. In the case of the American system the public struggle for political power involves a few thousand odd positions at the top. Regardless who gain these acclaimed titles, the dedicated career Subteranean keeps pushing the same programs he had thought all along to be for the "good of the country"—at rates discreetly adaptive to the permissiveness and perspicuity of the political supernumeraries.

The expert old-timer bureaucrat is well practiced in a variety of power-preserving techniques. The most effective is servo-bureaucratic viscosity. He or she is able to titrate just the right amount and kind of laws, executive orders, regulations, security factors, red herrings, pet peeves, unofficial commitments, what-happened-to-whom-whens, we've-tried-it-befores, conflicts of interests, jurisdictional disputes, coordinations, and the like to dictate the organizational sluggishness required in defense of his or her domain. The inertia seems to increase geometrically as the proposal encroaches closer upon what has been traditionally delimited as the bureaucrat's sphere of authority and power.

If the program directed by the political appointee has been developed in collaboration with the senior career civil servants and flag-ranked officers and the general conclusions and objectives meet with their concurrence, all obstacles are waved aside like magic, as it were, and the political boss is impressed with the speed of execution. If the program has been unilaterally conjured up by the political appointee with outside experts and friends and the general conclusions and objectives are completely antagonistic to the senior bureaucrats' desires, it could be bogged down in no end of administrative entanglements, coordinating contentions among agencies, or attenuating disputes over meaningless phraseologies.

Should the political appointee go about like a threatening bull in a china shop, he will soon find out how frustrating his "subordinates" can be. The more vigorous and impatient he becomes in trying to make an immediate mark for himself, the more frustrated will he become as he wades in the gradually deepening and thickening administrative molasses. So he finally quits in exasperation. That, of course, pleases the bureaucrats immensely, as they sit applauding his farewell speech at the going-away party. This is always the painless way of getting rid of an alien invader, who was trying to break their rice bowls.

Actually, most bureaucrats are sincere, talented, and loyal to the political appointees and do not resist changes in policies. More frequently than not, the impasse is primarily engendered by the over-conspicuous display of power on the part of the political tyros in power. They are completely unawares of the realities of governmental de facto power. The delegation of power by the citizens to the most recently elected representatives and their appointees in a democracy is only partly real and mostly symbolic. The fact is that the real exercise of power is shared between elected officials and the standing bureaucrats. The elected officials may represent the prevailing sentiments of the citizens at the time under illusions of the election campaign. But the bureaucrats embody the cumulative experience and mores of all the previous elected officials, civil servants, and citizen preferences of the past pre-election illusions and post-election realities, which impart the vector and momentum in the evolution of governments. They have the information in their files and the knowledge in their persons, which constitute an essential stuff of power. It is this historical momentum that is the source of the irresistible power in senior civil servants and ranking military officers.

The combined wisdom and empirical experience of all of the previous ruling personalites in government has formed into a consensus of the general relationships and rights among the parties involved and the norms of relationships with the ruled. A person freshly entering on the scene, whether he be a newly appointed civil servant or the president, should enter with a certain degree of modesty and high respect for the intelligence and experience of his predecessors and should not take it upon himself to destabilize the heritage and foundations of his government. In some respects this recognition is an adaptation of Edmund Burke's "developmental consensus" of the relationship of an infant entering the realm of an existing consensus by birth into it. "Duties are not voluntary," he said in his *An Appeal from the New to the Old Whigs.* "Duty and will are even contradictory terms. Now, though civil society might be at first a voluntary act (which in many cases it undoubtedly was) its continuance is under a permanent standing covenant co-existing with the society; and it attaches upon every individual without any formal act of his own." The long-time civil servant and military officer are steeped in this line of thinking.

To become identified with this historical momentum, the bureaucrat acquiesces in a certain loss of uniqueness and identity and merges himself as part and parcel of the infinite past. The running average of the national temper now resides in his nameless personage. His judgment becomes the de facto norm against which the direction of the political appointee is to be measured. The personal opinion of the newcomer is to be weighed against the refined statement of heritage. The collective of these thousands of nameless judgments and identityless actions is what is meant by the frustrating phrase that hits the wearied petitioner in the face: "Washington says . . ."

This discussion may raise a normative issue for those interested in the administrative philosophy of democracies. But for those concerned with power, the realities of how things actually work should not be confused with the platitudes of theory. Bureaucrats must be taken as a durable power elite in their own right. This is supposed to be somewhat of a secret, judiciously guarded by the senior civil servants and flag-ranked officers—who deferentially accord the elected officials and civilian authorities the full rites of office—and begrudgingly acknowledged by experienced political officials. Every once in a while someone will let the cat out of the bag, like the British Cabinet Minister Richard Crossman did in his diaries published in 1976. In the words of the book reviewer, Anthony Howard: "Even in hinting at that Crossman is, of course, blurting out the one secret about British Government that no one is ever supposed to tell. It suits the vanity of politicians to pretend that they are all-powerful; it equally suits the convenience of civil servants to maintain that they have nothing more than an occasional influence on the margin. But the truth is rather different: civil servants willingly yield to their political 'masters' all the rewards in terms of fame, glamour and publicity—in return for which they expect, and are conceded, a continuing power, regardless of the political color of the Government, over the decisions that are actually taken."

Sooner or later the rude awakening comes to every political newcomer. After fifteen months in office, the present American Chief of State could contain himself no longer. "Before I became President I realized and was warned that dealing with the Federal bureaucracy would be one of the worst problems I would have to face," said Jimmy Carter, as he opened his press conference of April 25, 1978. "It's been even worse than I had anticipated."

As someone had once noted, "Bureaucrats need have no fear of democracy."

28 **Opportunist** There is a bit of opportunism in most of us. We find it difficult seeing a free ride go by without hopping on the gravy train. In this discussion, however, we are not concerned with this kind of natural inclination. We are referring to professional Opportunists of power with unlimited appetite as to what they can squeeze out of the traffic. For them, people are not divided into good and bad, intelligent and stupid, but into milkable and not milkable. They are not cultists with lasting and nostalgic loyalty for last year's hero. Instead, they ask: "Who's going to be the next front runner?"

Between periods of peak activity, they often assume the role of middlemen, extracting bargains from both sides. Their cleverest skill lies in the shaping of circumstances, whereby the host has no choice but create opportunities peculiarly suited for their grasping tendrils and parasitic suckers.

The expert Opportunists look beyond sinecures and low-grade rewards. They seek princely recognitions of equality, to be worthy only of the highest exchanges of stature. This was the approach of the famous writer of the sixteenth century, Pietro Aretino, toward the Marquis of Mantua. In the words of his biographer Thomas Chubb, Aretino's "quilled pen was to make him not some prince's highest-paid hireling, but the human equal of whatever man that lived. What a better way of demonstrating this than the way that he instinctively chose? Not to sell his verses, but to offer them as free gifts. Not merely to accept presents from the tribe of rulers, but to make them presents of equally princely nature. The fact that the princes later so repaid these gifts— as indeed they were expected—as to virtually make them purchases did not change the situation. For if you accept a gift you more or less imply the giver's equality." Aretino then presented a Titian portrait of Hieronimo Adorno, whom the marquis loved dearly, another of Aretino himself, and a statue of Venus by Sansovino.

The ground-laying tactics of the Opportunist is the front-office watch. This provides primary intelligence and most important contacts. He or she keeps close tab of the comings and goings of the strong-man and/or strong-man-to-be, camps in the environs, assist in odds and ends with a smile, and ingratiates himself or herself with confidential and timely information.

Should the occasion demand he or she is able to bolt through the jealous palace guards so as to call direct attention of the big chief to his or her great talents. Photius, the Patriarch of the Byzantine Church, left us with a demonstration of how this can be executed. After being exiled in the year 867 by Emperor Basil the Macedonian, he drew up a genealogy in old lettering showing Basil to be a descendant of the ancient Arsacid Dynasty of Parthia. He then hired the scoundrel Theodore of Santabaris as an agent, who made arrangements to have the document placed in the Imperial Library and by "accident" come to the attention of the emperor. When asked about its meaning Theodore said that only Photius was sufficiently learned to interpret it. So the former Patriarch Photius was invited to Constantinople and prevailed on for a deciphering. He presented a lucid and convincing explanation, which impressed the emperor. Whereupon he was appointed tutor to the eight-year-old heir to the throne and finally succeeded Ignatius as Patriarch on the latter's death in 877.

The second characteristic tactics of Opportunists is hedge-betting. This is practiced during the earlier indeterminate phases of competition between the protagonists, shifting investments from one side to another as the tides of promise reverse themselves. Their eyes are glued to that big chance of committing an expendable portion of their resources to the losing side in a power play involving large stakes, thereby converting pending defeat into victory and reaping a handsome return.

Among the more socially respectable of contemporary hedge-bettors, although they should not be necessarily regarded as Opportunists on that account, are some of the contributors to political campaigns. In the 1968 presidential campaign, 294 corporate officials from forty-nine of the largest defense, space, and nuclear contractors to the government donated at least $1.2 million. With the Republicans favored in the election, they received the bulk of the money. Even then, some companies sent money both ways. The executives of a large automobile manufacturer donated $87,000 to the Republican Party and $53,000 to the Democratic Party; those of a large electronic and computer company, $104,000 and $32,000, respectively.

Given wealth, how can the front-office-watching, hedge-betting Opportunist lose? Given the need for money and connections, how can the aspiring, hard-pressed person of power not succumb?

29 **Permeator** Permeators recognize no national boundaries, no alien traditions, and no human sentiments as having the right to restrict their activities or supersede their authenticity. The mundane sectors of society must not intervene, they declare, inasmuch as their anointed mission rises above the petty materialistic concerns of the industrial, financial, and political domains. *Their* inspiration springs from the fundamental philosophical values of man—goodness, beauty, truth. Perfection is their appeal: *the* goodness, *the* beauty, *the* truth. Universality is their claim. Their institution belongs to the self-appointed: the church leaders, the art patrons, the intelligentsia.

"We have been chosen, called and invested by the Lord with a transforming mission," said Pope Paul VI to the fifth synod of Roman Catholic bishops in September 1977. He called for energetic propagation of their faith. "Evangelization has no geographical limits. Potentially it tends to and must include the whole world."

The masses are reminded that they are not able to think for themselves on matters of goodness, beauty, and truth. They are to be guided by the permeating authorities. In matters of religion, ecclesiastics with the divine inspiration; in matters of art, critics with the aesthetic eye; in matters of the intellect, scholars with the deep erudition.

How can the man on the street argue with what Mohamet is said to have related about what Allah had revealed to him? Or with the proclamation that the leader of one particular church alone is God-inspired and those of the others are much less so?

How can he say that the portrait of Genevra de Benci is not worth $5 million in 1968, when the National Gallery of Art paid that amount for it? Or that the Etruscan statue in the Metropolitan Museum in New York City was not an original until the museum admitted it as not being so?

How can he doubt the word of a Nobel laureate who said that the whole universe is made up of just two elementary particles—a proton and an electron? Or that of another Nobel Laureate sixty years later that perhaps there are no such things as elementary particles after all?

While the Permeator is striding about on the center stage of power, trying to dominate the very minds of all men and women, he or she disavows any designs upon the *usual* kinds of power and insists that the *ordinary* persons of power do not offer *his* or *her* kind of service to the masses. But material resources are inseparable from institutional growth in this worldly sphere. The more successful Permeators become in the distribution of goodness, beauty, and truth, the more guidance is required from them to the masses and the greater the assurance needed to keep up the faith, which in turn, calls for increased physical resources to maintain the institutional base. There is only one reliable avenue to the needed large resources and that is the *usual* kinds of power play with the proven methods and machinery. Thus it is that religious, aesthetic, and intellectual issues are intertwined with the materialistic, financial, and political; vice versa; and with each other.

The Pharaohs heeding well the words of the Egyptian priests as they chanted the wishes of the god Osiris in the Hall of Maat, the Moslem Sultan Firuz Shah burning alive Brahmins practicing the Hindu rites in the fourteenth century, the Attorney General of the United States referring to newspapermen as "you bastards" in 1969 and the leading American newspaper referring to him as "the evil influence" a month later, the Soviet government suppressing the writers Boris Pasternak and Alexander Solzhenitzen and the Swedish Nobel Committee awarding them the Nobel Prize in literature, the 300 formal religious sects in North America trying to convert each other, orthodox Christians harping on the materialism of scientists and scientists fingering the factual discrepancies of Christian doctrines—the permeators themselves are permeated.

Permeators and permeatees are all nibbling and devouring each other like barracudas in the same ocean of power.

30 Coalition History has shown that most one-time national allies become enemies sooner or later. It all depends on the exigencies of the moment.

In an analysis by Melvin Small and J. David Singer of fifty interstate wars and forty-three colonial and imperial conflicts between 1816 and 1965 in which more than a thousand battle fatalities occurred, a fifth of the 209 pairs of opposing enemies had previously been allies. Of the 136 nations with more than one experience in war, four-fifths of the ninety-five pairs with some experience as enemies had been allies at least once. Citing hundreds of treaties between 1535 and 1968, Laurence Beilensen showed that political treaties will be broken if it is in the national interest to do so. He concluded that no reliance should be placed on the long-term honoring of treaties by any nation.

Even more common is the simultaneous cooperation of two parties in one sphere and antagonism in another. Scientists join together in transnational defense of their common demands for intellectual freedom, yet in their respective countries are engaged in competitive weapon development toward mutual destruction. Religious leaders join together in fighting the rising trend of agnosticism and atheism, yet proselyte members from each other. Artists jointly decry the government's inadequate subsidy of the arts, yet savagely criticize each other's artistry.

In view of the infidelity of expedient collaborators, you should consider appropriate precautionary measures before voluntarily joining alliances, such as the following:

(1) Make a prior determination as to whether outside help is essential for your specific purpose at hand. The temptation of proffered assistance is hard to resist, especially if you find yourself a little short on resources. Unless circumstances leave no alternative, it is preferable not to seek allies. The offer for help might come from the wrong quarters with shady ulterior motives, be of the wrong kind, or prove unreliable at a critical moment. You should be wary of an alliance with

a party who can do without your help, who may well end up disproportionately more powerful than before, leaving you exhausted in the
process. You might then be reduced to the status of being a satellite or
even being completely assimilated by him or her. In general, it is also
prudent not to join a strong movement, which seeks only your
supplementary presence to add mass to its attack on a common opposition for demands of its own. Even if it is willing to add your demand on
the list, yours will still remain an afterthought and might be the first
to go as a bargaining chip during the subsequent negotiation.

(2) If you do plan to participate in a coalition, establish a prior
agreement among all members as to what each is expected to contribute and receive at various points along the way and at the end. Be
suspicious of those who refuse to be committed to anything, as well
those who are willing to promise the moon. Both types are unreliable
when the going gets difficult. Do not rely on either of them for critical
input.

(3) Maintain a continuous followup to ensure that the sequence of
events is unfolding along the agreed pattern. Should some member of
the coalition appear to be intentionally getting too far out of line, take
immediate and effective compensatory moves. Should unforeseen problems necessitate a revision of the allocation of contributions, roles, and
rewards, reopen the original agreement formally with all of the collaborators present.

(4) Protect yourself against the two-on-one strategy pointing your
way. If you contemplate using it yourself against others, then go on the
assumption that your erstwhile collaborators are already suspicious of
the situation. The Russian Communists followed such a strategy during the buildup of their revolutionary power. They first joined with
enemy number 2 to eliminate number 1, then with the next number 2
to eliminate the succeeding number 1, and so on until all their enemies
were destroyed. At the beginning, they united with the liberal
bourgeoisie against the Tsarists, then with the Mensheviks and
Social-Revolutionaries against the liberal bourgeoisie, then with the
smaller farmers against the large landowners, and finally with the
peasants against the kulaks.

(5) Conduct your operation in such a way that at the time of the
joint victory your own reserves and system are not so unbalanced that
your competitive position is impoverished. The closer to victory against
the common foe you stand, the more closely should you scrutinize your
own fortunes, adjust your balance, and toughen your resiliency.

Only in this way can you really reap the harvest of coalitions.

VECTORING RESOURCES

People and money per se are neither here nor there as far as power goes. It's how they are engineered into a thrust with a direction that gives them the essential vector. This section enlarges on the implementing methods. How do you make use of other people's resources? What must you do to get the maximum out of your lieutenants? Whom must you be careful never to cross up? What should you make of the nonviolent types? And what weight should you place on scientific analyses when it comes to the big decisions?

31 **Paraproprietary control** The prelude to power in modern times is the battle for social or organizational positions, which constitute the decision-making loci governing resources. No chief of state owns the men he or she directs; no banker the money he or she manipulates; no bishop the heaven he promises. But they all act as if they do. Such is the common state of affairs in a paraproprietary society.

P. P. Harbrecht described the paraproprietary society as one in which "a man's relationship to things—material wealth—no longer determines his place in society (as it did in a strong proprietary system) but his place in society now determines his relationship to things." The person in command then attempts to bring even greater amounts of resources within the compass of his or her position.

It is through this route that a handful of persons, who own less than a few percent of the voting shares of a company, can so arrange matters that the stockholder-owners cannot help delivering it up into their hands. By dominating the proxy committee and other key posts, they are able to appoint the board of directors, who select the officers of the company and adjust the administrative apparatus to continue their whip-hand in the proxy committee. The stockholder-owners of 97 percent of the company are kept happy at safe power distance through regular dividends.

There are two considerations to bear in mind as you try to move upward in the paraproprietary society. The first is related to the limited number of available positions within the inner circle. When you are on the outside trying to get in, the easier approach sometimes is convincing the powers-that-be to enlarge their membership rather than to displace one of their own to make room for you. When all the vice presidencies in your corporation are ably filled with relatively young encumbents, you should search for ways of creating a new one, for which you have a strong chance.

Alternatively, you may press for a partial equivalent of an extension of power from the governing inner circle by decentralization of authority. In pursuing this avenue, it is safer in general not to ask for increased authority for you alone, except for very special and specific projects, but for all of the persons at your echelon. You would then not stand out for easy retaliation. Just as the English barons called for a greater share of the power of the monarch in the thirteenth century, so are the Catholic bishops of today calling for a greater share of the power of the Pope as an extension of the "collegiality rule" of the church. At the same time the association of priests was pressing for further decentralization of decision making, coolness developed during the 1960s between the National Conference of Catholic Bishops and the National Federation of Priests in America. The West German theologian-priest Hans Kung published a book questioning the century-old doctrine of papal infallibility, which is tantamount to an attempt at decentralizing the religious power over the mind.

Once you are a member of the inner circle of power, however, you should support moves to restrict the membership. Sharing power is not only a loss in personal power but also a threat to what power is left. From the standpoint of a person of power, this factor alone constitutes a strong argument for holding headquarters, boards of directors, college of cardinals, vice presidencies, deanships, and the like to the smallest feasible size. The decentralization of independent authority should be restricted to that essential for the execution of assigned responsibilities. Tendencies at lower echelons in a contrary direction should be discouraged. Thus the School Sisters of St. Francis in Milwaukee was criticized by the Cardinal Prefect of the Sacred Congregation for Religious and Secular Institutions in Rome for its "exaggerated cult of freedom" and "uncontrolled experimentation" in religious life.

The second consideration is related to the great variation in the opportunities for growth in power among positions within the inner circle. Some are accorded relatively strong powers but lead nowhere. Others are given relatively weak powers but are good springboards to the very top. There are a select few with both advantages. You should keep your eyes especially on those positions astride the social switching functions. Not only do these intersections provide access to resources but also to critical information, both of which can be siphoned off and withheld by the persons in charge for their own advancements. Their ancestors have been steadily increasing their power without portfolio since human communities began to form.

The ancient civilization of the Indus valley is a case in point. It was sustained by a complex irrigation system. The flow of water through its canals was regulated by a series of gates. The farmers found it necessary to assure equitable distribution of water among themselves. So a group of gatekeepers was hired and trained to apportion water in accordance with the instructions and requirements of the farmers. According to historical accounts, not too many decades later the keepers of the gates became the rulers of the farmers.

32 **People**   The first step on the path of power is the assembling of a well-knit cadre, backed by followers beyond that in numbers adequate for the attainment of the next two milestones. Until you have developed this necessary base, do not dream of going anywhere. Conversely, do not reach for power beyond the strength of the platform you have constructed.

Julius Caesar made extensive preparations in building up a firm foundation of followers before he launched his serious moves to power. According to Plutarch, as translated by John Dryden, "In his pleadings at Rome, his eloquence soon obtained him great credit and favor, and he won no less upon the effectations of the people by the affability of his manners and address, in which he showed a tact and consideration beyond what could have been expected at his age; and the open house he kept, the entertainments he gave, and the general splendor of his manner of life contributed little by little to create and increase his political influence." He was lavish in his personal expenditures toward this end. Before he even held a major office, his parties became well known. His gladiatorial festivals would involve over 300 combats. His processions, shows, and feasts "threw into the shade all the attempts that had been made before him, and gained so much upon the people, that everyone was eager to find out new offices and new honors for him in return for his munificence."

In general, the magnitude of power in your hands is a direct function of the size of your constituency. The Lanchester law of warfare engagements, which also applies qualitatively to other types of confrontations, points out that success varies linearly with the capability per person of the force and exponentially with the size. A force of 1400 men, for example, will draw a force of 1000 down to zero in an exhaustive battle, but will also lose much fewer men in the process. It will only go down to 980. Should the smaller force of 1000 be able to split the larger force into two parts and engage each group separately, then the 1000-man force will overwhelm the first contingent of 700 with only 286 casualties. With the remaining 714 men, it will reduce the second half of 700 men to zero and emerge victories with 140 combat survivors. If the remaining 714 men were able to be re-equipped between the two battles so that it has twice the combat quality per soldier, then it would end up with a much higher residual force of 514. Although both size and quality are essential in a strong competitive force, your first attention must be the size.

If you are the leader of a nation with a small population relative to your designs, there are many historical examples of how to go about increasing this aspect of your resources. In Sparta of the sixth century B. C., children were encouraged by both family and state. Laws were enacted to motivate their begetting. A father of three children was exempted from military service; a father of four from all burdens of state. A married woman without children would often be directed by the state to see whether some other man might be more productive than her husband; history recorded no objections on her part. Rome granted citizenship to all conquered peoples. The United States opened her ports to worldwide immigrants. Israel is pressuring for Jews from Russia and other lands.

If you are an established black or religious leader in America intent on power, your strongest long-term instrument as far as your institution is concerned, especially within a democratic one-man-one-vote setting, is to encourage your followers to multiply. Rather than distribute abortion subsidies and contraceptive advice, you should advocate more generous child support, free education through college, and higher welfare payments for the poorer people who form the broad base of your support, so that it will become broader still.

Because of the diversity of personalities among your constituents, you should take special pains to spread the sense of belonging to the organization. As chief, you should never so act as to give the slightest feeling on the part of the lowest members that you are not one of them. The sense of belonging to each other is far more important for social stability than the actual distribution of wealth and rights. During the feudal era, the baron was not only the lord and master but also very harsh and arbitrary at times. But he belonged to the masses. He spoke their language, thought their way, and got drunk with them. He shared their superstitions, their habits, and their good and bad times. There was no uprising against him. Revolts broke out in the Middle Ages, when the nobility got sophisticated in social polish and separated themselves from the rest.

Likewise, you should minimize the overt expression of superiority by one segment of your followers over another. The action of Tiberius Gracchus in this respect is worth emulating. In his campaign against Carthage, the Roman commander had to induct slaves to swell his army, whereupon he ordered that no soldier, under penalty of death, was to cast aspersions on his fellow soldier's servitude.

This does not mean that you should attempt to eliminate all traces of conflict within your organization. For one thing, this cannot be done, human nature being what it is. For another thing, perfect harmony connotes a weak and stagnant organization. It may mean that no one cares strongly about anything. It may be that the various functional assignments do not overlap sufficiently for proper seaming between functions. Overlap means tension, if the parties involved are achievers. A certain level of tension, then, is an indication of liveliness. This must not be smothered. Yet the level of tension needs be kept within limits. Without the cooperation, your organization will be pulled apart by internal tensions. But without the internal tensions, your organization will gradually doze into a pleasant somnolence.

In the harnessing of people, you should understand as much of their behavior as the engineer knows of the tensile strength, ductility, expansion coefficient, and other properties of his structural materials before designing and building a bridge. Human beings should be appreciated in each of four distinctive roles, namely, as resources, target, opposition, and milieu. They behave radically differently in their hotch-potch of inconsistencies in each of these roles and under varying circumstances in each case.

Just as an engineer does not count on his suspension cables to stretch beyond their elastic limits without breaking, so should you not expect people to act in ways other than their nature allows. This kind of knowledge is technological rather than humanitarian. It is important that the two not be confused. The former is knowing how to use people as tools; the latter is knowing how to care for them as human beings.

Your skill in using people rests ultimately on your ability to fashion circumstances such that their own treasured values of the moment dictate an action on their part which ineluctably advances your interests. This is exemplified by the powerful Arabian sheik who lost one of his horses during a long journey. So he directed the requisition of another horse from the next town on the way. Two horses were brought forward for his final selection. Since the owners did not want to lose them, each one exaggerated the age and weaknesses of his own horse and how it will never meet the high standards of the sheik. "Very well," said the latter. "Let's have a race. I'll take the winner." "But your Highness," whispered his aide. "This will not decide the best horse. The owners will not push their horse to their very best." "Ah, but they will," said the sheik. "Order each man to ride the other man's horse."

A continuing effort should be made to strengthen your immediate cadre. Be on the constant lookout for capable lieutenants, especially capable individuals who fit well into your personal style of doing things. These are relatively scarce. Should you find one but have no personnel vacancies at the moment, create an opening. If this cannot be done, then hoop him or her into your circle as a part-time advisor for the time being. In general, promotions from within will always constitute your main source of close deputies. This would hold particularly if the institution itself fosters such a policy. Even if it does not, you should think twice before going outside to fill most of your top positions. Whenever an attractive vacancy opens up under you and some candidate within your group meets your criteria and enjoys the whole-hearted endorsement from the rest as being most deserving, do not pass him or her over in favor of some outsider who happens to be apparently more qualified on paper. This would alienate your team. Yet, too much reliance on the inside source will insidiously weaken your organization from inbreeding over time. You must therefore open it up to outside infusions to a reasonable degree. They will not only bring new ideas and vigor but also disrupt internal cliques from becoming overly pervasive.

One kind of talent often undervalued by the so-called tough persons of power is the intellectuals. They may not be of great importance for competition at the lower and middle levels. But they are indispensable at the higher hierarchies. Brute force over animal instincts no longer suffice as the main weapon. It may even be counterproductive. You must deal with the higher human mind. For this you will not do well without the contributions from intellectuals. Napoleon Bonaparte's treatment of Johann von Goethe provides an illustration of the kind of appreciative approaches some of the more astute persons of great power follow in this respect. When the emperor visited Erfurt, Germany to meet Tsar Alexander to complete the humiliation of Prussia, whose army he had crushed at Jena, he invited the eminent German author to the palace. Napoleon pleased Goethe no end by speaking most knowledgeably about his book *The Sorrows of Werther*, asking him all kinds of questions about Tacitus, suggesting he could write a play about Caesar that would be more powerful than Shakespeare's, and inviting him to move to Paris. When Goethe learned some days later that he had been made a member of the French Legion of Honor, he expressed his gratitude with a pledge of "complete devotion."

The effective utilization of intellectuals as adjuncts to power requires considerable percipience. On the one hand, they can be extremely valuable. On the other hand, they can be much of a nuisance and at times quite harmful. It all depends on your judgment in selecting them and your skill in dealing with them. Some of the more brilliant but less matured become overimpressed with their own significance, as they review the troopings of sycophants yes-sir-ing them right and left. As a result, their former meticulously scholarly inputs often become gradually transformed into assertive opinions. Some of them might even forget their expected advisory anonymity in the scheme of things and strike a leadership position of their own. The primary difficulty is not their challenge to your power, but their growing tendency to formulate programs not in accordance with your policies and practical plans, but more in consonance with their own discordant academic theories. Should this happen to you, do not vex anyone but yourself for your poor selection of personnel. Ease them out with appropriate face-saving honors and start all over.

What all persons of power attempt to build in their cadre is a completely responsive apparatus, based on individuals in whom can be imparted what may be called faithfulness. In the words of Georg Simmel, this corresponds to the psychic and sociological state, "which insures the continuance of a relationship beyond the forces that first brought it about; which survives these forces with the same synthesizing effect they themselves had originally . . . An erotic relation, for instance, begun on the basis of physical beauty, may well survive the decline of the beauty and its change into ugliness . . . Sociological connectedness, no matter what its origin develops a self-preservation and autonomous existence of its form that are independent of its initially connecting motives."

Faithfulness is a nebulous trait, which is expressed in various ways. At times and in some individuals it expresses itself as a kind of unique respect for the leader. It is a mixture of awe, consecration, and fear—a touch of sacred dread. There is a consciousness of the absolute superiority of the leader and a self-depreciation before the higher being—an idea akin to the holy. The result is a code of complete loyalty. We read about its presence in the Samurai of the fifteenth century, who dedicated himself to the death in defense of his master. We see it today in men like G. Gordon Liddy, who was imprisoned for over four years for his part in the Watergate burglary in 1972 that led to the downfall of the President and for keeping silent before the judge and prosecutor. Upon his release, he was questioned by the reporters as to what he would say if asked by the President "to do that kind of work again." "I would say yes," he replied without hesitation. "When the prince approaches his lieutenant, the proper response of the lieutenant to the prince is 'Fiat volutas tua.' . . . Thy will be done."

In some cases it is associated with a deep conviction that the leader is the only hope. A prior sense of desperation is induced either by others or by the person of power himself. People respond to crises. Want to avoid economic chaos? then elect me—there is no other person. Want to avoid torture by the enemy? then go into battle with me— there is no other safety. Want to avoid eternal hellfire? then join me in my church—there is no better avenue to salvation.

At times, it results from an unshakable belief in the righteousness of the leader's cause. This personal persuasion communicates itself to members of the collectivity, which, in the words of Robert Michels, "gives them the aplomb and energy which they need to achieve their goals. This is as much to say that those critics who estimate that in their aggressive actions national groups are fundamentally ferocious and savage are fundamentally wrong. At bottom, this ferocity and savagery which cause people to trample under foot and wipe out the interests and aspirations of others are only the forms in which the missionary—and almost always the visionary—conviction manifests itself. Missionary peoples are ferocious and savage not in their feelings but in their actions."

The ones in whom faithfulness is often found in greatest intensity are the selfless and psychopathic heroes. Such a personality has been described by Norman Mailer as follows: "The decision is to encourage the psychopath in oneself: to explore that domain of experience where security is boredom and therefore sickness; to exist in that enormous present which is without past or future, memory or planned intention . . . The life where a man must go until he is best, where he must be with it or doomed not to swing." There is an ample supply of this type in the world, and you should not have much difficulty in recruiting an adequate and expendable number to do the dangerous work. Allen Dulles informed us that in his ten years as director of the American intelligence operations, he could recall only one instance out of many hundreds where an agent felt any scruples about carrying out an assignment. Looking for kamikaze pilots? Assassins? Martyrs? The eager stress-seekers are just waiting for a nod from some aggressive person of power.

33 **Money** When the emphasis on fitness for public office is on virtue, as had been the case during part of Roman history, then wealth is not decisive for great power. Men like Marcus Regulus and

Cincinnatus held high positions and wielded immense influence, yet had never been personally wealthy, both before and after public life. They remained frugal and law-abiding as they tended to their small holdings.

In contrast, when corruption is the order of the day, then wealth is all important. In such circumstances, aspirants with modest means should resist any temptation to move prematurely against the entrenched. Even those with considerable wherewithal need be extremely cautious in selecting the grounds of challenge. This was the situation in Florence during the life of the enormously wealthy Cosimo il Vecchio. When a clique of powerful opponents was planning to get him out of the way, Niccolò da Uzzano reminded them of the facts of life: "If you plan to put him to death, never by way of magistrate will you succeed, because his money and your corruptible minds will always save him."

While the United States is nowhere nearly as corrupt as the Florence of Cosimo il Vecchio, it is not being unduly modest to admit, in the light of Section 11, that it is probably not as virtuous as the Rome of Marcus Regulus. Money still talks in America and Wealth still commands, within limits. As it has been as far as man can remember, power rolls smoothest on wheels of gold. If you do not have the requisite dollars, then borrow, beg, and/or steal you must; or else slow down your climb to power. All men of great power in America had to go through this experience time and again. Hubert H. Humphrey was especially bitter about his having to raise money from the "fatcats," as he confided to a newspaper interviewer in late 1974:

"Campaign financing is a curse. It's the most disgusting, demeaning, disenchanting, debilitating experience of a politician's life. It's stinky, it's lousy. I just can't tell you how much I hate it. I've had to break off in the middle of trying to make a decent, honorable campaign and go up to somebody's parlor or to a room and say, 'Gentleman and ladies, I'm desperate. You've got to help me. My campaign chairman is here and I'm going to step out of the room.' You even have to go through all that kind of fakery. . . . You must have to grovel around in the dirt. And you see people there—a lot of them you don't want to see . . . out of the twenty-five who have gathered, four will contribute. And most likely one of them is in trouble and is somebody you shouldn't have had a contribution from."

Yet when the chips are down, persons after great power rarely refuse to demean themselves to the necessary level to acquire the essential money. This is simply part of the accepted personal overhead that one must pay to get into the main arena.

As far as institutions are concerned, their power parallel the state and magnitude of their controlled wealth. This obvious statement needs no elaboration. We need only remind ourselves of this point by way of few titbits of historical interest.

In the twelfth century B. C., according to the *Great Harris Papyrus*, the Egyptian priests during the reign of Rameses III owned 113,433 slaves, 493,386 heads of cattle, 88 barges and galleys, 169 towns, and one-seventh of the land. Their holdings brought an annual income of over 2,000,000 jars of incense, oil, and honey; 1,000,000 jars of wine; 500,000 jugs of beer; and many other returns.

A single American company today, A T & T, earns a net income after taxes greater than that of the national income of Sweden. Between 1939 and 1969, American equity in British industry rose fifteen-fold. American managed companies in Britain employed 500,000 workers and accounted for a tenth of the nation's production.

Banks came into their own beginning with the seventeenth century. After the Bank of Amsterdam issued the first bank notes in 1609, they became quasi-official monetary institutions. A standard practice has since been adopted through which bankers are able to achieve earnings and control destinies without endangering their own fortunes, just as government officials operate on the citizens' resources. A customer with a reputation for meeting his debts and with adequate security in the form of stocks, land, buildings, or other assets to cover the loan will be extended an amount of credit as mutually agreed upon. This is entered into the bank's books and the customer can then draw on this sum. On the average, however, large borrowers conduct over 90 percent of their financial transactions by checks. In effect, bankers have thereby increased the amount of money in circulation. They draw interest from its use while the value owed is being fully covered by securities. Wihout risking their own money, bankers are theoretically capable of drawing interest on as much as the total worth of the private sector itself at any given time.

As a consequence, today's bankers stand on a higher rung in the ladder of social power than do the wealthy, just as the loan shark does over the gangster. The New York City Police Department's expert on organized crime testified to this effect in 1965: "It is a demonstration of power. . . . It seems an unwritten law that even if you are a criminal, even if you are a top guy, you always pay the shylock. . . . You borrow money, you pay it back. [Members of the Gallo gang] weren't afraid of the shylock. But they didn't know when they might need him again. So they very diligently paid the shylock."

During recent decades the administration of pension trust funds has become a vehicle of considerable economic power. In 1969, the top ten American trust banks controlled assets of $102 billion, and the total trust assets managed by all insured commercial banks approximated $300 billion. These funds are invested by the management primarily in stocks. The executors can thereby acquire controlling voting positions without investing a cent of their own money. The pension fund itself may be invested in the corporation's own stocks. A closed loop can thereby be generated with the fund management determining the corporation management, which in turn selects the fund management. At the same time, trust operations can be very profitable. In 1969 the top ten trusts received over $300 million in fees, quite apart from the personal power of the executives. This is an example of the zeromax principle: zero risk with maximum gain.

Ever since King Gyges struck the first coin in the seventh century B. C. governments have controlled monetary transactions as a system. It formulated the taxation policies, which bracketed the financial opportunities for all. Because the instrumental value of money is stabilized by this institutionalization of the control and disposal of property, the management of large investments in a capitalistic economy is intrinsically interwoven with national and international affairs. It was through legal arrangements that much of the great fortunes, for example, had been accumulated around the turn of the century in this country. A typical illustration was an innocent-looking law that the railroad barons had guided through Congress. It stipulated that title to the government land allocated to the railroad will not be signed to them until they had paid a small fee. But the fee was not paid by the railroaders until there was a buyer ready to advance a generous downpayment on a very profitable sale. In this way, the government carried all of the investment and holding costs and the barons made the money.

To protect their financial stakes, corporation executives and people of wealth must devote considerable attention to strengthening the political scaffoldings on which their fortunes hang. They must make their desires felt in the highest councils of government across national boundaries. Otherwise they will remain neither solvent nor powerful for long. Political skill is essential to persons of great power of any kind, and political involvement is their daily fare.

34 **Identitive inducements**   Monetary rewards constitute an important inducement for capable talent. As the American saying goes, "If you pay peanuts, you get monkeys." But they are not always the critical factor. The balance sheet keeps the business person fairly well in line over the long run. But reputation as a fierce competitor, feeling of achievement, publicity, and status symbols are often decisive in a particular situation.

The use of prestige symbols is identitive, in contrast to utilitarian, which pertains to the granting and withholding of material things, and coercive, which pertains to threats or injury.

In general, you can attract greater commitment from a follower who is actuated by identitive motivation than utilitarian, and in turn more by utilitarian than by coercive. In the motivation of lower-ranking subordinates, coercive means should always be visible as potential, while utilitarian means should be emphasized for most of the day-to-day actions with intermittent identitive stimuli. With the perennial junior-executive category, utilitarian means should be stressed with occasional application of coercive and identitive in roughly equal proportions. With persons of high aspirations, utilitarian means and identitive should be applied in roughly equal proportions, with coercive more implied than actual. With individuals of considerable intellectual, aesthetic, and spiritual leanings, coercive means are more frequently than not counterproductive. Identitive means should prevail with an acceptably low-key but ever-present utilitarian.

You should so manage your dispensing of inducements, so that not only will you be effective in your employee relations in general but also be respected for your firmness by those specifically moved by firmness and for your understanding by those specifically moved by understanding.

35 **Push-pull** Instruments for inducing action can be divided into the push and the pull.

Instruments of push deter an action through inciting the fear of punishment or injury: the sarcastic slur, discharge from work, multiple warhead independently targeted intercontinental ballistic missiles, and eternal damnation.

The amount of bodily punishment that is socially acceptable on an individual basis has declined over the centuries. During the days of the Roman army a guard who was found guilty for falling asleep on duty was punished by the *fustuarium*. The tribune of the court martial would touch the condemned soldier with a cudgel. On that signal the other soldiers would pounce on him with clubs and stones. He was usually killed on the spot. A comparable offense today would be met with a few days in the stockade and a loss of a stripe or two at most.

Although punishments dealt individual human beings have become on the whole less severe, the same cannot be said for people *en masse*.It is within recent memory that a nation systematically decimated millions of nameless Jews in nameless production-line gas chambers over a period of several years and a single bomber killed a hundred thousand nameless Japanese over a few seconds. The instruments of push are being refined and amplified nowadays more for power on a grand scale than for power on individual coercions.

In contrast, the instruments of pull attract an action through appealing to the appetite for gain: the gentle compliment, performance bonus, foreign aid, and eternal bliss.

As democracy and socialism widen the opportunities for self-expression, the pull instruments are becoming progressively more subtle and complex. Inducements for the individual are so cunningly alloyed with the goals of the institution that the two are confounded by the unsuspected as one and the same. Individuals are led without their knowing. The more selfish the subjects in their confusion, the more useful they are to the institution in pursuing their own gain as embodied in the pull instrument. At the same time the more selfless and community-conscious they are, the greater effort they exert in achieving the institution's objectives on their own steam. As a consequence of astute application of the art of the pull, either motivation leads to the same practical result of institutional advancement, which in turn enlarges one's own springboard for power. Subjects are being pulled when they think they are pursuing.

The progressive series in the push-pulling of power is: (1) killing the target individuals, (2) eliminating them, (3) damaging them, (4) threatening them, (5) cajoling them, (6) bribing them, (7) persuading them, (8) seducing them, (9) attracting them, and (10) educating them to your view. In general, you should lean toward the nonviolent pull end of the spectrum as options of first preference. If effective, they are more acceptable to the public, more economical all around, and less injurious to yourself. When the big chips are down, however, you will frequently have to fall back toward the violent push end as the old reliable.

There are a few individuals who are immune from push or pull of all kinds. Men who have subdued anger, pride, and craving cannot be enticed or pressured to do your bidding.

A typical historical figure famous for his independence was Shihman I-liao of the fifth century B. C. When Sheng Po-kung and Shih Ch'i plotted to assassinate the two senior cabinet officials to gain control of the government, they felt that 500 men would be necessary.

They were stymied as to how such a number could be recruited in secrecy. Shih Ch'i suggested that the collaboration of I-liao would lend the equivalent strength. So they called on him and revealed their plans. I-liao refused to participate, even at the point of their swords. Fearing that I-liao would divulge the plot, Shih Ch'i wanted to kill him. But Sheng argued that a person unmoved by threats of death and promises of gain would not let out their secrets just to curry favor with a king. So they left him alone and departed.

A more familiar display of independence has been recorded in Macedonian annals a century later. When King Alexander traveled to Corinth in his newly conquered land, nearly every Greek of consequence came to pay his respect or ask for favors. Diogenes did not. His fame as a philosopher, playwright, and teacher was so great that Alexander decided to visit the legendary old man instead. As Alexander approached the half-naked man in ragged clothes, Alexander asked, "Is there anything I can do for you, Diogenes?" Whereupon Diogenes replied, "Yes, stand to one side. You're blocking the sunlight." Alexander immediately grasped the significance of his inability to make meaningful contact and walked away. As he did so, he muttered to his retinue: "If I were not Alexander, I should be Diogenes." His aside was interpreted by Gilbert Highet to mean: "He knew that of all men then alive in the world only Alexander the conqueror and Diogenes the beggar were truly free."

Do not waste your energy working on the likes of I-liao and Diogenes. Leave them be.

36 **Nonviolence** Develop a capability for nonviolence for specialized uses. This is more a matter of inner resolve than outer resources. Learn from the bamboo.

Some among the apparently peace-loving people are sincerely so; some are only wily so. A nonviolent person without a purpose in mind is indeed a person of peace. A nonviolent person with an objective in mind may be pursuing power. A nonviolent person with a dedicated objective in mind may be a threat. A nonviolent person with a dedicated objective in mind to the point of death may be a mortal threat.

Like the bamboo, the nonviolent person can easily be pushed to the very earth. True. But this does not mean that he or she has been subdued.

37 **Gut feeling** One of the chief weaknesses of forceful young managers brought up in the modern scientific techniques of systems theory, games theory, cost-effectiveness analysis, and operational research and suddenly catapulted into positions of considerable social complexity is their entrancement with rationality and the so-called scientific management. They have yet to appreciate fully the forte and limitations of science and logic. They fail to use scientific approaches when they should be used and fail to disregard them when they should be disregarded.

Two simple stories are sufficient to caution against the intrinsic uncertainties of the scientific method when inappropriately applied. The first concerns the law of cause and effect. It lies at the root of scientific work and has served science well. Actually the law itself has never been proven rigorously. This is shown by the story of the little chicken that ran away in fright at its first sight of a man. After the man left, the chicken came out of its hiding place, only to find some corn on the ground, which it then enjoyed eating. The sequence was repeated over and over again—999 times. In terms of the law of cause and effect, this would mean that whenever the man appears, the corn must also appear. So when the man came out the thousandth time, the scientific chicken ran forward to thank the man for the delicious corn—only to have its neck wrung for supper that night. Obviously, the assumed law of cause and effect failed the chicken miserably the last go-round.

The second story concerns the fundamental issue of objectivity. Most scientists claim objectivity as the foundation of their observations and conclusions. There are many situations, however, in which objectivity simply cannot be invoked. This is shown by the story of the Mormon graduate student who wrote a critical thesis on Mormon history. Came the day of the final oral examination, one of the professors asked the student, "Do you think that you, who are a Mormon, can be objective enough to write a fair critique of Mormon history?" Whereupon the student replied, "Yes, if you, who are not a Mormon, can be objective enough to judge it."

These stories are sufficient to indicate why it is that astute persons are seldom overawed by rational arguments, scientific theories, and computerized models as the final arbiters on matters of considerable social consequence or critical corporate significance. They recognize that effective executive actions include, to be sure, the science of management—the objective, the verbalizable, the systems analytical, and all the other quantifiable factors that are being so well covered in the current literature on "modern" management. But they also include the art of management—the subjective, the ineffable, the holistic synthetic, and the infinite concatenations of cascading sensed unknowables. Small executive decisions are weighted toward the former polarity; big executive decisions are weighted toward the latter. When it comes to the scrambling for power, vulnerability is often not a matter of the magnitude of the consequence in terms of reverberation so much as the criticality of the crack. For this reason, even small flaws can be fatal. In the game of power then, all decisions are potentially big.

Ultimately, it all comes down to, not rationality, but gut feeling. Trust it. And do not try to outsmart it.

SHAPING COMMUNICATIONS

Whoever controls the fabrication and flow of information controls the distribution of power. This section offers a digest of some of the more relevant know-how. How much information should you entrust to whom? And for what purpose? What kind of privately personal channels to and from you should be set up? How can you guard against incoming raw data misleading and/or confusing you? How do you shape information to stimulate the effectiveness of your own cadre and the support of your mass constituency as instruments of your personal power?

38 **Need to know**   Just because a piece of data may be useful to the recipient does not necessarily mean that you should have it transmitted to him. From the standpoint of organizational efficiency, the volume of data to be forwarded to a particular echelon or individual should not exceed the processing capacity at that point. If more data are poured into it than can be handled, the net result of the glut would be progressive inefficiency.

Besides intellectual and physical capacity, there is the further consideration of a need to know. Does the individual need the data to do the particular job you have assigned to him? If so, let him or her have it. If not so, then not. This guideline would minimize the chances of sensitive data falling into the hands of the opposition. In the competition of power, all data may be sensitive, depending on the situation.

Placing as much data in somebody else's hands as in your own may lead to undesirable consequences. The subordinate with much data but little ability to act on them may become frustrated and thereby become a weakened member of your team. On the other hand, the subordinate with much data and much ability to act with them beyond the confines of official duties has enhanced his or her value to others seeking to topple you from power, should he or she be so recruited. As a person of power, therefore, there is not much point in passing data down the line willy-nilly.

The same kind of consideration operates in the upward direction in the event you are contemplating challenging someone upstairs. The less data in his or her hands, the more vulnerable he or she becomes. The more he or she is kept in the dark without suspecting it, the less knowledgeable he or she becomes as to what is afoot.

The manipulation of information to the constituency is also an essential measure for durability in power. When the future is predictably and routinely secure and prosperous, people tend to be less willing to surrender power to their leaders, especially in a democratic institution. A certain degree of uncertainty must be sustained through a carefully adjusted flow of information about a future that may in fact be most promising. Sustained power is nurtured through doses of anxiety.

It is for these reasons that a power structure always entails censorship, selectivity, and metering of public data. The person out to augment his power always distorts the communiques from his office to varying degrees. The dilemma posed by governmental manipulation of news in a democracy is a corollary to the issue: How much of the power, which the chief executive and his cadre had schemed and fought so hard to acquire, should voluntarily be distributed back to the people and those very competitors, who are trying to seize it from both them and the people at the same time?

The answer depends on who is in office and what he or she can get away with. In any case, it would be unexpected of him or her to be overly generous. He or she would not have gotten to the top had he or she been so inclined by nature.

39 **Private channels** The formal communication network of your organization should be tested from time to time to make sure that it is, in fact, keeping you in touch with your constituents, whom you serve and who comprise the ultimate source of your power. The worst insulation often turns out to be the immediate circle of personal aides around you. The well-intentioned assistants understandably try to protect you from being bothered by what appears to them to be trivia. The selfishly clever ones pass only those outsiders, who are willing to pay deference to their derivative power or exhibit opinions consonant with their own. The applause of this well-placed claque might easily mislead you into thinking that you are hearing the unanimous voice of your constituents at large.

You should consider the traditional practice among the wise ancient Eastern kings, who were always open to direct appeals from the least of their subjects. It is essential that you maintain a redundant system of private channels completely bypassing your own staff and reaching any desired nexus of concern. This conduit must be responsive to and usable by you alone. The inner workings, involving professional confreres, acquaintances, friends, rumor mills, newsmedia men, "misplaced" documents, "denials," trial balloons, hot lines, and the like, must remain a mystery to others, even though everyone may recognize that something like it is in existence, as the currency of your knowledge of events so clearly attests.

Not only will your private network ensure the secrecy of your personal thinking and critical messages, transmit them faster, and keep you in intimate touch with the true feelings of your constituents, it will also enable you to calibrate the reliability of your formal network. Furthermore, it will prove quite an incentive to the latter, which is forever faced with the challenge: Get the news to the chief before he gets it via the grapevine!

40 **Data translation** One of the weakest links in dealing with human beings is the translation of raw data into usable information. Until your data can be converted into action, they remain as just so much noise. Yet should your data be translated into an unwarranted basis for your decisions, you would be worse off. No matter whether you are a manager striving to do a good job or a person of power seeking to augment it, the first task at hand is to ensure that this translation is not faulty within your unit.

To begin with, all data come with varying degrees of validity, reliability, and variability. It is only empirical experience to recognize possibilities of pure fabrication. During the Vietnam War in the 1970s an American four-star general intentionally ordered his subordinates to falsify battlefield records, so as to permit his continued bombing of the enemy homeland against the explicit directives from his superiors in Washington. In any case, always attach an appropriate "standard deviation" to all incoming data and handle them accordingly.

In these days of a plethora of data, considerable judgment and skill in the use of computers and data-handling techniques are required, especially in large and technologically sophisticated operations. In taking advantage of these modern aids to management, you should allow ample leeway for the continuous distortions and errors during the course of processing and transmission. One of the principal sources is associated with the necessity of summarizing lengthy inputs into the limited channel capacity for relay to successively higher echelons. Various aspects of the original message are deleted, and more concise but less precise substitute phrases passed on. New accents are unconsciously introduced. Personal biases enter the picture. Skewing in the direction of the successive bosses' likes and away from their dislikes along the line is a natural offshoot.

Since success and failure often rest on the clear understanding of the more subtle features and intentions behind a given dilemma or confrontation, you should never rely on a single message, no matter from what source, as the sole basis for a major decision. The accuracy should be ascertained through repetition in different forms of inquiry through independent and qualitatively distinct avenues and authorities.

Besides the accurate translation of data into information, there is the equally important synthesis of the bits of information into a proper perspective of the state of affairs. Unless your envisioned pattern of events is true to reality and your present location and objective are accurately positioned within it, you will find yourself in the troubled company of so many of our philosophers and writers of history. They are enmeshed, as Allan Nevins informed us, in a probable "bewilderment and anxiety in the loss of old landmarks, and the overturn of long-accepted truths. They are stunned by the rapidity, multiplicity, and immensity of the revolution of our age, and baffled by the enormous enlargement of knowledge. The historians have suffered particularly because the value of all good history depends upon a clear sense of perspective and a strong grasp of the tools of research and interpretation. And how can these be kept available when perspective whirls incessantly and new tools constantly replace old?"

41 **Intelligence** A person is often bothered in the gathering of intelligence by the gnawing reflection of the reasonable democratic and moral limits in the invasion of the privacy of others. Actually, as Alain F. Westin had remarked, "the notion of societies in which people happily 'mind their own business' and 'let everyone alone' is a fantasy of some libertarian's imagination, not the condition of men in either primitive or modern societies." Most persons of power have never hesitated to overstep the conventionally touted bounds of propriety and fairness in order to guarantee an extra margin of safety. A vast array of modern devices, from electronic bugging to satellite photography, has been added to the old-fashioned method of informers. The uprooting of potential challengers in an organization, revolutionaries in a country, and heretics in a church is always relentless and merciless. In the late 1960s and early 1970s, the Office of the President directed the burglary of a psychiatrist's office and wiretapping of its own high officials and others for "national security" purposes. The President himself ordered the bugging of his brother's telephone conversation for a year for "protective reasons."

The same kind of activities has been going on in a less sophisticated way in business and labor. Testimony by a labor organizer in January 1937 before a Senate Committee, chaired by Robert La Folette, presented some forty affidavits of admitted spying for a trade association and a company in the electrical and machine industry. The hired spies operated in companies in which open shop existed or in which a union was about to be formed. These agents filed weekly reports and vouchers identified by numbers. In the words of one of the sworn depositions, "I was to make reports concerning the type of men I was working with, whether any of the men were constantly complaining about conditions, to get to know what my fellow workers were thinking about, and their attitude toward their pay and working conditions. I was also told that when I incorporated any of the complaints of the men I was to make sure to state the name of the man."

The bulk of intelligence activities does not involve such sleuthings but careful analyses and judgments of openly available data. Such public sources provide a fairly accurate picture as to the pulse of the community in which you operate. In this connection your assessments should go beyond purely economic considerations, even for relatively straightforward business competitions. As Milton Kotler puts it, some of the broader sociological issues of direct significance for corporate surveillance are: "How are corporations relating to other forces within the city, like the professions and political machines, and for what exchange of interest? Whom do they oppose and seek to weaken? How are they winning the institutional support to develop and establish a durable rhetoric to protect their power? Which institutions and sectors of the public will object and resist?"

It should be understood that intelligence gathered under normal conditions provides only data for the adversarial baseline. The true mettle of the opposition is largely determined by his generalship and will under stress. This cannot be known until you have tested his main body in actual conflict. For this reason, a sizeable contingency factor should be melded into your estimate of the situation. The initial stages of any engagement should be considered to be as much an intelligence-gathering phase as an initiation of active confrontation.

Except on a selected basis, do not reveal your possession of a significant piece of intelligence. Avoid the temptation of showing off your knowledge about diverse topics of conversation. The shrewd operator even goes to some pains to mislead his rivals into believing that his information is of a contrary character. This dissembling achieves the dual purpose of keeping the information to himself and transmitting noise to others. The nineteenth century Rothschilds were artists at this. The five sons of Mayer Rothschild stationed themselves in Frankfurt, Naples, Vienna, Paris, and London and maintained an efficient intelligence liaison among themselves. Focus was directed to news that could prove profitable at the stock market and the commodity bourse.

While the Battle of Waterloo was underway, England was kept wondering about the outcome for thirty hours. If the British had lost, the English consols would drop in value. If she had won, they would rise. So the speculators were watching like hawks for any sign of early indications. Late in the afternoon of June 19, 1815 a Rothschild agent with a Dutch gazette just off the press but not yet delivered to the stands boarded a boat at Ostend. Nathan Rothschild was at Folstone Harbor in England waiting in the early morning fog. He glanced at the headlines, informed the government in London many hours before it received word from her own messenger, then went over to the money exchange. Instead of buying consols, as a novice with such a hot tip would have done, he sold and sold. The traders felt that Rothschild had the inside information about Waterloo. So the price of consols dropped and dropped. At the last moment, he bought a hoard at the lowest price. Nathan Rothschild became the boss of the British Stock Exchange overnight.

42   **Integrative principle**   No matter how well administratively knit your supporting organization, it is never sufficiently solid a base for great power, unless at its very core stands one or more living integrative principles associated with conducive preconditions. You must bring your cadre back to these principles at the earliest signs of deviance. Reinforce them with each reorganization.

In primitive African communities, where terror had proven successful as a binding factor, Eugene Walter had identified five preconditions. These are: (1) An accepted system of beliefs lends justification of violence, such as ancestral license of terror. (2) Victims are expendable. (3) The agents of terror and their victims are kept apart from contemporary social activities at times by means of devices such as masks. (4) Incentives for cooperation are employed at the same time. (5) The terror does not destroy the cooperation necessary for social order and function.

One of the continuing problems facing the leader of a tightly controlled organization, which has prospered heretofore on the basis of a well integrated doctrine, is the doctrine's gradual loss of appeal to the members, who are being increasingly influenced by the outside world.

When a basic mismatch of integrative principle and reality exists, the power of the leader becomes questioned. When the leader does not budge in the face of the breakdown of the previously effective integrative principles, a second reaction often sets in among his people. There arises a tactical ignoring of the old doctrines on a selective basis and an adoption of activities outside of the doctrinal areas as the commanding centers of interest in their day-to-day preoccupations.

A drift of this nature is visible in the Catholic Church. During the late 1970s many educated lay Catholics chose to abide by certain approved practices, such as attending Sunday mass, and to disregard certain proscriptions, such as birth control.

In addition, there is an increasing entry of priests and nuns, while still wearing the robes of the church, into boards of directors of corporations, civil rights movements, and political campaigns in the United States. On the last Sunday in April 1972, no less than a dozen nuns disrupted a mass celebrated by the cardinal himself in St. Patrick's Cathedral in New York City to protest the Catholic Church's apathy on the Vietnam War, then prostrated themselves in the central aisle. The managing editor of the Catholic Commonweal magazine commented in reference to the incident "that the peace witness is but one aspect of a widened social apostolate which has taken more nuns into the inner city (sometimes living in rooms or an apartment), onto campuses in pastoral capacities and to assignments in housing projects, prisons and drug clinics. While nuns long have worked in hospitals and among the poor, today the numbers going into these activities and more radical social pursuits are unprecedented."

Should the center of active moral interest continue to shift from the afterlife to the secular sphere, the Catholic Church will have to find a way acceptable to the modern mind of increasing the magnetic power of her traditional integrative principles and/or provide theological extensions to encompass the diverse yearnings in this-worldly ethics, thereby subsuming them over time. Otherwise it will be faced with a series of insidious departures in this-worldly weightings, which are often as debilitating to the vigor of an institution as outright secessions.

The task of fashioning an effective integrative principle to bind together people who happened to associate out of expediency is, at times, almost an impossible one. This seems to be the case with large cities. These centers of culture are of greater service and value to nonresident artists, patrons, and audiences, it often seems, than to the residents themselves. The mayor's channels of communications usually lead not to the people but to the leaders of special-interest blocks, such as labor unions, business, ethnic groups, churches, and political machines. Each of them is committed to the perpetuation of its respective narrow integrative principles, rather than the nebulous one of "the common good" being bruited about by the mayor. This lack of a collective cohesion led Jan Habberton to despair when he said in 1899 that "A great city is a great sore—a sore which can never be cured."

Before constituting your cadre and massing your constituency, therefore, be sure you have thought through your integrative principles very carefully from the standpoint of both its initial attractivity and its long-term viability and adaptability.

43 **Orthopraxy** During former centuries, the elite was able to subjugate people through sheer force, intellectual superiority, and/or wealth. With the awakening and educating of the labor and peasant classes in the twentieth century, these methods alone no longer suffice. A tacit consent from the ruled for the ruler to rule seems necessary. There is an increasing need as time goes on for a voluntary surrender of freedom on the part of the people at large or at least for a relative passivity toward encroachments on it. An essential instrument for bringing this predisposition into being is propaganda. The purpose of your propaganda, then, should not be sympathetic education but subtle manipulation.

Public debates are getting increasingly popular. Whenever possible, you should avoid entanglements of this sort with a professional intellectual. His purpose on such occasions is subconsciously often to show how intellectually superior he is to the other fellow, while yours is not the converse, but to achieve a certain practical objective, which may have no necessary relation to the outcome of a contest of words. You have all to lose and nothing to gain in most exercises of this kind. If you are not as clever-tongued as the intellectual, the audience will think your cause unworthy of its support. If you are every bit as clever, your supporters will only become confused by the haranguing intricacies and lose the intensity of their original ardor. Your debating opponent would have enjoyed the stimulation of the exchange, but you would have only succeeded in braking your own momentum to power.

Even a learned scholar like Desiderius Erasmus disdained grappling with disputatious men of the intellect. "Perhaps it were better to pass over the theologians in silence, and not to move such a Lake Camarina, or to handle such a herb *Anagyris foetida,* as that marvelously supercilious and irascible race," he concluded. "For they may attack with six hundred arguments, in squadrons, and drive me to make a recantation which if I refuse, they will straightway proclaim me a heretic. . . . They are protected by a wall of scholastic definitions, arguments, corollaries, implicit and explicit propositions. . . . The methods our scholastics pursue only render more subtle those subtlest of subtleties; for you will escape from a labyrinth more quickly than from the tangle of Realists, Nominalists, Thomists, Albertists."

In point of fact, many of these individuals subconsciously yearn for power of their own. They are not intellectuals of the truth but intellectuals of power. They seek domination of the minds of people. They will not let you, as a person of power, sidestep their attacks so readily. Consequently, you should maintain your own phalanx of hair-splitters to throw into the forensic breach. The object of the participation is not to convince the debating opposition of the validity of your own position but to obtain the support of the audience for some practical goal in mind. If losing a given debate would help the cause you have in mind, for example, then do not hesitate to lose it.

Orthodoxy should not comprise your primary objective in propaganda, but what Jacques Ellul has called orthopraxy. This is "an action that in itself, and not because of the value judgments of the person who is acting, leads directly to a goal, which for the individual is not a conscious and intentional objective to be attained, but which is considered such by the propagandist." Knowing the real action to be taken in furtherance of the objective behind the informational barrage, the propagandist "maneuvers the instrument that will secure this action."

Propaganda is the prime prop to power.

44 **Propaganda methods** The subject is a broad one, about which much has been written. This is not the proper place for a detailed exposition. But because of its central role in your progression to great power, it is essential that you develop a keen sense of most of its ramifications. We shall touch on a number of aspects to provide some flavor of its multimasking agilities.

Controlling media. The more widespread the empire concerned, the more significant is the role played by the public media. They package the issues. They select the data for the people to see. They mold the predilections. They editorialize. They command a large fraction of the average person's nonwork waking hours. A good index of the propaganda value of the public media is the cost of advertising. In the 1978 professional football championship game in New Orleans, Louisiana, the available advertising time for the television broadcast was over-subscribed at $400,000 per minute.

It is because of this overwhelming influence that the press and the broadcasting stations are always among the first to be seized in a revolution and controlled in a totalitarian state thereafter. Adolf Hitler held Max Amann, the Reich boss of the press, in highest esteem because of his bringing the German newspapers into the Nazi orbit. Beginning in 1920 Amann built up the Nazi's own publishing domain to direct ownership of 80 percent of the German press in 1942. The Marxist publishing houses were liquidated outright in 1933. The Amann ordinances of April 1935 took care of the middle-class journals. The Reich Chamber of Culture was given the authority to promulgate requirements for institutions in cultural activities, to open and close enterprises in them, and to overview their conduct. As president of the chamber, Amann eliminated the independent presses in short order.

The same degree of domination of the news media has not happened in democratic countries. Nevertheless, those in power continue to insinuate themselves on the freedom of the television, radio, and the press by the more subtle means of controlling the flow of information to them rather than the release from them.

In making use of the mass media, you should recognize their limitations as well as their strengths. Even though they may diffuse information widely, the average person does not take action based on their say-so alone. He usually makes a personal, even though cursory, check on a face-to-face basis with some other individual who fills the role of opinion leader. You should always have your own representatives in the flesh on the ground to retain the confidence of your constituents and assure them in person. This is why missionaries will continue to be the backbone in the propaganda of any faith and why office holders will continue to make frequent public appearances among their constituents. After they have planted the seed or confirmed the message by dealing directly with their followers or potential followers, the massive wave of the media can then take over for a while. They are particularly effective in following up on specific issues based on supposed facts, appealing to emotions, focusing on limited-interest groups, and discussing personalities.

Adapting messages. When beaming to the opposition, your message should convey the advantages of coming around to your point of view. At the same time, the disparaging attacks from the other side must be vigorously displaced.

When beaming to the peripheral members of your own movement, the propaganda should stress the "fact" that they are on a winning team with a good cause, led by an inspired tradition-maker, a man or woman of the times. Furthermore, the word is to be spread around that it is futile to buck the tide in your favor in any case.

When beaming to the relevant public, your spokesmen should stress the similarity of your positions to its traditional values and mores and the identity of what you are trying to do to what it wants in the long run.

As the power struggle rises in intensity, considerations of fairness usually become progressively elastic. This is commonly seen in political campaigns. The one waged against Herbert Hoover in 1932 is not atypical. As described by Arthur Krock, the Democratic Committee's "smear Hoover" machinery "had been supremely well oiled by financial contributions obtained by National Chairman John J. Raskob and put in charge of one of the ablest political propagandists since the days of Andrew Jackson's pamphleteers and journalists, Charles Michaelson, formerly of *The World*. The daily output of personal attacks on Hoover's presidential capacity—including a deluge of ghost-written speeches for Democratic spokesmen—fixed as a fact in the American mind the thesis that Hoover's presidential incapacity was to blame for the outbreak and prolongation of the Depression." Over a century ago, Henry Clay had already proclaimed, yet again, that "The arts of power and its minions are the same in all countries and in all ages. It marks its victim; denounces it; and excites the public odium and the public hatred, to conceal its own abuses and encroachments."

Employing sign stimuli. A given symbol may mean different things to different people. You should be clear about the fitness of the symbol to the target audience before using them. Do not be overly taken by advertising gimmicks dreamt up on the spur of the moment by Madison Avenue agencies. Six-fingered hands, naked damsels, and talking stomachs may be appropriate for high school class rings, bath soaps, and antacids. But there are so many well-proven symbols available for your kind of propaganda purposes that there is little need to risk your cause on adolescent novelties.

If properly chosen, sign stimuli can be counted to trigger predictably definite behavior patterns. The male robin, for example, will attack a bundle of red feathers but not an exact replica of a robin without the characteristic red breast. The male silver-washed fritillary butterfly begins courtship responses in reacting to a rotating cylinder painted with orange and dark stripes. The more rapid the rotation of the cylinder, the more sexually excited the male becomes. The artificial sex partner stimulates the same emotions as the fluttering wings of the female butterfly with their orange and dark stripes.

Human beings are likewise susceptible to spontaneous actuation. One of the more dramatic of the sign stimuli is the severed head. It has been used throughout history to strike fear into the hearts of the enemy. The same recoiling has been observed in laboratory investigations with untrained primates. A sudden paroxysm of terror occurs at being shown a model of a detached human or chimpanzee head. An innate releasing mechanism seems to be involved in the anthropoid nervous system itself.

Second-order associations are also useful. Rasputin found his peasant clothes of greased boots and belted shirt and his unkempt beard to be of considerable advantage in his relations with the czar and the czaritza. When listening to him, they had the feeling that they were hearing the voice of the people. When listening to the members of the Duma in fine attire, they had the feeling that they were hearing the voice of the gentry.

Rallying allies. Among the closest of natural allies in America are members of certain minority religions. The same goes for a few minority races. Should you belong to one of these groups, your propaganda should contain subtle allusions that attract such otherwise neutral individuals to your side, without alienating their enemies who do not happen to be yours. Those who are naturally kindred to at least one aspect of your propaganda will usually stop to listen to the rest. This is half the success. Should you not be naturally allied to the audience but your opposition is, then your propaganda should refrain from mentioning the matter at all, so as not to drive the listeners into his camp. In this connection, the minority should not be written of simply because it is relatively small in numbers. This is shortsighted. If properly inspired, minority members are more willing to undergo greater sacrifices for a common cause. Their impact per capita is far greater than members of the majority.

Another group of logical allies involves the military and industry. During times of peace, industry prospers from military procurement; during times of war, industry relies on the military as the only means of protecting its facilities from destruction. Conversely, during times of peace, the military requires the support of industry as a logistical mobilization base; during times of war the military depends upon industrial output for combat superiority over the enemy. Under our present social conditions, no military leader can afford to weaken industry, and no industrial giant can afford to dismantle the military. If you are using either as a power base, you will find the other an amenable auxiliary, and accordingly, your propaganda should never unwittingly give cause to injure that solidarity.

Even more of a Siamese twin are the head of state and the military. In order to placate the civilian sector, the closeness is played down by both parties. But the irreducible fact remains: no head of state can remain powerful for long without strong military backing; no military chief of staff can be strong for long without the political and financial conduits of a generous head of state. He who controls the military controls the nation. The American Constitution theoretically recognizes this point by designating the President as Commander-in-Chief of the Armed Forces. South American politics repeatedly have demonstrated their empirical inseparability.

Solidifying biases. Once you are fairly well entrenched, the immediate objective of much of your mass communications should be reinforcing favorable opinions in contrast to changing unfavorable ones. Those who are disposed to follow your lead are given a rationalization for doing so. In view of the continuing conflict between private conscience and institutional requirements, the propaganda should salve the friction so that the individuals will fight for your institution's welfare without reservation. This would strengthen their resistance to the opposition and offer justification for their emotional excesses.

A helpful technique toward preventing the erosion of faith by rival ideologies among your followers is alerting them to the probability of such attempts. This in itself would arouse the spectre of a threat, which warns your disciples to ready their own defenses. The message might be sharpened by citing an anticipated argument or temptation of the opposition's, even if it is not accompanied by a refutation and even if the opposition uses a completely different line of attack later on. The followers have already been conditioned to close their ears to such quarters.

Exploiting foibles. Effective propagandists know just how to limn their line with attachments to some basic human susceptibilities. As an advertising agent once remarked, "The cosmetic manufacturers are not selling lanolin; they are selling hope."

For the Japanese, shame and mockery constitute strong attention-getters. For the Americans, guilt and anxiety.

A rather profitable opening for appeal to affluent populations, such as Americans, had been portrayed by the Scythian Babouc in Voltaire's tale. He was sent by the god Ithuriel to see whether the Persian city of

Persepolis should be destroyed because of its evil. During his investigation, Babouc bought a toy. Finding that he was grossly overcharged, he jotted down the merchant's name for special punishment. Just then the merchant himself appeared before him, returning his purse which Babouc had left in the store. In his surprise, Babouc inquired as to how an honest man like him would charge four times the value of his commodities.

Whereupon the man answered: "There is not a tradesman of even very small reputation in the city, who would not have returned your purse; but whoever said that I sold these bric-a-bracs for only four times their value is very wrong. I sold them for ten times their value. . . . But nothing is more just. It is the ephemeral fancies of men that puts the value on these things. It is this fancy that keeps the hundred workmen whom I employ. It is this fancy that gives me a fine house and a beautiful chariot and horses. It is this, in fact, that stimulates industry, fashions taste, promotes circulation, and produces prosperity."

After thinking over what the merchant said, Babouc scratched his name off the list.

Pettifogging truths. Thomas Hobbes conceded that "I doubt not, but if it had been a thing contrary to any man's right of dominion, or to the interest of men that have dominion, that the three angles of a triangle should be equal to two angles of a square; that doctrine should have been, if not disputed, yet by the burning of all books of geometry, suppressed, as far as he whom it concerned was able."

The suppression of the basic documents of the opposition has been common historical practice by all organizations with any pretense to power. The early church fathers attacked the *Mishma* of the Jews as a menace to Christianity. The fact that the *Mishma,* second in importance only to the Bible to the orthodox Jew, made no mention of the founders of Christianity was taken to mean that the authors denied Christianity. Emperor Maximilian ordered the *Talmud* burnt. In many regions of Europe during the Middle Ages, it was purged from public distribution.

Hannah Arendt speculated about the prevalence of general misinformation in our times. "Is this because organized lying, dominating the public realm, as distinguished from the private liar who tries his luck on his own hook, was still unknown? Or has this something to do with the striking fact that, except for Zoroastrianism, none of the major religions included lying as such, distinguished from 'bearing false witness,' in their catalogue of grave sins?"

Truth has been irrevocably compromised in Western society by the adoption of adversary proceedings as a social convention in conflict resolution. In the court of law, neither the prosecutor, nor the defense attorney, nor the jury, nor the judge is charged with revealing the complete truth at all times. Even the witness is enjoined from testifying the truth, as he sees it; he is only permitted to state the partial truth as strictly delimited by the specific questions put by the adversary attorneys in court. The prosecutor becomes famous for the jailing of people, not for the elaborating of truth. The defense attorney becomes famous for the keeping of people out of jail, not for the elaborating of truth. The jury is not permitted to search for missing pieces of the complete truth but must determine guilt solely on the basis of the evidence selectively placed before it by the adversaries.

In this connection a professor of law in Washington, D.C. posed the following three riddles for attorneys in 1966: "Is it proper to cross-examine for the purpose of discrediting the reliability of an adverse witness whom you know to be telling the truth? Is it proper to put on the stand a witness who you know will commit perjury? Is it proper to give your client legal advice when you have reason to believe that the knowledge will tempt him to commit perjury?" The correct answers, so the professor taught, are "Yes" to all three. Not only was the professor not admonished for such teachings by his peers, he was promoted to dean before too long.

In some respects, practical justice in our system of jurisprudence may be regarded as the statistical average of pettifogged truths, fractionally distilled by well-schooled alchemists in the art.

The most artful pettifogging uses the target recipient himself as the agent. Carefully selected raw data are furnished to the exclusion of others. The listener is then given all the independence of decision in the world. But he can come to no other honest conclusion save the one of the perpetrator's own predetermined prototype. At no time had any preference been mentioned, and the subject feels certain that the decision was entirely his own.

This approach bears some resemblance to the theory of painting developed by George Seurat in the latter part of the last century. After studying the physics of optics and color he came up with the concept of pontillism. The colors are broken down into their component hues, which are then put on the canvas as tiny brush dots or strokes. The spectator's own retina then reconstitutes these into the actual color and object that the artist had intended him to see all along.

Spreading innuendos.　In the field of propaganda, few devices are as insidiously effective as the innuendo.

Ralph Turner and Lewis Killian divided the commonly employed techniques into the following categories: name calling (use of unpopular or unsavory terms to tinge the belief or person without justification), glittering generality (use of lofty or noble phrases to attach respectability to one's position or self), plain folks (identification of one's sentiments with the solid common people), testimonial (association of a despicable person with the ideas of the opposition and an honorable or heroic person with those of oneself), transfer (association of an odious thing with the ideas of the opposition and a revered thing with one's own), card stacking (selection and omission of facts to present a formidable array of data against the opposition and a formidable array for oneself), and bandwagon (implication that the large majority is rushing to one's own leadership and the listener should not be left behind).

Remaining silent.   During periods of grave uncertainties or delicate balance, you should refrain from public utterances, no matter how tempting it is to reply to the things being said. Do not let your own propagandists, who are being paid to do something, goad you into making statements against your better judgments.

You may wish to memorize the four short speeches suggested by Edward Hale, which might prove useful for many occasions of this sort. These are: (1) Very well, thank you. And you? (2) I am very glad you like it. (3) There has been so much said, and, on the whole, so well said, that I will not occupy the time. (4) I agree, in general, with my friend at the other side of the room.

ORCHESTRATING CEREMONIES

In some respects, living itself can be described as nothing more than a sustained succession of ceremonies. Society runs smoother when pleasing ceremonies prevail. Impatient amateurs often forget this essential facet in the scheme of power. This section expands on the theme. What are the nine varieties of ceremonies which you must keep performing on a regular basis? And how do you go about each one?

45 **Strategy reinforcement** Life without ceremony is like a gift without wrapping. Even brute force is often accompanied by a fitting ceremony. In the past wars were usually preceded by a formal declaration. Today, the last instruction by the referee to the boxers in the ring before the opening bell is: "Now, shake hands and come out fighting."

This superficial kind of ceremony is well understood. What is meant by ceremony in the context of power is much more. It is, above anything else, strategy reinforcing.

Observe the negotiator casting a feigned sigh of impatience with just the right grimace and loudness, as if to intimate that unless the unwarranted concessions are extended the entire deal will be called off. Observe the politician presenting the picture of a cool-headed steadiness with solid judgment during periods of normalcy and that of a decisive leader with passionate drive during periods of unrest. Observe the Kiwai Papuans conducting emotion-packed ritual in preparing young warriors for battle—feeding them eyes, talons, beak, and tongue of the large hawk, so as to sharpen their ability to find, seize, and kill the enemy; and male and female sex organs of the enemy, so as to strengthen their determination to slaughter both sexes alike.

There has never been a person of great power who failed to recognize the indissoluble relationship between ceremonial reinforcement and social control.

When Charlemagne penetrated the sacred sanctuary of the Saxons in the year 722 as King of the Franks and entered their Holy Hearth in Westphalia, he cut their Irminsul down. This was their ancient symbol of the bearer of the universe. There was no misunderstanding among all present as to his message.

The old Norman chronicler outlined how meticulously Duke William of Normandy planned the binding ceremony to strengthen his claim to the throne of England. When rival Saxon Harold was in his castle, Harold was made to understand that his very life depended upon his obeying the wishes of the duke. One day the duke cordially disclosed to the Saxon that King Edward of England had promised the duke that he would be the successor to the crown. The duke added that he would appreciate Harold's help when the time came. Harold agreed; he was in no position to do otherwise. William also obtained Harold's consent to marry his daughter Adela and to send Harold's own sister to Normandy to become the wife of one of William's barons.

After that conversation the duke proceeded to cloak the promise in a form appropriate to his purpose. He collected all the bones and relics of the saints kept in various churches and monasteries in Normandy and placed them in a chest, which was covered with a golden cloth, in the council room. A missal was placed on top. Harold was asked to repeat his private agreement in public before the assembled nobles. Taken by surprise and unable to go back on his word, Harold placed his hand upon the missal and repeated his promise under oath. "So help me God," he ended. And the assembly cried: "God grant it." Whereupon duke William pulled off the golden cloth, lifted the lid of the chest, and revealed to Saxon Harold the holy relics upon which he had solemnly swore. Harold was stunned.

In modern times we are witness to how Charles de Gaulle went through considerable effort, ingenuity, and circumvention to outmaneuver General Dwight Eisenhower and the Allies to dictate the ceremonies accompanying the liberation of Paris on August 25, 1944. Despite the expressed orders of the High Command that the Americans and not the French were to take over the city, de Gaulle felt that the vital political interest of the French government, as well as himself, was at stake. So de Gaulle out-schemed and frustrated everybody and marched at the head of the French Second Armored Division down the Champs Elysees. Two days later, General Eisenhower paid him an official call to show that "de Gaulle was the boss of France." The ceremonial trooping down the Champs was an essential part of the strategy upholding the primacy of France and de Gaulle. In his mind, the American planned ceremony would have greased the skids for the setting up of an American military government, which would open the way for the Russians to move into the vacuum on its departure.

If a course of desperation is inevitable in any case, then the strategy-reinforcing ceremony can be depended on to facilitate making the best of a bad bargain. Such is the magical spell cast on a girl in

Guadalcanal embarking on a career of prostitution. The ritual usually takes place after an initial scandal, which forces the girl into the profession. A mixture of rough leaves, burrs, thorns, and smooth bark is placed beneath the girl's sleeping place. The incantations begin with the straightforward statement that "she seeks men always. . . . She is without shame." She is already a prostitute, so let her excel in it. "Let the rough leaves make staying at home uncomfortable so the girl will go out and search for men. Let the burrs and thorns stick the desire for men in her mind. Let the smooth bark make her skin beautiful." Then a mat is placed by the magician over the leaves. After several nights sleeping on it, the girl becomes attuned to her new life. She is emotionally ready. She will serve her clients well. She has become a pro.

46 **Participation** What is needed more than anything else for your acquisition and retention of power in a democratic institution to look right is conveying a sense of citizen participation. A pervasive feeling of participation soothes the anguish of being used on the part of the subjects. To foster the feeling, you should encourage their substantive participation with power of decision on all matters that do not jeopardize your power. On those issues that are decisive with respect to your power, however, you should be most adroit in fostering a convincing ceremonial substitution.

What the participation by the constituents actually amounts to in the latter instances is signing their proxies over to you, in effect, and vicariously enjoying your power. Much of the practical processes of the wheeling and dealing of corporation chief executive officers fall into this category. They never cease to remind the stockholders at the annual ceremony that they are working for *them*.

The vicarious participation on the part of the citizens in the exercise of raw power by the district attorney has been dissected by Edmond Cahn. He told about a store robbery in New York City, involving two masked men who shot a policeman during the 1950s. The unemployed young men of the neighborhood were rounded up, and the woman of the store identified two of them as the bandits. They were taken to court, tried, found guilty—despite credible evidence that they were someplace else at the time of the incident—and sentenced to ninety-nine years in prison.

The mother of one of them put an ad in the newspapers, offering a reward of $5000—representing eleven years of savings as a scrubwoman—for exonerating information. Intrigued by the notice, reporters investigated the case and found that the woman of the store had refused to identify the youths but was forced to do so by the police, who had threatened to send her to jail for selling liquor illegally. The conspiracy was led by the district attorney, who wanted to assure the international customers and visitors attending the exposition, which was to open in the near future, that the city was perfectly safe. For the merchants' sake, someone had to be arrested and convicted in a hurry. When the facts were finally published in the newspapers, the public pressure brought about a pardon and release of the two innocent young men.

The ceremonial masking of calculated ruthlessness is older than the Bible. "It is older than the death that came to Uriah the Hittite because a king desired to possess Uriah's wife, or the death that came to Naboth because another king desired to possess Naboth's vineyard," noted Cahn, "and there is no comforting reason to assert that any city or state is today immune from incidents of this kind." But something new has come into play since the dawn of democracy. The new factor is that "we citizens find ourselves identified with the *district attorney. . . .* Representative government has implicated us. We are participant-accomplices, if we will—in the deeds that are done in our name by our authority. . . . As human beings, it has always been possible to connect ourselves with the victim of the wrong; as citizens, the new, democratic experience is that we find ourselves unexpectedly connected with the inflicter of wrong. What can this experience do but tighten and intensify our involvement in Joe's mistreatment at the hands of the law?"

Your continuation in power rests on social respectability. And social respectability calls for a judicious blend of actual and ceremonial participation by your constituency.

47 **Credibility** Your constituents must have faith in your credibility. They must not only believe your data, but they must also believe you.

The greater the consequences of the issues under contention, the more urgent is the need for trust on the part of your followers. During the days of the Hittite Empire in the thirteenth century B. C. the sovereign signed no obligation to his vassals. But they trusted him to do what was right by them. As recorded by George E. Mendenhall, the Hittite suzerainty treaties "established a relationship between the two, but in its form it is unilateral. The stipulation of the treaty are binding only on the vassal, and only the vassal took an oath of allegiance." The Hittite king does not have to bind himself by a legal formality. His very position takes it for granted that he would protect his subjects from claims or attacks by others. "Consequently for him to bind himself to specific obligations with regard to his vassal would be an infringement upon his sole right of self-determination and sovereignty. A most important corollary of this fact is the emphasis upon the vassal's obligation to *trust* in the benevolence of the sovereign."

Newsmen in Washington began popularizing the phrase "credibility gap" during the mid-1960s. As construed by William McGaffin and Erwin Kroll, "they were too shy to speak of lies—the lies that increasingly, alarmingly, emanate from their government through its official spokesmen, including the President of the United States." They pointed to many incidents.

For two days after the Russians shot down a U-2 espionage plane, American officials insisted it was a weather observation plane that had accidentally strayed off course from Turkey. When Secretary of State Foster Dulles met with Foreign Minister Vyacheslav Molotov and violently disagreed on every point, the communiques said that their meeting was "friendly" in order to give the impression to the world that the United States and the Soviet Union were settling their differences. When the ill-fated American-sponsored invasion of the Cuban coast occurred in 1961, a deliberate falsehood was passed on to the press by the White House. When the President was proclaiming to the world America's absolute respect for Cambodia's neutrality in the late 1960s, American planes were bombing it all along.

The American people have so frequently discovered that they have been misled that the old appeal of "Honest, believe me" no longer suffices. Your credibility requires concrete confirmations on a continuing basis. You have to produce convincing demonstrations. There are many ways of doing so. The best foundation on which to build is absolute integrity on all matters not critical to your personal power. If at all possible, avoid pure fabrications. There are many other ways which are more effective and safer. These generally fall into two categories.

The first is exemplified by the Chicago alderman in 1970. He would often visit his favorite pawnshop, pay cash for a hundred-dollar watch, and immediately pawn it for thirty dollars. He would then redeem it within a short time. After this cycle happened several times, the pawnbroker became curious and asked the alderman as to the purpose of the routine. The latter explained that his political friends were continually pressuring him for contributions. So he simply tells them that he doesn't have any money and whips out the pawn ticket to prove the point.

The second category is exemplified by Shang Yang, a minister of the Court of Ch'in during the fourth century B. C. Lord Shang had planned a drastic revision of the social order. Definite ranks were to be instituted. Each of these was to be assigned stipulated rights, duties, and privileges in the hierarchy. The community was to be organized into family groups. Members within each were to be responsible for each other's behavior, sharing all rewards and punishments. Before promulgating the radical edict, however, he set out to solidify his own credibility among the people.

A thirty-foot pole was placed near the south gate of the capitol. The people were assembled around it. He then announced that he would give ten measures of gold to anyone who would move the pole to the north gate. No one believed his ears and no one ventured forth. "Fifty measures of gold," Shang raised the offer. One man stepped forward and moved the pole to the north gate. Whereupon Shang Yang promptly paid him the fifty measures of gold.

From that day on, his words were accepted throughout the land at face value.

48 **Reasonableness** A reputation for being reasonable is essential when your acquisition of power is to be based on a long-term accumulation of increments using means other than brute force. Objectives can often be more efficiently gained through accommodating than through mutually damaging. Such an approach goes smoothly only if there is a modicum of respect for moderation on both sides.

One of the most esteemed persons of power during the 1930s in this regard was Sidney Hillman. He was leader of the Amalgamated Clothing Workers of America from its inception in 1914 to his death in 1946. Not only did he raise wages and improve working conditions for his union members, but also significantly influenced the President in national social policies. He was well-known for his reasonableness even among the bargaining corporate executives. In 1934 the trade journal, *The Daily News Record*, wrote that "Mr. Hillman enjoys the confidence and respect of employers with whom he has dealt. It is generally said of him in employer circles that he has never made demands on an industry that it could not meet economically and he has been known to make concessions where the realities of the situation proved irresistible."

If a person were reasonable by nature, he or she would not have to worry about artificial means for shoring up the reputation of reasonableness. It would naturally show through his or her actions as a matter of course. But most individuals pursuing power with any degree of tenacity are naturally one-sided in their distribution of say-so over others. Power, after all, rests on an unequal equilibrium of command.

It would appear likely that the internally obtuse man, although it may not show externally, who keeps inching forward and grabbing every parcel of power on which he can lay his hands, will become a man of greater power in a shorter time than a man willing to relinquish that little extra increment for the sake of reasonableness. Nevertheless, it has been shown time and again that once a person in high position loses all semblance of reasonableness, his downfall is imminent. Even his intimate cadre soon deserts him.

Your ceremonies of reasonableness must be carefully adapted to the situation at hand. When the target individuals are totally unfamiliar with the issue or at least slightly disposed in your direction, then advancing only evidence supporting your own side is usually most persuasive. However, when the target individuals are opposed, then the better way of winning them over would be the inclusion of the contra arguments as well. Of course, you must be discriminating in selecting and phrasing the pros and cons so that the overall weight is not prejudicial against your own case.

Under certain circumstances it is preferable to present the arguments of the opposition *after* your own. The forceful elucidation of your own position will then induce the audience to discount the others. This holds especially when the opposing points are not very cogent and no time elapses between the two presentations.

On the other hand, when the target individuals are somewhat suspicious of your position but are conversant with the opposition's argument, then it might be more effective to present the opposing argument first. You would then have first conveyed the picture of reasonableness, while giving your own arguments the benefit of recency at the same time.

On occasions, an artificial competition espousing a diametrically opposite extreme is fostered and kept under surreptitious reins, like the bogeyman. The presence of this phantom threat would thereby make your own position appear so much more reasonable by contrast.

One of the most disarming conveyors of reasonableness is a sense of humor. A shared chuckle and laughter during the intermission of power plays often make a person appear not only reasonable but also genuine and lovable.

In any case, you should always try to lean over backward in situations when the outcome does not subtract from your power. Being considerate and even solicitous outside the arena of power also relaxes your own tensions, dissembles the opposition, and engenders a valuable goodwill among your broader base of support. Fierce competition for everything else leaves little energy for the fierce competition for power.

49 **Consensus** It is through consensus that organizational strength is enhanced and the troublesome minority neutralized. Without consensus, law itself, the guarantor of legalized power, is ineffective.

Never begrudge the time and effort spent toward gaining consensus among your constituents. Embarking on innovative and major programs is inevitably accompanied by controversy. Some individuals anticipate gains; others anticipate losses. The importance of the highest feasible consensus lies not only in increasing the support for your activities but also in decreasing antagonisms to your person. The relatively small amount of extra patience expended in converting someone over to your view and projecting a public appearance of consensus on the issue at hand is well worth the prevention of what may turn out to be a large amount of effort needed to defend against attacks that would not otherwise arise.

Depending on the scope of your interests, you would be involved at any given time in not just one large consensus issue but with many different consensuses involving various constellations of individuals. Some individuals may belong to more than one group. Your gaining their concurrence on one issue makes it easier to gain their concurrence on another. The greater the fraction of issues on which you gain agreement, the less likely will you be challenged on those actions taken by you, for which, for reasons of your own, no consensus is sought in fact but consensus is projected in ceremony. Let all issues not impinging significantly on your power therefore be decided by genuine debate and consensus. Let it be known ahead of time that you will abide by the decision of the group. The only thing you have to ensure against in such cases is that potential opponents are not exploiting the occasion to capture followers from your fold. This can best be done by your administrative guidance of the proceedings.

It is important that your constituents at large, who may be divided among themselves on various matters, get the feeling that no dissension exists within your leadership unit. Only on rare and transient circumstances should you permit persons who refuse to show loyalty to you by a public act of some kind into the very center of your movement. The astute biblical statement about vomiting the lukewarm from one's mouth is reflected in the instinctive utterance of the young rioter in

Watts of California in 1966. He went up to a black assemblyman standing nearby and demanded his expression of solidarity with the black people by throwing something at the police car. The gentleman refused, saying: "No. I'm for peace." The boy snapped back: "No. You're with the man."

The ceremony of consensus should ring with assertions of unity from the person of power and reverberate with reaffirmations from his constituents.

50 **Objective expertise** One of the commonly conducted ceremonies to assure the masses that the decisions have been arrived at openly, expertly, and objectively is the use of a "blue-ribbon" panel, a board of visitors, or such suitably labeled body. There is a large membership of professional committeemen from which to select. Through a judicious culling from the pool, a group can be assembled, which would be respected by the public to provide knowledgeable assessment and yet be depended on not to upset your applecart. In those infrequent cases of an unwelcomed report, the recommendations can be tabled through another ceremonial statement, such as lack of funds, the necessity of coordination with other studies underway, and being superseded by the emergence of new information that was not available at the time of the investigation.

The typical panel report, confirming what you have in mind to do, assumes a characteristic format. It begins with an assertion of the critical importance of the issue at hand, embellished with some choice cases of the horrible things which allegedly have happened or can happen because of insufficient attention to the problem. The ramifications, we are told, go significantly far beyond the narrow limits of the immediate question. In addition to the institution, the nation and mankind itself are affected. Then follows a voluminous compilation of data, which are related to the subject at hand to varying degrees and are conventionally attached as tabs A through X. About an inch of documentation is usually collected for each ten man-months of committee staff time. The discussion enumerates all the possible things that can be done, leading to the conclusion that pitifully little is underway. The recommendations call for greatly increased effort along the path paralleling the general objectives of the sponsor. To do anything short of this, we are again told, is to endanger the welfare and security of the institution, especially in the light of the latest intelligence that the competitor has been extremely active in the same field of late.

This consideration does not imply that most committees are assembled solely for cosmetic purposes. It is only to say that when they are manipulated for ceremonial purposes they do pay off handsomely—much more so than testimonials by believers in revival meetings and endorsements by celebrities on television.

A few pertinent comments about the value of ad hoc committees may be in order at this point. Properly constituted committees do find feasible solutions to knotty problems. They also coordinate the emerging plans among key elements of the organization. As a matter of fact, most large corporations are run by committees rather than individuals nowadays. Almost always do specially convened committees publicize one's resolve to do something about a crisis, take the pressure off the leader for a cooling-off period, float trial balloons for various options, recruit supporters of one's endeavor, and soften up the constituents toward acceptance of the impending course of action. Finally, committees often assist the chief executive officer should he or she prefer a more speculative and aggressive posture for his or her future plans. It often happens that given suitable encouragement, individuals are much more inclined toward higher risk options as members of a group than as individuals reacting separately. The ceremonial function of committees should not blind one to these substantial contributions to a smooth implementation of programs. Even the least of them, therefore, should not be dealt with in a cavalier fashion.

51 Legitimacy The less legitimate your designs and actions, the more impressive must be the accompanying or follow-on ceremonies of legitimizing. Although illegal power may be seized through force alone, it cannot be long sustained without the blessings of legitimacy.

During the days of ancient Greece a proposed plan was automatically approved by the masses as legitimate if it had the blessings of the Oracle of Delphi. Even then a ceremony had to be performed and a sign received. Oracles soon got out of fashion, and men have had to resort to less divine devices. Each kind of activities adapts its own set of proprieties to convey the impression that what is being done is not improper.

When Jugurtha bribed the Roman army commanders Calpurnius and Scaurus to halt their march into Numidia, they arranged a formal surrender by Jugurtha with the payment of thirty elephants, a number of cattle and horses, and a sum to the Roman quaestor. This ceremony convinced the Romans back home that everything was above board.

When the American President wanted to escalate the war in Vietnam during the early 1960s, he got the United States Senate to pass the 1964 Gulf of Tonkin Resolution. The overwhelming passage with only two dissenting votes out of a hundred provided the legal justification. By the time the Senate woke up to what it had done and repealed the resolution in 1969, the President had already committed half a million troops in a full-scale war. The succeeding President then claimed that *his* authority for continuation of the war does not rest on *that* piece of paper but on *others*. He would not object at all to see it repealed. In the meantime, it had served the intended purpose of legitimacy well.

Should legal documents prove impossible to come by, they can be faked. This practice was more commonly employed in the past, when forgeries were more difficult to detect. Among the more famous of the historical forgeries was the Protocols of Zion, which served as a basis of European antisemitic propaganda for several decades. It was first distributed by a Russian mystic, Sergei Nilus, during the early part of the twentieth century, purportedly as a record of some twenty meetings by a group of Jews in collaboration with the Egyptian Ritual of the Masonic Lodge to replace the Christian civilization with a world state of Jews and Freemasons. Even when it was exposed in 1921 as an obvious distorted plagiarism of Maurice Joly's *Dialogue*, it continued to influence public opinion for a couple more decades.

A rather primitive but time-proven technique at imparting legitimacy to the extension of one's power over another's domain is covertly stimulating a call for help within it. I recall the street gangs in Honolulu during my childhood. When spoiling for a fight they would send a small boy wandering about the neighborhood provoking an assault by an older boy. At times he would parade about with a small chip on his shoulder and dare someone to knock it off. If he were ignored, he would resort to something more drastic, like kicking the older boy in the shins. At the first sign of physical contact, the little fellow would yell for help. Whereupon the gang with brass knuckles, knives, and sticks would come rushing to his "rescue."

The same basic approach is often used by adults, albeit with far greater sophistication. There are always internal enemies to the party in power. The subtlest of signals on the possibility that help will be forthcoming if requested on a sufficiently high-sounding basis will elicit the desired pretext. If it is slow in coming, someone can be bribed to feign an appeal. As a last resort, secret agents may be sent into the territory.

On occasions, however, there appears to be no ready means available for conferring the cloak of legitimacy upon one's intended actions. In such cases, some leaders have resorted to the expedient of passing the dirty buck to some willing subordinate. A ceremonially graceful example is found in the annals of the second to the last of the Burmese kings, Meudoume-Men.

The king was a conscientious disciple of Buddha, diligently adhering to the precept of nonkilling of man or beast. No capital punishment was permitted in the kingdom. Now and then, some person would incur the wrath of the king. He would then turn to his prime minister and inquire, during some off-moment of relaxed conversation, whether or not So-and-so was still of this world. After several repetitions of the same query over a period of time, one day the prime minister would finally reply: "No, Your Majesty. I respectfully regret to report that So-and-so is no longer of this world."

And King Meudoume-Men would smile.

52 **Loftiness** "Reasons have to be given for the burdens that are variously proposed or approved," declared Louis Eisenstein. "In time the contending reasons are skillfully elaborated into systems of belief or ideologies which are designed to induce the required acquiescence. Of course, if an ideology is to be effective, it must convey a vital sense of some immutable principle that rises majestically above partisan preferences. Except in dire circumstances, civilized men are not easily convinced by mere appeals to self-interest. What they are asked to believe must be identified with imposing concepts that transcend their pecuniary prejudices." His statement summarizes a long series of human experience.

When King Akbar of India issued a decree in 1579 that he was to be the final authority in religious as well as civil matters, it was done "for the glory of God and propaganda of Islam."

When a group of young Russian nobles and army officers revolted against Czar Nicholas in the Decembrist Movement of 1825, they organized an "Association for Public Welfare."

When a group within the R. Hoe and Company took on the majority of the board in a proxy fight a century later, it mailed out solicitations to the stockholders in the name of the "Stockholders' Protective Committee."

When the Teamsters Union president keynoted the 1969 meeting of the Alliance for Labor Action to enlarge the union membership among the agricultural trade, and service activities, he announced that "We just want to do our thing in waging a war on America's social ills."

When the American public finally learned in 1974 that the Central Intelligence Agency had indeed been involved in the overthrow of the Chilean Marxist Government, despite earlier official assurances to the contrary, the President defended the action of his predecessor, asserting that it was "in the best interest of the people of Chile."

Following these precedents, instead of admitting that you are reaching for more power, solemnly state that you are seeking "more responsibilities so as to better serve the people with the talents you have." Instead of admitting that you are eliminating your opposition from ever contending your designs, solemnly state that you are "doing your duty in upholding justice." Be sure to invoke the universally appealing altruistic principles in protecting your privileged status and established power—peace, order, and harmony. Such a doctrine, as observed by E. H. Carr, "is the natural assumption of a prosperous and privileged class, whose members have a dominant voice in the community and are therefore naturally prone to identify its interest with their own. In virtue of this identification, any assailant of the interests of the dominant group is made to incur the odium of assailing the alleged common interest of the whole community, and is told that in making this assault he is attacking his own high-interests." The thesis thereby constitutes "an ingenious moral device invoked, in perfect sincerity, by privileged groups in order to justify and maintain their dominant position." The situation is true to the extent that harm to the dominant interest might also bring harm to the community as a whole. Yet the alleged natural harmony of interest is basically a rationalization by privileged power and provides yet another example "of the Machiavellian maxim that morality is the product of power."

In part, the euphemistic tendency may be a carryover from the conventional niceties of everyday business behavior. Typical of these are letters of recommendation on behalf of marginal performers. One is often entertained by the glowing expressions, although many a naive recipient who does not know the code may be pleased at the promising prospect. Instead of frankly stating: "He's a man of limited ideas," the letter says: "He's an excellent team worker." Instead of frankly stating: "He's a yes-man," the letter says: "He's a staunch supporter of his superiors." Instead of frankly stating: "He's a big mouth," the letter says: "He's a vigorous speaker who really sells his ideas." Instead of frankly stating: "He's afraid to make decisions on his own," the letter says: "He's one of our most active management committee members."

In today's large corporations, words such as incentive, individualism, and progress take on a special association. They border on secular piety. There is a new look, as Edward Ziegler phrased it, of "sacerdotal bureaucracy" in the executive corridor. "Ceremonial luxuriance is in many ways the most interesting aspect of the contemporary vested interest, as corporate ritual has much of the flavor of group magic."

It is well to remember, however, that appeals to lofty ideals and euphemisms work only with people who have satisfied most of their basic physiological needs. Do not try to recruit the unemployed on the basis of human rights, the sick on the basis of freedom, or the poor on the basis of the pursuit of happiness. Rally them under your banner on the basis of down-to-earth jobs, medical treatment, and food. Only after they have progressed out of physiological desperation into the American middle-class status should you preach about lofty ideals. In the meantime, do not rub salt into their wounds.

When Gerald Clark met Padre Antonio Costa in the village of Cabo in Northeastern Brazil, where Francisco Juliao was organizing his revolutionary Peasant Leagues in the 1950s, he asked the priest about the people's sentiments. "They do not believe in Juliao; they do not believe in the Church; they do not believe in anything," answered the Padre. "They are too hungry to believe."

53   Higher authority   "There is no law for God," said the Devil to Ivan Karamazov in Fëdor Dostoevsky's *The Brothers Karamazov.* "All things are permitted."

When a person is able to wrap his actions with God's blessings, things usually go much more effectively. A moving ceremony implying that what he is going to do or what he is calling on others to do has the highest approval of God Himself is to conduct a public prayer. It is not surprising to learn therefore that the crews of the B-29 and observation planes that atom-bombed Japan in 1945 had attended religious services before they took off from Tinian.

Or better still, a person can claim that what he wants to do has been directed by God. When Hung Hsiu-ch'uan organized the Society for the Worship of the Almighty in the early 1800s in southern China, he declared that God had entered his room in a dream, placed a sword in his hand, and commanded him to exterminate the devils. The movement destroyed temples, ordered people to pay tribute, and turned into the Tai-Ping rebellion against the Manchus.

For day-to-day affairs, the religious invocation cannot be overworked. Lesser and more visible authorities are often more quickening. A good example in the proper selection of gods is John L. Lewis's building up of his union in 1934.

During the 1929 depression the United Mine Workers was in a sad shape. Membership in the Pittsburgh bituminous district dropped from 45,000 to 293. Lewis tried desperately to revive the union. His friend Senator Robert F. Wagner attempted to pass the coal stabilization bill in vain in 1928 and 1930. A similar Davis-Kelly bill failed in 1932. Lewis switched support from the Republican to the Democratic Party, in which he saw sympathetic labor backing. In 1933 he succeeded in inserting a clause giving labor "the right of collective bargaining through representatives of its own choosing" in the National Recovery Act. With the passage of the Guffy-Vinson Act and the National Labor Relations Act, which established the legality of unionism in mining, he sailed forth in his membership drive with the slogan: "The President Wants You to Join the Union!"

Within a year the enrollment rose from 150,000 to 515,000. Lewis became the nation's most powerful labor boss.

54   **A winner**   To be a great leader is to be a shaman. You must be seasoned in the art of using images to instill an unshaken belief among your followers that you will always succeed in whatever you undertake.

A person would be in a much better position to look like a champion, of course, once he has established a track record of some kind. Given some accomplishments of note, they can be incorporated in the subsequent ceremonies with impressive impact. In his battle against the Samnites, the Roman general, Valerius Corvinus, sent his troops into a few light skirmishes to feel out the situation. Their performance did not please him. So he called them together before the main battle, reminded them of their valor when compared against the enemy, and added: "Consider then, under whose command you are about to go into battle, and whether your commander to whom you are listening is merely a big talker, terrible only in words; or whether he is a victorious fighter in military combat. I want you to follow my actions, and not merely my words; not the orders only, but the example of a man who by his own right arm has thrice achieved the consulate and the highest glory."

Saul D. Alinsky described how he staged a "cinch fight" to build the confidence of his followers in him as a winner and in themselves as a group, when he tried to organize the Back of the Yards in Chicago in the late 1930s. The demoralized people of the area were plagued with, among other things, a very high rate of infant mortality. They needed the medical services of the Infant Welfare Society. Alinsky looked into the situation and found that the community itself had driven out the

Infant Welfare Society's medical services about a decade earlier under the leadership of the local churches, because stories were being rumored about their dissemination of birth-control information. All that was needed to get them back was merely asking for it. But Alinsky kept this secret to himself, called an emergency meeting, and led the agitated citizens through his carefully staged maneuver. The strategy was simple: march into the office of the Infant Welfare Society, bang on the desks, demand infant medical services, without allowing the officials any chance to explain except to say, "Yes" at the end—and that was all they would be allowed to say. "With this careful indoctrination we stormed into the Infant Welfare Society downtown, identified ourselves and began a tirade consisting of militant demands, refusing to permit them to say anything. All the time the poor woman was desperately trying to say, 'Why of course you can have it. We'll start immediately.' But she never had a chance to say anything and finally we ended up in a storm of 'And we will not take "No" for an answer!' At which point she said, 'Well, I've been trying to tell you . . .' and I cut in demanding, 'Is it yes or is it no?' She said, 'Well, of course it's yes.' I said, 'That's all we wanted to know.' And we stormed out of the place."

The appearance of a winner, however, must at all times be kept within certain bounds, especially for the person on the rise. Unless you are prepared to draw your sword against your chief and throw the scabbard away, you should keep your light well dimmed below that of his. A warning as to what can happen to a person who does not adhere to this advice is the fate of the Minister of Finance to Louis XIV.

Nicolas Fouquet built a magnificent chateau, the Vaux-le-Vicomte, outside of Paris. The young king of France and all the nobility were invited to the housewarming. It was a gala of grandeur. The fountains were more brilliant than any in the world, including those of the king at Fontainebleau. The gardens were more beautiful than those of the Tuilleries of the Louvre. Jean de la Fontaine served as poet laureate for the occasion; Molière composed a new play for the evening; Jean Baptiste Lully conducted music written specially for the festivities. Dinner was prepared by Vatel and served under ceilings painted by Charles Le Brun. The finale displayed the most gorgeous fireworks ever witnessed in France, accompanied by the roar of cannons and the blare of trumpets.

The king declined to spend the night in the royal chambers and thought about the affair as he fell asleep journeying back to his palace at Fontainebleau. The ostentatious celebration convinced him that Fouquet's enemies were right. Jean-Baptiste Colbert had been whispering into the king's ear for some time that the minister had been denuding the treasury.

Within three weeks, Fouquet was arrested and thrown into jail for embezzlement. His estate was confiscated.

The necessary obverse of the coin of a winner is not to give any hint of being ruffled or afraid in a crisis. Nor should one show signs of being endangered or emasculated. This will shake the morale of one's intimate circle and impair its effectiveness.

One of the classical Chinese examples of cool-headedness in this respect is Liu Pang, the founder of the Han Dynasty in the second century B. C. During his military campaign against Hsiang Yu, the latter captured his father and threatened to boil the old man in oil if he did not surrender. Whereupon Liu sent off the following message: "Hsiang Yu and I had once been brothers-in-arms. My father is therefore also his father. If he chooses to boil our father, inform him to save a cup of soup for me." When Hsiang Yu received this reply, he let the father go.

A corollary of the avoidance of manifestations of insecurity is the avoidance of acts of cruelty. When a person is cruel in his actions, people will suspect that he is insecure. Quite apart from the public hating him for his inhumanity, his followers will desert him for his insecurity.

In contrast, an act of mercy can be a most impressive sign of greatness. To rescind someone's dismissal at the last moment as he is worried stiff about his next meal and to pardon someone's death sentence as he stands before the firing squad is unmistakable evidence of power. It is the power not only to take life but also to grant it. It is the ultimate gesture of a winner—of a winner in grand style.

MANEUVERING AND STRIKING

"Talk does not cook rice"—so goes the old proverb. More than anything else, persons of power are persons of action. Not just action, but adroit action. This section describes what adroitness calls for. What are fifteen most useful techniques to be developed to enhance this capability? And what is the characteristic hallmark of the Master of Action?

55 **Ready flexibility** The Roman slave Publilius Syrus had said, "Bad is the plan which is not susceptible of change." In other words, be sure that your operations are sufficiently flexible. This generality is well understood by managers. The trouble is that many of them mistake flexibility for a lack of specificity of objectives. This is not flexibility but fuzziness.

The particular kind of flexibility that is desired is the freedom of tactical movement within a given strategic thrust. Do not commit yourself to a single tactical target from the very beginning. This would lock you into a rigid course of advance, which would be much more readily frustrated by the circumstantial changes in the interim. Ready flexibility is ensured by the principle: Maintain at least two tactical targets within attainable range until the last moment of final commitment.

General William Sherman's march through the South during the American Civil War demonstrates the point on the battlefield. The Confederates never did know which of several towns he was going to strike until he turned at the last minute from his general direction of march. By then it was too late for the defending forces to respond effectively.

Another illustration is provided by the story of the prisoner of the Sultan of Persia. The sultan had sentenced two men to death. One of them, knowing how much the sultan loved his stallion, offered to teach the horse to fly within a year in return for his life. The sultan, fancying himself as the rider of the only flying horse in the world, agreed. The other prisoner looked at his friend in disbelief. "You *know* horses don't fly. What made you come up with a crazy idea like that? You're only postponing the inevitable." "Not so," said the skilled tactician. "I have actually given myself *four* chances for freedom. First, the sultan might die during the year. Second, I might die. Third, the horse might die. And fourth, you know, I might just teach that horse to fly!"

When on the defensive, even the smallest business person today recognizes the necessity of ready flexibility in the face of the open-ended competitive processes in America. The merchant is competing not only with the buyers against the supply-demand equilibrium but also against other sellers to the same buyer at the same time. As one of thousands of small proprietors, he or she is subject to the economic whirlwinds generated by the several hundred massively financed, tightly organized large corporations, which dominate our industrial society.

A single person in a key position in any one of these economic giants or other extensive political networks can bring pressure from all directions to bear on an opponent. An edifying example has been passed on by Congressman Otto C. Passman, Chairman of the House Appropriations Subcommittee in charge of foreign aid during the 1960s. Secretary of the Treasury Douglas Dillon testified before his subcommittee "with his usual smile and personality." The Democratic National Chairman called on officials all over the country to put pressure on Congress. Secretary of State Dean Rusk sent letters to Passman. His department briefed editors of newspapers. Ayub Khan of Pakistan in this country at the time spoke up on its behalf. A Citizens for International Development was established to bolster the campaign. Twenty-four hundred mayors were asked by the House Majority Leader to add their weight. The Director of the Peace Corps Sargent Shriver personally called on every Congressman's office. Business groups in every state were contacted by the White House. Passman recalled how after he scribbled some figures down to clarify his own thinking on possible cuts, they were leaked to the President by a subcommittee member. "While I was presenting the subcommittee report in the full committee meeting, administration agents continued to place phone calls to committee members in the room. In the same meeting letters from an Assistant Secretary of State to members of the Committee, all calling for more funds, were actually slipped under the door."

Maneuvering and striking effectively within such a fast-moving scenario leave no room for time-consuming deliberations. A wavering of the will, a slip of the tongue, a hesitation of the hand can be disastrous. Your reflex repertory needs be slaved to the exigencies of the moment within the long-term trajectory, as Prince Huei's cook had instructed us over 2000 years ago. "I have had this chopper for nineteen years. Although I have cut up thousands of bullocks, it is as sharp as if fresh from the whetstone," he told his admirer. "Since the joints always contain interstices and the edge of the blade is without thickness, there is much room for it to slowly move about and cut. Yet when I come across a knotty part, I am all concentration. I fix my eye upon it and steady my hand. With a *hwah* of my chopper, the part separates like earth crumbling to the ground. Then I carefully wipe off my chopper and put it away."

56 **Propitiousness**   There is nothing more important in imparting elegance and style than the art of being propitious. The essence of propitiousness is good timing. More failures in the exercise of power have been due to poor timing than any other single factor.

When Catherine the Great ascended the throne she tried to introduce the liberal ideas of Charles de Montesquieu. But the Russian state of mind was not receptive. Her ministers balked, and the peasant uprising of Emilien Pugachev of 1773 forced her to drop the idea. It took another 120 years before the time was ripe for even a semblance of parliament.

In our own day, there are relatively few executives who possess a really keen sense of timing. Most of them do not know how to use the instrument of time. They are unable to allow precisely for lead time, lag time, incubation time, time to build up a head of steam, time to forget, time to get bored, time to stop talking, and so on. They do not have the feeling for matching the duration of different acts to come into fruition against their respective times of need. They fail to lay the basis for the resolution of conflicts before their actual onset. As a result, they only struggle with the fortitude of facing crisis after crisis. They never glide with the art of de-existing them.

A frequent variety of poor timing is premature closure. Many junior executives and quite a few senior ones are very impatient in mapping out a course of action or implementing a given plan. They want to arrive at a decision or a consummation as soon as possible instead of when the decision or consummation is required and/or when the time is ripe. As a result, they do not have time to reconnoiter the situation thoroughly, acquire complete data, or examine more complex options that might be more profitable. They do not even allow sufficient time for the problem to go away on its own, when such might well occur. They keep making tentative fixes when the essential data are not yet at hand. The net effect is a continuous defending of successive tentative fixes along the way, thereby biasing themselves when faced with the final decision.

One of the worst kinds of premature closure is exhibited by the impatient leader who seems to be winning. He launches into the final push when the opposition has not yet been sufficiently unbalanced internally. He charges forth before he has gained a psychological advantage. The favorable outcome, if attained under such circumstances, is always extra costly. And he may very well fail.

Another common deficiency is failure to pay adequate attention to the optimal sequencing of actions. The significance of proper sequencing can be shown by the Condorcet effect. In 1785 Marquis de Condorcet in Paris stated that an intransitive ordering in group decision may arise from members with transitive orderings. For example, consider 60 voting members confronted with the ultimate selection of one alternative out of three mutually exclusive choices: 23 members preferred $a > b > c$; 17 preferred $b > c > a$; 10 preferred $c > a > b$; 8 preferred $c > b > a$; and 2 preferred $b > a > c$. Voting by pairs, $a > b$ by 33 votes to 27; $b > c$ by 42 votes to 18; $c > a$ by 35 votes to 25. Thus there is a circular group ordering resulting from individual transitive orderings. The outcome of majority rule in successive decision pairs would depend on the order of consideration. If a and b were first matched up against each other and the defeated alternative dropped from further consideration, c would emerge as final choice. If c and a were first matched, then b would emerge as final choice. If b and c were first matched, then a would emerge as final choice. You should be careful then about the sequencing of actions in activities like public relations, group decisions on alternative options, and multiparty confrontations.

For best results, your thrusts for power should also be timed with the social cycles of crisis and prosperity. In general, do not make conspicuously sudden moves toward increased personal power when times are good and peaceful. People are more amenable to your grab for drastic power during chaos and emergencies. Be certain, however, that the apparent crises are not isolated cases during basically peaceful phases of the social cycle. This will not allow sufficient time to consolidate your acquisition of new powers. The more propitious moments occur with specific crises during depressed or anxious phases of the social cycle. When the opportunity presents itself, you should move fast to fan the need and obtain the assignment of new authority. It might even be necessary to create an incident-crisis, as many national leaders have done to lead their countries into war. Should you sense at the initial stages that the constituents are still wary of granting the new powers, you should exhibit some degree of reasonableness before flexing your new powers. Exercise it expeditiously and decisively to the satisfaction of your constituents in a few cases. After another period of restraint, you may then increase the frequency of your assertion of authority as they become progressively used to your directives as standard procedures.

As to the specific moment during generally favorable circumstances to strike, Lev Trotsky made the following apt statement: "Between the moment when an attempt to summon an insurrection must inevitably prove premature and lead to a revolutionary miscarriage, and the moment when a favorable situation must be considered hopelessly missed, there exists a certain period—it may be measured in weeks, and sometimes in a few months—in the course of which an insurrection may be carried out with more or less chance of success." The key responsibility of the leader is the choice of the precise time for the decisive overt attack. "It can with full justice be called the key problem, for it unites the policy of revolution with the techniques of insurrection—and it is needless to add that insurrection, like war is a continuation of politics with other instruments."

If Trotsky's estimate of weeks and months for power struggles on the national revolutionary scene is reasonably accurate, how much shorter must it be—hours and days perhaps—for office coups in corporations? It may well be that the subconscious appreciation of this possibility accounts for the reluctance of many an insecure executive to go on extended trips and long vacations away from home base.

57   **Three sets of three questions**   The three sets of three questions each have been devised especially for junior executives as an essential quick check on the soundness of any major proposal, over and above the careful staff studies that may go along with it.

The first set of three questions is a personal series. Before you forge ahead on any serious move, ask yourself during one of your more relaxed periods, the following three simple questions: (1) Does the proposition add up? (2) Does it sound okay? (3) Does it feel right? If the answers to all three questions are yes, then there is a good chance that you are on the right track. But if one or more are no, then you had better rethink the whole affair.

After a decade or two of experience, you probably would have relatively little difficulty with the first of these three questions. You would have acquired a grasp of the ball park of the kinds of technical know-how, money, and personnel required for propositions of various kinds within your sphere of responsibilities. You will probably have greater difficulty in arriving at a correct answer to the second question. The proposal may sound okay to you, but will it sound okay to the persons who must go along? Can you put yourself in their respective shoes and be convinced by the kinds of different stories you are planning to put out from their points of view. The third question is the hardest of all. This is the real test as to whether you can reach into a mass of conflicting data and arguments and pull out the right thing to do.

The second set of three questions focuses on the ramifications of a proposed action. This is the three-so-what-then-what test. Whenever a lieutenant of yours comes up with a complicated course of action, ask him or her the question: "So *what?*" What will it bring, good and bad, in terms of the objectives of your operations (while you examine the reply in terms of your own growth in personal power)? If the answer (answers) makes sense, ask next: "*Then* what do we do?" If the answer (answers) to that second question also makes sense, you should follow with: "And so what?", "And then what?" Another two times around. If you cannot see your way through at least two cycles of the so-what-then-whats, then you ought to mull over the proposition some more before sallying forth.

The third set of three questions pertains to contingency factors. This is the three what-ifs. Assuming the plan is approved and is being implemented, (1) What if the boss or an essential ally suddenly changes his or her mind? (2) What if the competitor or the community does such and such? (3) What if the person on whom you are counting to spearhead the drive suddenly goes elsewhere?

58 **N-cushion billiard** Passing the test of three sets of three questions is based in large part on your skill at N-cushion billiard. When the cue ball is stroked in a northeasterly direction, it heads northwesterly after bouncing off the first cushion, southwesterly after the second, southeasterly after the third, northeasterly after the fourth but along a path usually different from the first, and so on.

Unless a person is skilled at a high-N game, he or she faces great difficulty in predicting the ultimate effects of his or her actions. The capability of the opposition must also be taken into account, especially the particular N to which he or she is pointing for the given contention. The higher N at which you are adept, the more effective can your indirections be. Your offensives against the opponents can be indirect without any deception on your part. You may openly neutralize or eliminate someone from whom that opponent draws essential patronage and resources without public knowledge. You may openly weaken or destroy the assumptions on which the doctrines undergirding your opposition's claims are based.

You should also be aware, of course, of other indirections, that are not so openly performed. Your competitor might whisper into the rumor mill so that the news reaches your ears just before your interview with top management that it is looking for an encumbent who will not rock the boat, when in fact he knows that it is looking for some one who will shake the place out of its doldrums. Similar acts of indirection among corporation executives jockeying for higher positions were reported by the *Wall Street Journal* in 1957 as follows: a vice president plugging the carburetor of his new competitor's car to make him late for his first meeting; another official of a conservative Pennsylvania company planting "rumors that his principal rival had 'fallen for a New Dealish line,' thus ruining his chance for the presidency;" still another who "waited for his rival's special project to flop, then submitted to the boss a series of memos (carefully back-dated) to show he's opposed the project all along." They were practicing, as the reporter puts it, "the most delicate of all arts of self-advancement—throat-cutting."

The higher the stakes being pursued, the greater the number of players, the more irregular the cushions involved, and the greater the demands on your finesse. In advocating independence from the British Empire, George Washington and Samuel Adams were banking on entirely different N-purposes. The former was one of the wealthier of the colonists, although deeply in debt at times. He envisioned liberation for the building up of an empire to exploit the great opportunities in America for the big planters. Adams, on the other hand, was more of a radical. He and others, like Patrick Henry, had hoped that a change in the social order could take place with the war, in order to be more successful in opposing the restrictions on land, money, and the vote controlled by the conservatives under the protection of the British Crown.

Furthermore, many N-cushion games are going on at the same time in which a person with even a modicum of power is engaged. Their N-consequences interact with each other and create new vortices, which issue forth emanations of their own. The weaving of the economic, military, and political strands, for example, is typified by the arms trade. As summarized by George Thayer, the armament business "can be used to balance international accounts and create prosperity. They are capable of cementing international relationships more effectively than any other human endeavor. They can—and do—provide work that challenges all the skills that man possesses; they create wealth for the manufacturer, the seller, the nation; they stimulate economic and social stability by the maintenance of a high and continuing level of production; and they can create an atmosphere of a security and a sense of national unity, purpose and pride that is often reflected at every level of a nation's experience. In one sense, armaments are mankind's most continuing good business." Political outcroppings of the arms trade are many. The American cancellation of the expensive joint development with England of the Skybolt missile helped speed Prime Minister Harold Macmillan's resignation in 1963. In large measure, the purchase of American arms by West Germany, for which it could ill afford to pay, led to the collapse of the Erhard Government in 1966.

Whether cultural penetration or military invasion comes first is at times a debatable question. The fact that they are intimately conjoined is not. The colonial conquest of America by the Western Europeans is an example. By the end of the sixteenth century during the reign of Philip III of Spain, there were already five archbishoprics, twenty-seven bishoprics, about 400 parishes, and a comparable number of monasteries in Latin America. The first documented intervention of American troops in Vietnam in 1845 is another example. When the American Captain "Mad Jack" Percival was cruising in Asian waters in the old *U.S.S. Constitution*, he received word that a French bishop Dominique Lefèbvre was to be executed in Hue. He steamed into Danang, landed a contingent of marines, and captured several high Vietnamese officials as hostages. The bishop was let free. Had there been no bishop, there would have been no marines.

Despite repeated manifestations of the interconnectedness of *N*-games, when the Southeast Asian Ngo Dinh Nhu stated in a speech in the 1960s something to the effect that both Communism and American foreign aid were forms of colonialism, even highly perceptive American writers expressed hurt surprise. The inseparability of money, culture and religion, and guns in the furtherance of national political interest, especially on the international scene, is apparently neither openly admitted by countries of great power nor explicitly taught in their schools. People on the receiving end in the weakest countries, however, are very sensitive to the anastomoses of reality. For generations their children have been taught that there are three kinds of imperialism, namely, military, economic, and cultural. All three are to be regarded as equally dangerous, regardless of their initiating intentions. No matter which comes first, if allowed to get out of hand, the other two will not be far behind.

One of the outstanding *N*-cushion players of power was the union leader Walter Reuther. While applying his leverage to a given situation, he was also prying another farther down the line. This was the way in which he used one of his negotiations with Ford Motor Company to pressure favorable Federal legislation on higher pensions and Social Security. He had been trying to make union gains in pension and Social Security unsuccessfully for twelve years under the favorable climate of Franklin Roosevelt and the New Deal. So Reuther said to himself: "Okay, we've got to use our leverage at the bargaining table to try to facilitate greater progress through legislation." An implementing plan was carried out. As he described the results: "And in Ford, which was the first pension plan negotiated, we tied together the private benefits with the public benefits and within forty-eight hours after we adopted the Ford pension system, where we required the employer to pay the total cost of private pension, as contrasted to the worker paying half and the employer paying half in the public system, we got action out of Congress that we were unable to get in twelve years." Using the first bounce off the Ford cushion, the union was able to realize much greater benefits in its public Social Security than it could ever have been able to achieve by aiming the cue ball directly at the government.

Having been hurt many times by the boomerangs of power, the established leader is usually reluctant to rock the boat or make too drastic changes at one stroke. Nothing is trivial in the game of power with its vicissitudes. A tiny spark may light an explosion; a small envy may topple an empire. It is for reasons of this kind that the superpowers throughout history have always been so concerned about the eruption of little conflicts around the globe, which have not been of their own doing. They expend considerable effort toward eliminating them if possible, or keeping them localized if not. Expansion of the disturbance might well upset the balance of world powers at a time when they are not ready to respond.

In the tergiversation of power, one does not wait until the intended danger is clear and present. Intention or no on the part of the opposition, activity per se constitutes a threat. For it may well bounce off the fourth cushion as an intention.

59 **Injected hopelessness** Injecting a sense of hopelessness just at the right moment often leads to a collapse of resistance on the part of the opposition, leaving you to go about your business freely.

The tactics is always accompanied with danger to oneself and should not be attempted by amateurs. It requires an unusual combination of craft and will. It is the strong suit of refined persecutors. On a short-term basis, it has proven successful by the brazenly entrenched with compatible personalities. Senator Joseph McCarthy exhibited such a trait-set during his drive against the Communists in government agencies during the 1950s. In the words of Peter Ustinov, McCarthy "had trained the very shortcomings of his equipment into weapons. His own evident lack of wit makes him impervious to the wit of others; his own inability to listen makes him immune to argument; his own tortuous train of thought wears down the opposition; his crawling reflexes, his unnaturally slow and often muddled delivery force quicker minds to function at a disadvantage."

How to induce such a state among the citizenry has always been a forte among political bosses. The techniques are many, each tailored to the situation at hand. A typical case in point was the city boss of Philadelphia during the early 1900s.

The reporter Lincoln Steffens managed to obtain a frank interview with him and expressed puzzlement in trying to understand how it was that the then municipal administration would risk a burst of "steals" and "jobs" in a very short period of time. Why did he not play it safe, like other big-city bosses and pull off only one at a time, or spread them about the country a bit. The city boss cleared up the muckraker's bewilderment. "If we did any of these things alone the papers and the public would concentrate on it, get the facts, and fight. But we reasoned that if we poured them all out fast and furious, one, two, three—one after the others—the papers couldn't handle them and the public would be stunned and give up. Too much."

Whereupon Steffens surmised the reason why all the people with whom he had discussed the problem had said "there was nothing to be done."

"Yes," Ivy Durham answered. "The Bullitt charter was a great thing for us. It was the best, last throw of the reformers, and when we took that charter and went right on with our business, we took the heart out of the reform forever."

60 **Concomitant blame** Never punish out of vanity or vengeance, but out of hope for conversion on the part of the target individual over to your way of thinking.

To be effective for this purpose, the instrument of compulsion needs be more than mere infliction of pain. There must be concomitant blame. As Joseph Rikaby commented nearly two centuries ago, "To punish is not simply to pain: it is to pain and to blame together. Though it be sometimes just, for a man's own benefit and for the protection of others, to make him suffer pains for what he cannot help, it can never be just to blame him for what he cannot help." The term punishment is improperly used when children and animals are involved, since moral reproach is not understood by them. "It is from an exclusive study of this improper sense that utilitarians have evolved their theory of punishment, a theory supposing that a wicked man, a 'naughty boy,' and a restive horse, are all on a level as objects of punishment." But this is not so. "Man, boy, and horse receive stripes alike; but the man is blamed severely, the boy perhaps slightly, the horse not at all."

The attaching of blame and the administering of pain must both be felt and accepted by the person punished. The Inquisition had consistently given equal weight to indoctrinating the subject toward repentance while escalating anguish. The same pairing of blame and pain had been practiced in the treatment of prisoners by the Chinese Communists during the 1950s. As recounted by R. Guillain, "The regime desires unanimous approval even in prison camps. We must not imagine that the pariahs can fulminate against the system within their cell walls or under the sun of the Gobi desert. The pressure on them is so great . . . that the prisoners are zealous to bow to the warders, accusing themselves of all manner of crimes and thanking the People's Republic which has reformed their way of thinking."

In contrast, the modern penal system in America is not compulsion but vengeance. When apprehended, blame is not attached; when attached, often not just; and when attached and just, usually not acknowledged. For the inmate it is not punishment—just torture. There is no rehabilitating—just hardening.

61 **Adaptive centrality** The farther from the center of gravity of your movement you sit, the more readily can you be spun off it. The farther out on the limb you perch yourself, the more readily can you be sawed off. This is why the old Chinese adage advised: Maintain the mean of centrality, so as to touch the four corners of the universe.

It is true that there have been extremists throughout history who have massed great power. But these regimes have not lasted. The durable persons of power have nearly always carried the main body of their constituents along with them, rather than surged too far ahead as a pioneering element. The latter is a function of scouts; and scouts—as is well known—are expendable and often expended.

In order to effectively assume the position of centrality, a person must be accepted by the relevant community. This was one of the principal reasons why the Islamic conquerors of India around the eighth century had failed to either convert or govern the Hindus. As long as the population remained Hindu, despite the tolerance of its philosophy, the rulers were foreigners. The persecution of the Hindus, who were regarded as idolators by the Moslems, created a permament separation between the two. Hinduism continued to develop its doctrine with Sankara and other thinkers of the period, as the passive resistance by the citizenry led to a rapid decline of the country as a political power.

The same fate continues to plague the police in our present-day slums. Despite the dedication of most of the police to the public good, his very presence seems to be an acerbity to those he is trying to help. His badge, gun, and club are symbolic of oppression. To borrow James Baldwin's description, "he is facing daily and nightly, the people who would gladly see him dead, and he knows it. There is no way for him not to know it: There are few things more unnerving than the silent accumulating contempt and hatred of a people. He moves through Harlem, therefore, like an occupying soldier in a bitterly hostile country; which is precisely what, and where he is, and is the reason he walks in two and three's."

One of the more impressive institutional transformations in attitude toward accommodation within the larger community of man had been brought about by Pope John XXIII, elected in 1958. He began to move the Catholic Church steadily toward doctrinal and day-to-day neighborliness with the rest of the Christian world. He directed the avoidance of ceremonies that might be interpreted as offensive by other religions. He embarked upon tension-relieving official relations, beginning with regular visits to Italian prisons. His earthly humor endeared him to the people as "one of us." Ever since the sixteenth century, so Francois Mauriac noted, "the Vatican had been immobilized, as if spellbound, as if condemned to an eternal pomp, an incurable ostentation. Its guard with their doublets, helmets, and halberds had become the guards of the Sleeping Beauty and had waited for more than four centuries for the gouty hand of an old man to come and wake them up. That splendor to which the popes of the Renaissance had sacrificed close to half the Christian world (since the basilica of St. Peter was built with the money of those same indulgences which aroused the revolt of Luther), that splendor encircled Holy Church, and the Vatican, isolated in the midst of the world, became literally a prison . . . until the advent of Pope John."

You should therefore stand in the midst of your constituents, in touch with all, balancing the antagonists, adjudicating their differences, protecting the rights of those in contention, and moving the center of gravity along your direction of greater personal power. Although you may eventually associate yourself with one side or another in your adaptative centrality, you should not begin as a contender at the extremes within your own constituency, even though you may be antagonistically extreme vis-a-vis the external opposition. If you do, some internal competitor will preempt the position of centrality. Your days as leader are numbered.

62 **Multifaceted speed** We are all familiar with the importance of physical mobility in combat, such as that of the buccaneers of the sixteenth century. In sacrificing size for speed, the five ships of Francis Drake's squadron ranged only from 12 to 120 tons. He easily caught up with and captured the Spanish *Cacafuego*, laden with a million and a half ducats of gold, silver ballast, and jewels. Such speed made Sir Francis the wealthiest of admirals—even bribing the queen, it has been said, with a diamond cross and an emerald coronet. His raids around the Indies broke the confidence of the Flemish and Italian bankers in Spain's ability to make good on her loans, collapsed the bank of Seville, and drove the king of Spain into military desperation.

For maximum effectiveness, physical mobility must be accompanied with speed of another kind. This is the speed of insight and decision. It is akin to an element of creativity present in geniuses like Lope de Vega, who authored 1500 plays in his lifetime, and Christopher Wren, who designed St. Paul's Cathedral in twenty-five minutes.

Especially useful in the thick of power plays is the speed of dissimulating and dismasking. To tear the mask off a smiling person in the lair of power is to disclose an enemy. A lightning and certain move of this kind is dangerous but often decisive. Occasionally, an innocent person is embarassed and injured by the mistaken suspicion. But the determined seeker of power remains uninhibited; he only wants to make sure that he and nobody else gets away with it. In the meantime he himself resorts to a rapid exchange of masks, when called for, out of a well-variegated stock. As Elias Canetti depicted the ruthless practitioners of the art in former times, "A ruler invites civil or military notables to a banquet and then suddenly, when they least expect an act of enmity, has them all butchered. The change from one form of behaviour to another exactly corresponds to a rapid change of masks. The performance is carried through with the greatest possible speed, for on this depends its whole success. A despot must always be conscious of his own sustained dissimulation and will always, therefore, expect the same from others. Any means of forestalling its effects will seem to him permissible, and indeed obligatory. The fact that in his speed he may crush the innocent does not trouble him: in the complex world of masks there must always be errors. What does disturb him profoundly is to let an enemy escape by failing to move fast enough."

Tearing off masks often unleashes a fury of passions, which had been previously held in check by their pretenses. In undertaking such measures, therefore, be prepared to cope with the repercussions. Bernard Shaw regarded this to be one of the fearful ramifications of wars. "What really happened was that the impact of physical death and destruction, that one reality that any fool can understand, tore off the masks of education, art, science, and religion from our ignorance and barbarism, and left us glorifying grotesquely in the license suddenly accorded to our vilest passions and abject terrors. Ever since Thucydides wrote his history, it has been on record that when the angel of death sounds his trumpet the pretenses of civilization are blown from men's heads into the mud like hats in a gust of wind."

At the same time, speed should be guided by compatible pace. Maneuverings should be adapted to the limiting factor of the situation. As a reminder, an episode in the life of Chou Yung, the celebrated Ming painter of the seventeenth century, is worth retelling. One winter evening he and a little boy with an armful of books and papers took a ferry boat across the river to the town of Chiao Chuan. As the boat neared the mooring, Chou inquired of the ferry boatman whether they would be able to reach the town a mile away before the gates closed for the night. "Oh, yes," he replied, as he looked at the boy with the loosely tied bundle, "if you do not walk too fast."

As they stepped on land, the sky was overcast, the wind was brisk, and it was getting dark. Chou and the boy became apprehensive about being locked out for the night and left at the mercy of the bandits roaming the countryside. As the sun went over the mountain top, they began to run. After ten yards, the string around the bundle broke, scattering books and papers all over the place. By the time they succeeded in gathering the pieces, tieing them together again, and reaching the city, the gate had closed down on them.

Chou never tired of repeating the story to his newly made friends and extolling the wisdom of the ferry boatman.

63 **Surprise** Much of the groundwork that sets the stage for the visible manifestations of power is laid in secrecy. In contrast to the neophyte, who likes to talk about his exploits and relishes the spurious adulation of his knowledge and cleverness, the professional

persons of power prefer the slightly mysterious mien in dimmed al-
coves. The more complex the encounter, the more taciturn they become. They guard the decisive secrets of power as something terribly
personal. One of Saadi's charming stories is worth relating in this
connection.

There was once a wrestling master who was versed in 360 feints
and holds. He took a special liking to one of his pupils, to whom he
taught 359 of them over a period of time. Somehow he never got around
to the last trick.

As months went by the young man became so proficient in the art
that he bested everyone who dared to face him in the ring. He was so
proud of his prowess that one day he boasted before the sultan that he
could readily whip his master, were it not out of respect for his age and
gratitude for his tutelage. The sultan became incensed at the irrever-
ence and ordered an immediate match with the royal court in atten-
dance.

At the gong the youth barged forward with a lusty yell, only to be
confronted with the unfamiliar 360th feint. The master seized his
former pupil, lifted him high above his head, and flung him crashing to
the ground. The sultan and the assembly let out a loud cheer.

When the sultan asked the master how he was able to overcome
such a strong opponent, the master confessed that he had reserved a
secret technique for himself for just such a contingency. Then he related the lamentation of a master of archery, who taught everything he
knew. "No one has learned archery from me," the poor fellow be-
moaned his naivete, "who has not tried to use me as butt in the end."

There is much of the wrestling master in every person of great
power. The closer to the top they get, the more skillful they are in
shrouding the sacred mystery and the more valuable it becomes to
them.

The last of the powerful dukes of Milan in the fifteenth century,
Filippo Maria, was famous for the ways in which he disguised his
thinking. He would talk to someone at length about working in a high
post in his court at an early date but then let the matter cool off. Just
about the time the eager aspirant had begun to lose all hopes, the duke
would call him up again. At times he would compliment people whom
he dislikes or criticize someone to whom he had just decorated with
honors. He would even complain about the executions he had personally decreed.

An allied technique of retaining one's true sentiments to oneself is
being off the point. Prime Minister Stanley Baldwin of England was
clever in its use. The following incident is typical. In 1925 a group of

right-wing Conservative members wanted to alter the basis for the political levy of trade unions. When they met with Baldwin, he said that he regretted the division within the party but one or the other side will have to be let down. But he was not prepared to state his views at the time. Two days later he spoke against the bill in the House of Commons. As recorded in the diary of Duff Cooper, "The Prime Minister's speech had a wonderful effect on the House. It was vague and rather off the point, and although I liked it myself I was afraid that it wouldn't impress other people. But it did; and completely silenced all those who were most vehement for the bill. I saw a Member sitting near me with a carefully prepared speech on many sheets of paper, tearing it into little pieces and throwing them on the floor."

Baldwin thereby refrained from aggravating the division within the ranks of his party. Neither did he provide the opponents an advanced opportunity to lobby against his position. Finally, by being unclear and off the point, he did not give the legal argument of the lawyer who prepared the bill a solid basis for refutation.

Although resourceful tacticians may be vague at times, they do not keep the opposition in complete darkness all the time. This frequently arouses suspicion and places him on guard. He may flail out in fear and upset the timetable. Instead they let their overt maneuvering attract his interest and guide him along a logical pattern of thought away from the intended climax, like the intriguing author leading his reader astray in a detective story.

One of the most clever ruses of this kind in modern warfare was that perpetrated by General Edmund Allenby in 1917. Because of the available water supply, the Turks expected that the British would attack their strongly fortified right flank at Gaza. So Allenby decided to attack the opposite flank, despite the scarcity of water in the desert. He would be able to accomplish this successfully only if he could rapidly overcome the resistance along the way and reach Beersheba with the wells intact, since it was the only oasis in the area. The plan and operation will have to be well camouflaged. The Turks must be made to believe that his attack will be directed toward Gaza. He worked out an elaborate deception.

A month was spent sending wireless messages using a code which was permitted to be broken by the Turks. A British intelligence officer got himself pursued by the Turk outpost guard near Beersheba, exchanged rifle shots, appeared wounded, and escaped, dropping a blood-smeared rifle and a haversack in the process. The next day the British sent a coded wireless message, which was decoded by the Turks, to the Desert Mounted Corps to send a party for search of the haversack, which was to be returned forthwith to General Headquarters without examination or explanation of its contents. The contents had been carefully prepared to include an order and battle plan to attack Gaza mixed with the usual collection of love letters from home and so on. The haversack was not found by the British, of course, since it was securely in the hands of the Chief of Turk Intelligence.

The Turks began to move more units behind Gaza. On October 27 massed British artillery began pounding the Turk trenches, with British and French gunboats joining in. The Turks, fully convinced in their prediction, wired their field commanders that a diversionary attack would be made by the British toward Beersheba but the main one would be at Gaza. Allenby did bring up his main force opposite Gaza. At the last minute the troops slipped away at night, with a few laborers left behind. These kept the camp fires burning, with the tents left standing and fake wooden horses alongside. Some mules kept dragging planks of wood around the camp, generating clouds of dust, which looked very convincing to the Turk reconnaissance planes.

On October 31 a powerful British force with 30,000 water-bearing camels drove toward Beersheba from two directions and captured it in a day. The Turks expected a diversionary attack there and found only too late that it was the main one. The left anchor of their line fell, and they had to retreat all the way back to Jerusalem.

The wider the field of operation involving a larger number of simultaneous competitors, the more essential becomes the element of surprise. Strategic postures must then be formulated to operate against an array of competitors rather than against a single one. The same plan is expected to be effective over a far more extended period of time. The fuzzier the outline appears to the potential oppositions, the greater is the probability of success in its consecutive usage.

It is for these reasons that the centuries-old Arabic *Book of the Crown,* which preserved many of the traditions of the Persian Sassanid kings, included the maxim: "It is the privilege of kings to keep their secrets from father, mother, brothers, wives, and friends."

64 **Chinese baseball**   The nature of the milieu in which persons of power operate is illustrated by the American debate over the deployment of the antiballistic missile (ABM) system.

Just before President Lyndon Johnson left office, he obtained Congressional approval for research and development on the Sentinel ABM system, but not for deployment. The purpose of the Sentinel system, so he said, was to provide a thin area defense for a few American cities against small-scale nuclear attack of the type that could be launched by Red China.

The Congressional opponents then began to shore up their arguments against the actual deployment as Richard Nixon was inaugurated in 1969. As anticipated, the new President soon asked for authority to deploy the ABM. He asserted, however, that the intended deployment was not to protect the cities against small-scale nuclear threat. That was impractical. It was to protect the American Minuteman intercontinental ballistic missile (ICBM) silos against the Soviet SS-9 missiles. The Sentinel's name was changed to Safeguard to emphasize the modified mission. This switch in justification unbalanced the anti-ABM foes, and the President won the inning in the Senate by one vote. It was agreed to deploy two ABM Safeguard sites to protect Minuteman ICBMs.

The anti-ABM forces then began to regroup and prepare their revised plan of battle against the next round of requests for further deployment of the Safeguard system to protect more Minuteman ICBM silos. They began to line up their cost-effectiveness analyses.

But the President again befuddled the opposition. He suddenly announced in a news conference that he intended to expand the ABM system not to protect more Minuteman ICBMs but to provide an area defense for the entire United States against nuclear attack. In his words, the system would be "virtually infallible" against this kind of threat and was "absolutely essential" if we were to have a "credible" foreign policy in the Far East. The name Safeguard was retained, but the mission was changed back to what the Sentinel's used to be but on an expanded basis. The carefully prepared counteroffensive on the part of the anti-ABM cadre was again caught off-base at the time and point of confrontation.

With this picture of the jousting grounds before us, one can readily understand why it is that the singularly essential art for the great players in the game of power is the so-called Chinese baseball.

The game of Chinese baseball is almost identical to American baseball—the same players, same field, same bats and balls, same method of keeping score, and so on. The batter stands in the batter's box, as usual. The pitcher stands on the pitcher's mound, as usual. He winds up, as usual, and zips the ball down the alley. There is one and only one difference. And that is: after the ball leaves the pitcher's hand and as long as the ball is in the air, anyone can move any of the bases anywhere.

In other words, everything is continually changing—not only the events themselves, but also the very rules governing the judgments of those events and the criteria of value. This kind of situation is alien to the scientific tradition of fixed boundary conditions, clearly defined variables, objective assessments, and rational consistency within a closed system. In the ball game of power, everything is flux and all systems are open. There is no such thing as a challenge, which can be met and put away for all times, like a mathematical problem of two plus two equals four. There are only issues—never fully delineated, never completely resolved, always changing, always in need of alert accommodation.

The secret of Chinese baseball is not only keeping your eye on the ball alone but also on the bases, and doing some fancy-footed kicking of the bases around yourself.

65 **Antisocial context** The essential precondition for a successful revolt against an established order is an antisocial undercurrent.

The situation often develops when the elite group extols certain symbols of success for everybody but maintains a status quo so as to put them beyond the reach of a large fraction of the population. A democracy, which professes the ideal of equality of monetary and other opportunities and has yet to realize it in practice is especially vulnerable. Those frustrated in their desires will seek avenues of escape; those with unrequitted ambitions will resort to illicit means. The resulting neuroses and hostilities make them susceptible recruits for overthrowing the regime in power for whatever convincing pretext that surfaces at the time. Since they feel that the approved means are denied them, ethical norms become meaningless to them.

At the same time, the desire for precedents expresses itself in a variety of strange ways in a democracy. E. H. Chapin voiced his disgust over a century ago: "Here, where everybody says all men are equal, and everybody is afraid they *will* be; where there are no adamantine barriers of birth and caste; people are anxiously elusive." He went on to condemn the forms of this competition for wealth and style of living: "such gorgeous nonsense as here—turning home into a Parisian toyshop, absorbing the price of a good farm in the ornaments of a parlor, and hanging up a judge's salary in a single chandelier. . . . It is one way of getting a head taller than others upon this democratic level. It is a carpet contest for the mastery in what is called 'society.'"

In the light of these ostentations, many Americans of the present generation are rather uncertain as to what precisely is the social promise proclaimed in the Constitution. There is some resemblance of today's disharmony to that described by Alexis de Tocqueville a century ago on the crumbling of the employment relationships in Western Europe. The traditional subordination of workers to their masters was disintegrating. But the master continued to believe in his superior position, while the servant rebeled at the idea of a divine duty. They were secretly suspicious of each other within their inner selves and remained ever rivals: "The master is ill-natured and weak, the servant ill-natured and intractable; the one constantly attempts to evade by unfair restrictions his obligation to protect and to remunerate, the other his obligation to obey. The reins of domestic government dangle between them, to be snatched at by one or the other. The lines that divide authority from oppression, liberty from license, and right from might are to their eyes so jumbled together and confused that no one knows exactly what he is or what he may be or what he ought to be. Such a condition is not democracy but revolution."

Such preconditions of internal revolts should be distinguished from their precipitants. "Phenomena which precipitate internal war are almost unique and ephemeral in character," explained Harry Eckstein. "A bad harvest, a stupid or careless ruler, moral indiscretion in high places, an ill-advised policy . . . They are results of the vagaries of personality, of forces external to the determinate interrelations of society, of all those unique and fortuitous aspects of concrete life which are the despair of social scientists and the meat and drink of narrative historians."

Crane Brinton had examined the preconditions of revolts in America, France, England, and Russia. Although these have been studied for their impact on political revolutions, their analogies would also apply in general to any large organization, whether it be a corporation, a church, or a labor union. The five preconditions are: (1) The economy is on the upgrade, and the discontentment of the not-unprosperous people, rather than the outright oppression of the downcast, gives the primary force to the revolutionary movement. (2) Bitter class antagonisms exist, primarily against the privileged aristocracy by those who have enough to live on but feel bitter about the imperfections of the society. (3) The intellectuals are neglected by the power structure. (4) The governing machinery is clearly inefficient. (5) Members of the old ruling class lose confidence in themselves and their heritage, with some even going over to the attackers.

Not infrequently, persons in power become so preoccupied with the passing attractions and troublesome problems of the day that they are insensitive to the early signs of storms gathering strength over the horizons for years, to which their very behavior and actions had been contributing. Should you be the chief of an institution of major size, you should maintain measures to protect yourself against your own failure in this direction.

One of the simplest arrangements would be having at least one highly perceptive and visionary personal advisor. He or she is to be free to roam wherever and talk to whomever he or she pleases, without any operating responsibilities whatsoever. He or she is to be charged with one and only one function, and that is to speak whenever he or she feels necessary to you frankly, directly, and privately regarding matters threatening to degrade your power significantly. It is essential that this function and advice be kept secret between the two of you. A suitable cover for his or her activity will have to be fashioned. Otherwise you might well end up receiving not his or her perceptions but those of your cunning opposition, funneled through your advisor's mouth by way of N-cushion billiard.

66 **Interpretive prerogative** The power of the prophet lies not in his bringing the word of God to mankind but in his interpretation as to what the purported word of God means. Truth, it seems, does not determine what the prophet says; instead, what the prophet says determines what truth is. The fight then is over the privilege of interpretation. To take a passage from Oscar Cullman, in the fixing of Christian canon of Scripture, "the *Church herself* at a given moment traced a clear and firm line of demarcation between the period of the apostles and the period of the Church . . . in other words, between apostolic tradition and ecclesiastical tradition. . . . By establishing the principle of a canon, the Church . . . declared implicitly that from that moment every subsequent tradition must be submitted to the *control* of the apostolic tradition which constituted the Church, which imposed itself on her."

The issue of interpretive prerogative is also central in the secular arena. During the 1890s the socialist Eduard Bernstein began to reexamine the fundamental tenets of Marxism. He could not contradict the fact that the European worker in 1890 was better off than he was in 1850. This did not uphold Karl Marx's thesis that the worker would absolutely be worse off as time goes on under capitalism. In 1899, he put some of his doubts in a book, entitled *Evolutionary Socialism*. Even though Bernstein was the literary executor of Friedrich Engels and was highly respected throughout the Communist world, he was condemned by Lenin for revisionism. Yet two years later, Lenin himself suggested modifications to some of Marx's concepts. But these were not called revisions; they were accepted as desirable clarifications of orthodoxy.

"We are under a Constitution," Justice Charles Evans Hughes had once said. "But the Constitution is what the Judges say it is."

67 **Law of reversal** "When the sun reaches the meridian, if falls," said an old Taoist text. "When the moon becomes full, it wanes."

As the aggressive corporation approaches progressively closer to its objective of eliminating all competition, the progression reverses itself with the emergence of a new kind of opposition. John Kenneth Galbraith calls it a "countervailing power." In his words, "private economic power is held in check by the countervailing power of those who are subject to it. The first begets the second. The long trend toward concentration of industrial enterprise in the hands of a relatively few firms has brought into existence not only strong sellers, as economists have supposed, but also strong buyers as they have failed to see. The two develop together, not in precise step but in such manner that there can be no doubt that the one is in response to the other." Attempts to eliminate competition as a "self-generating regulatory force" give rise to countervailing power to take its place. As time goes on, the countervailing powers themselves no longer operate as independent powers but coalesce into higher orders of power.

Much of military planning based on strategic deterrence is plagued with difficulties emanating from this principle of reversal. Up to a point the massive display of force might deter the other side from major adventures. War can thereby be prevented for a while. At the same time, however, what also happens is a notification that one is expecting a war of the magnitude of his own deterrence. This will lead to matching military preparedness on the part of the adversarial nation.

A deterrence therefore often turns out to be an invitation to escalation in military expenditures by mutually suspicious nations. If one of the two backs down, the other might assume that she is too weak to fight and begin pressing inordinate demands, which might just prove sufficient to start a war. If neither nation backs down until they both reach the point of near economic unbalance at home, then they are both unfit to fight any more than the next large war to come. Their future has already been forfeited by strategic disorganization. They are already defeated before they fought. The third power is sitting back smiling.

"Stretch a bow to the very limit," cautioned Lao Tzu in the sixth century B. C., "and you'd wish you had stopped in time."

68 **Consolidation** Impatient persons of power have considerable difficulty in accurately gauging the special factors that need to be taken into account in the consolidation of their gains.

To begin with, various lengths of time are required for people to forget and forgive, depending on the nature of the transgression. Toppling one's boss in a corporation is generally forgotten in about six months, unless someone keeps fanning the gossip. Even then, the sting would have been dissipated. A small military conquest, such as India's annexation of Goa in 1962, may take a while longer. But if one has been successful and remains out of the limelight for about a year, the newsworthiness would have disappeared. A major encroachment, such as James Polk's one-sided war with Mexico in 1848 to clear the way for the acquisition of the southwestern fourth of the United States, may take a decade or two to be forgotten, but much less if the acquisitions are quickly consolidated.

In perpetrating ethically questionable power plays, therefore, you should shape events as close as practical to the following three conditions: (1) The probability of success should be high. (2) The time needed for consummation should be relatively short. (3) Another power play of the same dubious ethics should not be attempted during the time it takes your constituency to forget.

When the consolidation of power requires a concomitant acceptance of change in fundamental doctrines or ideas, considerable time is necessary for the change to take hold. Even creative scientists who pride themselves in their open-mindedness to innovation are no exception.

When Charles Darwin published his theory of evolution in 1859, a furor ensued. It was not limited to the religious authorities, like Bishop Samuel Wilberforce, who assailed its contradiction of *Genesis*. The scientists themselves were up in arms. Many, such as Sir Richard Owen, Superintendent of the Natural History Department of the British Museum and Louis Agassiz, Professor of Botany at Harvard University, rejected the thesis outright.

When the physicist Max Planck tried to introduce his radical concepts several decades later, which constitute the foundation of much of modern physics, he was ignored by fellow workers. He found nothing but apathy, even among physicists in the same field. Hermann von Helmholtz snubbed his paper. Gustav Kirchhoff disapproved. Rudolf Clausius did not reply to his letter. Carl Neumann remained unimpressed after a conversation. Planck later reminisced: "This experience gave me also an opportunity to learn a new fact—a remarkable one, in my opinion: A new scientific truth does not triumph by convincing its opponents and making them see the light, but rather because its opponents eventually die, and a new generation grows up that is familiar with it."

This natural refractory response to change has long been taken into account instinctively by revolutionaries. After taking over a country, they methodically purge those older individuals who continue troublesome resistance in acts or words. The others over forty are kept in line, leaving time to soften their antipathy without any illusion about their enthusiasm for the new regime. Patient indoctrination is reserved for the young.

69 **Instant focus of relevant totality**   Having considered some of the techniques of maneuvering and striking, we might ask the question: Is there one mark that distinguishes the great person of power from the rest? Yes, the answer would be: he acts from an instantaneous apprehension of the totality.

There is no need to belabor the common sense admonition of seeing the big picture or getting the full story. But some preliminary comparisons of the effectiveness of the so-called partist strategy versus the so-called wholist strategy in resolving problems may be instructive.

When faced with a decision, the partist strategy begins with a small group of factors assumed to be necessary and sufficient to solve the problem. As in model building, different combinations and permutations are then successively tested and discarded until the final equilibrium is reached. In this case, the tentative answer at any given time is always precisely stated but wrong until the correct one is found.

This step-by-step approach is reminiscent of the two Yankee tourists driving along the shore of a beautiful lake in Florida one hot summer day. As they came up to a boy fishing from the banks, the driver stopped the car and asked the youngster, "Son, are there any snakes in this lake?" "No suh," came the reply, "no snakes in de lake." Whereupon the men peeled off their clothes and enjoyed an hour's swimming. When they came out, the other fellow inquired, "How come there are no snakes in this lake?" The boy answered with a half-grin, "Becuz de alligators done et dem up."

In contrast, the wholist strategy begins with the totality, so that all possible factors are included within the net of consideration. The unnecessary and less relevant components are then successively eliminated, until the desired equilibrium is obtained. In this case, the tentative decision at any given time is always correct but imprecise because of the varying degrees of extraneous chaff and noise, until the final answer is found.

As discussed by Jerome Bruner, Jacqueline Goodnow, and George Austin in *A Study of Thinking,* the tests showed that given infinite time to complete the task, either strategy will deliver the correct answer. When only limited time is available, however, the wholist strategy is superior. When we take the game of Chinese baseball into consideration, the odds would be overwhelmingly in favor of the wholist strategy. Furthermore, as any professional football player knows so well, the big games are decided more often than not by the mistakes committed rather than by the yardages gained. Although the wholist strategy may not make as much yardage in any one play or in any one game, it is relatively invulnerable to fatal mistakes. In contrast, although the partist strategy may make a spectacular yardage in any one play or in any one game, it is invariably susceptible to fatal mistakes over time.

The master of power instantly transforms a mass of conflicting events and risks into a sure course of action, without thinking, without hesitating, without failing. Like a knock—the sound does not wait for the completion of the knock before issuing forth; knock and sound, cause and effect, plans and operations, means and ends—all merge in the instant of action. This trait was impressively manifested by young Temujin during the successful escape for his life.

Temujin was a prisoner of his murderous brother, Targoutai. He was awaiting his execution with a huge wooden yoke resting on his shoulders to which his hands were tied. As soon as darkness fell, Temujin slipped away with the guards in pursuit. He jumped into a river with his eyes barely above the water watching. As the soldiers roamed the banks, one of them saw him but said nothing. Temujin noticed it and then and there he knew exactly what to do. He followed the horsemen back into his brother's camp. Then he crept into the tent of the stranger who had not given him away. At great danger to himself, the soldier removed the yoke, burnt the evidence, and carted him away under a pile of loose wool. Temujin galloped off to freedom on a fresh horse.

There is no stopping such a man in a struggle for power. He became Genghis Khan.

NEGOTIATING AND PRESSING ON

During their confrontation with the Kuomingtang in the 1940s, the Chinese Communists coined the maxim: *"ta-ta, t'an-t'an"*— fight-fight, talk-talk. The same cycle holds for most battles for power of any kind that continue for any length of time. The earlier sections of this part covered the *ta-ta*. This section examines the *t'an-t'an*. When should you switch from *ta-ta* to *t'an-t'an*? What kind of representative should you send to the *t'an-t'an*? How should he *t'an-t'an*? Finally, what about the succeeding *ta-ta*?

70 **Cessation of active confrontation** The agreement to negotiate is dependent on the perceptions of the opposing leaders as to the advantages of reconciliation over confrontation. In making your decision to proceed with negotiation, you should not be unduly influenced by popular sayings, such as negotiation from strength. As Coral Bell had noted, the cliché has "the true mirage-like quality of some of the most effective political myths, shimmering promisingly, always a little farther off . . . keeping its distance at each apparent advance." What is essential is your being sufficiently well buttressed to undergo the particular exchange with all of its rules and traditions and come out ahead in your own clearly defined objectives.

One of the most binding of the customs is the need for all parties to give up something in the process. Do not go into a negotiation, therefore, unless you have something under your control that the other side wants very much. If you do not, you should develop it ahead of time. Some of the stronger nations have invaded or bombed territories to possess the bargaining chips of military withdrawal and bombing cessations. Some of the richer nations have driven the opposition into financial chaos in order to possess the bargaining chips of financial assistance. Some of the corporations have held back on increasing health benefits to the workers which they can afford in order to give in at the negotiations later on. The groundwork for negotiations must be well laid before it begins. Do not enter negotiations with whatever you happen to have and depend on your negotiating skill. You cannot negotiate unless you have something to negotiate with.

Your moves toward cessation of active confrontation should be initiated as soon as you feel that the course of events have assured high probability of your obtaining more than your minimum objectives at the negotiation table. If there is a good chance of obtaining the practical maximum, measures should be taken to move the events rapidly toward negotiation even from a position of apparent weakness. Your confrontational strategies should then be changed from defeating the opposition to attracting or compelling him to negotiate.

71   Conduct of negotiation   Negotiating is a highly specialized art. As a person of action, you would be better off, as a rule, being represented by someone else more naturally endowed and experientially polished than attempt to conduct the actual exercise yourself.

The representative is to have a very clear idea of your policies, attitudes, strategic overrides, specific targets with boundaries, and limitations of his or her own authority at the negotiation table. He or she should be given no independent judgment as to what will be given away and what will be taken, when the final agreement is signed. In this regard, negotiations should not be entered into merely to get as much as you can from the opposition on an ad hoc basis. Even if this is apparently remunerative, it is seldom prudent to press it too far. You might well gain forced concessions at the session, but these might drive the opposition into repudiating the entire agreement at an inconveniently early date and create a situation, which is highly undesirable at an inauspicious moment from your own point of view. Driving a hard bargain may be profitable at times, but never a greedy one.

Four reference estimates should be established before negotiations begin and revised as proceedings continue: (1) minimum objective for your own side, (2) irreducible minimum for each of the other participants, (3) key issues for each side and adamant position likely to be taken in each case and under what conditions, and (4) practical maximum realizable by your own side with and without lasting enmity on the part of the opposition, associated with the kind of damaging resurgence at a later date.

When it comes to day-to-day tactics and conduct at the negotiation sessions, the representative should be given considerable latitude—provided, of course, he or she possesses the commensurate talent. It might be well to get some feel about the behavior of the more successful negotiators, so that you might be in a better position to pick the right representative for yourself. The following glimpses provide an introductory insight into their abilities and personalities.

Expert negotiators are unfailingly equipped with that unerring ability of quickly sizing up the lay of the land with the minimum of clues and never letting on in the process. They sense the difference in tactics required in dealing with the respective representatives of an authoritarian opposition, a democratic, and a weakly led coalition. They can immediately sniff out the relative advantages of bilateral, submultilateral, or totally open negotiations and in what sequence. They possess a keen intuition as to the right moment to say an explicit "no" to a proposal or a more flexible "no" by way of talking around the subject, ignoring it, or keeping quiet.

Another essential is that continuing awareness on their part is being finely tuned to just the right amount and kind of information that should be given to the other side. They recognize that all parties come to the parley with considerable ignorance regarding the true interests of the others and at times even of their own. These generally come into clearer focus during the ensuing give and take. While there is a risk in the opponent's knowing too much about one's own situation, there is also the danger of his knowing too little. Keeping him completely in the dark is usually not the most fruitful basis for bargaining. Experience has shown that a bargainer takes a progressively more inflexible and tougher stand, demanding much, yielding little, attempting more deceptive maneuvers, and protracting the process as he or she possesses less of the relevant information. The delicate judgment involves providing the opposition sufficient information about one's own side as to enable him to be comfortable with his concessions, yet not so much as to reveal one's real strength and weakness, as well as hidden plans and objectives.

Negotiators are sticklers for facts and details. Nothing is taken lightly. Everything provided at the meetings, whether it be from ally or enemy, is verified through independent checks. Nothing is agreed to until all the facts on which it is based have been confirmed. They keep fastidious records and make sure that there is no misunderstanding on the part of any participant regarding every associated detail before signing, so that the agreement does not fall apart because some of the others might not have been as careful.

Talented negotiators can never be goaded, pressured, or tricked into an action at someone else's convenience or timing. They would rather lose a deal because they did not agree to close it without sufficient time to study and mull it over than to agree to it and regret later. If the other side pushes too hard in this respect, they are never reluctant to say no.

They are sparing but astute in resorting to threats. They understand well enough that a threat called signals the breakdown of negotiations and that is not what they have been asked to do. They also understand that a potential threat held in abeyance is effective merely by being recognized by the adversary. Yet there may come a time when the intimation of the threat might be just the ingredient needed to get the proceedings off dead center. Seasoned negotiators have precisely the right feel for this sort of timing. Furthermore, they also know how to accompany their threats with promises of reward should the other side go along. More frequently than not, a bare threat without a positive inducement for compliance is at best not believable and at worst it stiffens the opposition's back to an unyielding extremity.

When called for, accomplished negotiators are specially adept at conveying the idea that the stated rock-bottom offer is indeed rock-bottom. They may convince the opposition that their own hands are tied by the force of circumstances—politically, economically, religiously, or otherwise. Or that acceptance of the opposition's terms would be disastrous to them. Or that their own terms are not as unfavorable to the opposition as the latter believes. They put the message across with the greatest economy of time and motion.

As far as personal behavior is concerned, successful negotiators conduct themselves at all times like a "gentleman." They refrain from phrases and mannerisms that unwittingly annoy others, thereby raising the arguments to undesirable heat which inevitable makes delicate exchanges impossible. They never lose their temper, yet are fully capable of indicating their displeasure and disappointment in a civil but unmistakable fashion. On those rare occasions of necessity, they may even feign an outburst. But this is always well under thespian control. They are unmoved by personal attacks and are not irritated by blusterings and reprehensible behavior on the part of others. They recognize that the exhibitions might indicate a lack of experience, a staged performance for home consumption, or merely a ploy to get them rattled. They do not comport themselves as superior or inferior, but extend courteous treatment to all parties. They respect confidentiality. They utter no discoverable untruths without preplanned design. They are relaxed, unhurried, and unexcited; never complacent; and always vigilant. They can be as unyielding as a rock and as inscrutable as a sphinx.

72 **Consummation** As the negotiations draw closer to the final stages of give and take, you will be inevitably involved in intimate consultation with your representative on a day-to-day basis, not in the conduct of the sessions themselves, but on the decisions regarding the specific terms. Should the negotiations become stalled at a point when it is to your advantage to drive it to a conclusion, then there are two additional spheres of activities in which your personal power is required.

The first area is raising the cost of the stalemate to the opposition. The cost of negotiation, with the attendant freezing of normal activities, constitute the most significant pressure toward bringing the sessions to conclusion. In the case of a labor dispute, the probable loss of wage income for labor is pitted against the probable loss of profit for management. The losses are not limited to dollars, dissension in the ranks, and public confidence, but extend to the immobilization of the respective parties from embarking on other profitable ventures. Unless a person is increasing his resources and consolidating his gains, he is actually falling behind in relative strengths in comparison to the others on the sidelines. The longer the negotiations drag on, the relatively stronger the latter are growing and the greater the ammunition being given the competitor within his own organization to dislodge him from his home position of leadership.

If your own side possesses a firm power base at home, as compared to that of the opposition at his home base, you would then be under less pressure to seek an early consummation of negotiations. You would enjoy the option of prolonging them in order to extract greater concessions. In this case, your actions may be directed toward fanning the aspirations of the opposition's home constituents which may weaken his position at the negotiation table. The message might subtly imply inadequacies on the opposition's part as a leader. Yet you should be careful not to overdo this sensitive masquerade of opinion formation in somebody else's backyard. If the tactics become obvious, they will backfire. The opposition's home ranks might close behind him and you would lose most of what you had gained toward weakening the opposition's determination up to that point.

Increasing the cost of negotiations has been refined to a brutal degree in international relations. After four years of stalemate at the armistice conference in Paris, while the fighting dragged on in Vietnam, the American Air Force was ordered to resume large-scale bombing of North Vietnam in 1972. "I will only say that I have had some experience, and a great deal of experience as a matter of fact, in this past year with Communist leaders," explained the President. "I find that making a bargain with them is not easy, and you get something from them only when you have something they want from you. The only way we're going to get our P. O. W.'s back is to be doing something to them and that means hitting military targets in North Vietnam and continuing the mining of the harbors of North Vietnam." When progress in negotiation again did not satisfy the American side, the full-scale bombing was resumed during the Christmas season later in the same year.

In trying to stand pat on their own essential demands, the North Vietnamese leaders were counting on aggravating the cost to the United States in terms of financial and psychological disequilibrium at home and military and economic erosion in the rest of the world. During the period of her being bogged down in Vietnam, Russia had come to parity with the United States militarily. Japan had overtaken her on world commerce as far as trade balance is concerned. Communist China had become the moral spokesman for the underdeveloped nations. The longer the United States remained mired in Vietnam, the more difficult it was for her to regain her former domestic unity and world leadership.

While putting maximum pressure toward increasing the costs of delays to the other side, each side tries to decrease them for itself at the same time. Most labor unions maintain a strike fund. In 1961, fifty-seven out of 102 national unions surveyed in America paid strike benefits. These went as high as 60 percent of the day's work scale for typographers with dependents. Similarly corporations subscribe to loss-protection plans through premiums to an insurance company or an industry pool. In the 1962 strike of flight engineers against Eastern Airlines, the company's loss of $23.4 million was reduced to $7.6 million by contributions from the eight-member pool.

The second area for decision from you as the person in power arises when the proceedings are at an impasse because there is not enough to meet the minimum demands of both parties. In this case, consideration should be given to finding a third party who is not directly involved in the argument, from whom the needed differential amount can be extracted—unsuspecting perhaps, begrudgingly perhaps, but helplessly acquiescent when he or she finds out later on. You must then decide whether you are willing to join in the collusion, which would resolve your own dilemma. Persons of power usually have little difficulty in making up their minds on such questions.

International relations have been marked by a succession of these exploitations of the weak and the nonrepresented. The Yalta agreement among Great Britain, Russia, and United States is a relatively recent incident of this kind. In the absence of China, all agreed to Russia's joining the war against Japan, for which Russia would be given "lease" rights to Port Arthur, safeguards of Russia's "preeminent interests" in a "jointly operated" Sino-Soviet Commission for the Chinese-Eastern Railroad and the South-Manchurian Railroad, and "preservation" of the status of Outer Mongolia, as well as some territory from Japan.

On the labor-management front, we find the same device of absentee-third-party payment in the regular contract-bargaining sessions. Both parties know that ultimately they are bargaining not against each other but toward the same point of resolution, that is, how much of the increased cost of the new contract can be passed on to the consumer? In an industry-wide union, the answer is straightforward—all. For where else can the public buy a piece of complex hardware? In some respects, the strike and bargaining themselves constitute an elaborate ceremony of convincing the public and consumers that the increased costs in material and services have been levied only after all other avenues have been anguishly explored. The procedure has reached a high level of dramatic artistry. Besides extracting present payments for themselves as recipients from themselves as consumers through inflation, they are extracting payments from third-parties-yet-unborn through such techniques as increasing the national debt, deferred old-age pensions, and long-term mortgages. A secular and modern version, as it were, of the Original Sin.

73   **Continuum of power**   Just as you have been ambitious and grasping for additional power all your life, so have other persons of power. Just as you have rested when beaten, licked your wounds, regained your strength, and attacked again, so will those whom you have just defeated. Just as you have sought to eliminate those threats to your power whom you had only partially neutralized, so will others be looking your way with anxious eyes.

Once your continuum of power plays is allowed to snap, you are on your way out. It is preferable to abdicate gracefully while you are still in your glory to do so than attempt to ply your power intermittently. "The will disappears when its continuity is broken," wrote L. T. Hobhouse. "It is replaced by so many separate volitional acts, 'free' like beads scattered sparsely on a string, that neither pull nor push one another, but move or rest each 'of itself.' The 'I' which wills this now has nothing to say to the 'I' of yesterday or of five minutes hence. Each choice is a new fact arising out of the void and plunging into it again. There is no will which abides, whether changeless or growing by successive acts of self-determination."

For persons of power, the consummation of a negotiation is not the termination of a struggle. It is merely a transition from one form of competition to another. The thrust remains unabated.

REFLECTING ON MORALITY

No matter how ruthless a person of power may appear to be, he or she is always moral to a greater or lesser degree. The human mind cannot help wandering off now and then from the pressure of the moment into the realms of higher values. And so, this section closes our little book with a deliberation on some of the issues that have undoubtedly troubled the more statesmen-like persons of power from time to time. Are ends and means separable in the acts of power? Does bigness necessarily foster evil? Or depersonalization? What personal choices are there? How about one's duty to the institution? One's compassion for the people? Finally, what is the true measure of greatness for those perched at the peaks of power?

74 **Ends and means** With some justification, one might be inclined to brush aside the question of the morality of power on the premise that power is but the means to an end and therefore basically amoral. It can serve mankind for good as well as for evil. Only the ends have moral connotations. But the issue is not that simple.

Sheer wielding of force is not power. Power begins with a specification of purpose. The expression of power thereby entails a moral choice. The determination as to the kinds of resources, including spiritual motivation and physical coercion, to be used invariably interlaces means and ends. Excessive dedication to the ends disregards any limitation on means, which in itself raises a moral issue. Finally, in power plays of serious dimensions, innocent people are hurt. What would one say when the amount of innocent suffering is out of all proportion to the gains desired, good or evil? Especially when it is needless to their acquisition?

When a person becomes the head of an extensive organization, he or she can no longer be self-limiting in the choice of either means or ends. The disintegration of the empire through "goodness" will make him or her the laughing stock among historians. Without conscious awareness he or she has become proficient in most tricks of the trade and uses them as the circumstances demand. Even when he or she and the hierarchy are highly "good," they will rarely return the spoils which their predecessors have acquired through what they themselves would confess as "evil" ends and means—spoils, which now constitute much of the base of their prevailing power. That is why many thinkers like Bertrand de Jouvenal have been led to the conclusion that all power, whether for purposes good or ill, is corrupt.

"Seest thou not how not only God but man too accepts the principle that regard should be had not to the nature of an action, but to its purpose," said Saint Chrysostrom. Others have affirmed the same principle. This argument as to whether the ends justify the means has lost much of its cogency in these modern times of overwhelmingly powerful means. Unrestrained ambition—for God, country, or self; for virtue, honor, or wealth—leads men with "bags of tricks" to exploit them to the ultimate of their capabilities. The very existence of means capable of achieving certain ends creates a disposition to use those means toward those ends. Given a nuclear bomb, an annihilated city is certain to follow; given spacecrafts in the stratosphere, spies in the skies and weapons platforms in the heavens are certain to follow; given computerized memory banks, increased invasion of privacy is certain to follow. Ends realized are nothing more than means expressed.

The impossibility of the separation of means from ends is recognized even by novices in the game of power. This was brought out in a television debate on student riots in 1969. One of the moderate students took a firm stand against coercive tactics, although he expressed belief in the objectives of the movement. To which the militant student sharply dissented: "This sounds so much like so many things I know we in the black community have heard a long time. I remember, you know, very interestingly, people used to say to Martin Luther King: 'But is it right to break a law simply because you disagree with it? Do two wrongs make a right?' Now what you wind up saying is 'Well, I agree with the issues you're raising, but I don't necessarily agree with your means,' which means then you don't do anything about the issues . . . Poor people come into Washington, D.C. They said: 'I'm against poverty, but don't mess up the grass and landscape.'"

There is no way around it. Power is a thoroughly moral phenomenon. It is effective, defective, or deceptive morality—as the case may be.

75 Bigness Persons of power in corporations are often perplexed and annoyed at people's distrust of bigness, just because it is big, even though the benefits to them from the resulting increased efficiency are so obvious. The issue is worth pondering over.

Whenever a group of competitors are left alone without constraints, one of them usually gains dominance over the others in time. Each successful adventure on its part generates new wants, which in turn give rise to new adventures. Gradually, the giant controls a wide spectrum of diverse operations. Like the medieval church, it then becomes a state unto itself within a state. The concentrated resources bring with them a major voice in the policies governing the community at large.

In the lexicon of power, a giant corporation is not a producer of goods and services. It is not limited to a particular market or a given set of laws. It is concurrently a vehicle of power for certain individuals. The skill of these persons of power rests primarily not on their ability at generating corporation profits but at expanding extra-corporation influence. Whatever havoc they raise in the exercise of that extra-corporation power is not done, in the words of Ferdinand Lundberg, "maliciously . . . any more than an elephant feels malice when it rubs against a sapling and breaks it in two. An elephant must behave like an elephant, beyond any moral stricture."

As an individual, the head of one of the largest corporations may well be much more powerful in the affairs of the country than the average member of Congress. It is when this potentiality becomes apparent that the federal government becomes harshest in its control of nongovernmental bigness. Power prestige is at stake.

It was only natural that the federal government, populated by persons of power, explicitly declared that bigness per se is a threat on the part of any agency other than government. The Sherman Antitrust Act of 1890 stipulated that contracts, mergers, and agreements in restraint of trade are illegal. The Federal Trade Commission Act of 1914 prohibits unfair competition in interstate commerce. Under Section 7 of the Clayton Act, mergers are not permitted if they might substantially lessen competition. Under the Sherman Act the prosecution only needs to show that unreasonable restraint of trade had been exercised. The courts had been careful to apply the Rule of Reason since the 1911 case of *Standard Oil Co. v. United States.* Unreasonableness is to be proven in the context of actual and potential restraint, as well as the intentions of the individuals and the extenuating circumstances leading to the action. In the case of price-fixing, however, the Supreme Court has held for over thirty years that price fixing per se violates the antitrust laws for which no defense can be offered.

Besides the antitrust laws, other methods have been employed by governments to control the excessive extension of power by corporations: socialization through state ownership as in Soviet Russia, public and private enterprises operating side by side as in India and Canada, mixed companies as in France and Italy after World War I, and capital and labor sharing as in West Germany after World War II.

It would appear that the preservation of free economic competition within these various countries is not the driving motivation behind many of the governmental restraining measures. What shows through the various justifications is the common abhorence of competitors to state power. Corporations are to be kept competing against each other so that they will not be able to compete against the government. Even so, many individuals using corporations as their base of power have been more than able to compete against most officials of the government using their disconnected government platforms as personal extensions.

From the standpoint of the individual, the question arises as to whether severe limitations on the growth in power of any institution would not only minimize the probability for evil but also minimize the probability for good. We would have to grant that to be the case. What is uncertain is the net balance.

Some authors argue on behalf of severe limitations. They feel that it is important to curtail man's power for greatest evil, even though this will curtail his power for greatest good at the same time. The basis for their distrust of great power is the feeling that man is basically selfish and bad. Western religion taints him with the Fall. Even its God has been unable to erase evil from the face of the earth. The culture seems obsessed with sin. The twentieth century is regarded to be as cruel and as cynical as ever. According to their line of reasoning, safeguards should be maintained against this evil urge from running amuck with power.

What would happen to the argument, however, if we assume that man is intrinsically good? Mencius noted in the fourth century B. C. that when a man sees a child suddenly about to fall into a well, he will invariably rush forward to help. This he will instinctively do, not out of expectation of reward from the parents or praise from his friends, or fear of a bad reputation for not having moved, but out of his natural goodness.

Even so, other authors would consider the argument as to whether the human being is fundamentally good or fundamentally evil as irrelevant to the prudence of a severe limitation of the power of one person over the welfare of another. They base their conclusion on the belief that the amount of practical good that one person can do for another is limited for a considerable fraction of the population, no matter how great his power, whereas the amount of practical evil is unlimited for the total population even short of absolute power. Their rationale would run somewhat as follows:

The primary criterion of evil is the infliction of unwarranted pain and suffering to human beings. That of good is the removal of pain and suffering and/or the augmentation of happiness. With respect to pain and suffering, there is a certain minimum of biological need which must be satisfied, such as physiological necessities, rehabilitative treatments, and protection from mental and physical injuries. To the extent that increased power in an institution would lead to a more effective meeting of these requirements, to that extent are its contributions for good increased. To the extent that an institution restricts the available flow of biological necessities (such as subsistence and medical attention) or inflicts suffering (such as through wars and psychological double binds), to that extent are its contributions for evil increased.

Considering the present state of technology, the biological and psychological essentials for the minimizing of suffering can be met for the American people without any further concentration of power in any institution. This would be especially true for the *cronopios*, as they have been called by Julio Cortázar. When they go on a trip, the *cronopios* find that their hotel reservations have been given to somebody else; all the other hotels within ready access are filled; it is raining cats and dogs; the taxis pass them by; they are soaken wet. But they believe this happens to everyone. When they finally manage to find a bed and lay down to fall asleep, they say to one another: "What a beautiful city!" Their cheerful frame of mind is largely their own doing. Others may add increments of joy, but do not determine the baseline. Such people do not need more powerful institutions to make them happy. But they can be made to suffer through both indirect and direct means.

The indirect route begins with breaking down the philosophy of contentment of the *cronopios*. The cravings of the American people for goods, services, enjoyments, and statuses over and beyond those available are to be intensified. Happiness to them then becomes the fulfillment of that ever-enlarging gap. The abstract painter of Greenwich Village trying to be another Picasso, the descendant of Scollay Square laundryman Sam Wong competing with the descendant of Abbott Lowell for a deanship at Harvard, and the junior executive of forty making $26,000 a year driving to become a vice president at IBM are most likely destined for unhappy futures. The extent of dissatisfaction that can be infused through the entire population is a function of the power available in the hands of persons operating from large institutional bases. It is they who can tantalize human subjects with what the latter are missing in life, thereby spreading the gap between craving and having. If the gap is maintained such that the immediate goal appears conceivably within reach but actually receding with each approach, they would have succeeded in recruiting new dependent disciples and creating new dependent customers, who are thereby kept within their escalating influence.

The other route is the direct hurting of people being used in the game of power. The larger and the more powerful the institution, the more people can be driven to bleeding ulcers and aneurisms in striving for that everreceding unattainable goal. It is such an institution that can order human subjects to maim or be maimed, kill or be killed.

It appears therefore that given control of massive resources, there are greater opportunities for the expression of power toward the unhappiness of the individual in the twentieth century than toward his or her happiness. Unlimited potential to power seems to favor practical evil.

76 **Institutional power amplification** Institutions are the social amplifiers of power. As an individual, a person's power potential is quite meager. It becomes significant only through institutional amplification. The amplification is primarily effected not through the large amount of resources available, although admittedly this constitutes an important element, but rather through the substitution of transmoral standards of institutions for the moral ethics of human beings.

This explains, in part, why the out-and-out humanitarian liberals have never been able to attain power on a massive scale. They permit personal values surrounding the dignity of the individual to interfere with the growth of their own institutions. Aggressive institutions of power do not tolerate such sands in the gears of its machinery and as a consequence nearly always outstrip the completely liberal institutions.

The range of opinions on the man-institution dualism is exemplified by the results of *The New York Times* survey of various writers in 1967 regarding civil disobedience to participation in the Vietnam War.

One respondent considered "that the actions of our Government in Vietnam are illegitimate because they require citizens to violate their basic sense of human decency. When the price of loyalty is sacrificing of one's sense of morality and justice, then the very foundation of the Government's legitimacy has been destroyed." He appeared to be arguing that an institution should operate on the basis of personal morality.

Another contributor felt that "A free society can recognize and respect the scruples of a conscientious objector to war who civilly disobeys the law and accepts the punishment. But if he forcibly tries to prevent others from fulfilling their duty to their country he is neither a genuine pacifist nor a democrat." He appeared to be arguing that institutional standards should be applied to everybody's personal behavior but not his beliefs. Deviants for reasons of personal morality should be punished and quietly secluded from infecting the masses.

A third replied: "That which is anarchic within me . . . tunes in strongly on the ideas of a society in which people decide for themselves what taxes to pay, what rules to obey, when to cooperate and when not to with the civil authorities. But that which is reasonable within me . . . recognizes that societies so structured do not exist and cannot exist: an insight as ancient as Socrates, so patiently explained to Crito." He appeared to accept the realities of power at face value.

Many individuals in high offices are troubled by the dualism. Restraint in the use of power, which is considered as highly desirable in the treatment of one's neighbor, is usually regarded by the same individuals as undesirable in the institutional setting—a mark of executive weakness. There is a braking effect in private life, and a person tends to keep his or her behavior within the bounds of friendship and decency. On the other hand, forcefulness in institutional operations is considered worthy of praise. Personal ethics are to be narcotized by institutional interest.

It is this anesthesia of personal ethics by institutional interest that enabled an American physicist in 1960 to discourse in a popular book about thermonuclear war in blasé arithmetic: "If 180 million dead is too high a price to pay for punishing the Soviets for their aggression, what price would we be willing to pay? . . . I have discussed this question with many Americans, and after about fifteen minutes of discussion, their estimates of an acceptable price generally fall between 10 and 60 million, clustering toward the upper number."

Within the atmosphere of ethical license, institutions have grown spectacularly powerful, especially when led by a succession of persons of power, who have, besides high managerial qualities, been capable of grappling, countering, and/or excelling in whatever sanctimonies, hypocrisies, immoralities, viciousness, and meanness that are operative within their respective amphitheaters. These persons of power have risen to the top because they have demonstrated their superiority in deeds by vanquishing their oppositions enroute.

As people study their history books and observe the current world stage, they begin to worry for themselves and their descendants. Will their own leaders use their enormous powers and consummate skills against them at home, as well as against the enemies abroad? Are they being fatted for institutional sacrifices? Or have they been bled all along?

Anxiety is the paradoxical twin to modern prosperity.

77 **Depersonalization** To gain power over people, depersonalize; to gain absolute power, depersonalize absolutely.

The process of depersonalization begins subtly with a separation of "we" from "they." "We" are persons; "they" are impersons. "They" becomes the most important impersonal pronoun in the transformation equation of power. As Franz Alexander puts it, "Conscience may be regarded as that portion of the human personality by which we identify ourselves with other people."

The so-called "tough" decisions come much easier when thinking in terms of impersonalities than personalities. Management is no longer viewed as exploitation of flesh and blood but as efficient use of materiel and resources. The engines of power always run smoother when built of impersonal modules than of personal beings.

When Ajatasaru murdered Bimbisara to become King of India in the fifth century B. C., he did not kill a personal father, but an impersonal king, who should give way to a more capable one.

When a religious leader in the twelfth century sent word to his bishops to "cause the princes and people to suppress them with the sword," it was not personal human beings who were being tortured and slaughtered but impersonal heretics.

When the director of budget and management was explaining the possible reductions in welfare programs in August 1974 as part of the President's drive to curtail inflation, he said, "these are the old, sick, handicapped, children and veterans—you can think of the politics of it." As spokesman for an encumbent of power up for reelection in two years, he was concerned not with the personal suffering of human beings so much as by the impersonal "politics of it."

Depersonalization is permeating the modern setting, which makes it so conducive for the acquisition of great power. Erich Fromm has contrasted the treatment we used to receive in the small neighborhood country store and the kind we now receive in the urban department store. "The customer who went into a retail store owned by an independent businessman was sure to get personal attention: his individual purchase was important to the owner of the store; he was received like somebody who mattered, his wishes were studied; the very act of buying gave him a feeling of importance and dignity." The big-town department store has changed all that. The customer is of no importance as an individual. He is merely "a" customer. Of course, the department store does not want to lose him as "a" customer, "because this would indicate that there was something wrong and it might mean that the store would lose other customers for the same reason. As an abstract customer he is important; as a concrete customer he is utterly unimportant. There is nobody who is glad about his coming, nobody who is particularly concerned about his wishes."

As the impersonal urban-industrial combine grows in magnitude, it becomes what C. Wright Mills calls "the biggest bazaar in the world." It is hard to say who owns it. "It began when a petty capitalist left whaling ships for retail trade. Then it became a family business; some partners appeared, and they took over; now it is a corporation, and nobody owns more than 10 per cent. From a single proprietor to what, in that curious lingo of finance, is called the public. The eldest son of an eldest son has a lot of say-so about its working, but if he went away, nobody doubts that it would go on; it is self-creative and self-perpetuating and nobody owns it. . . . There are managers of this and managers of that, and there are managers of managers, but when any of them dies or disappears, it doesn't make any difference. The store goes on."

The rate of depersonalization is being accelerated by our technological emphasis. We need mention only two of the major contributing factors.

The first is the central attraction of technological advances. There is no more impressive a tour de force than Apollo 11, which landed two men on the moon in 1969. Accomplishments of this kind require an extremely complex system—not of men with men—but of men with machines. The term man-machine system has become commonplace in America. For the man-machine system to function smoothly, a compatibility must exist between the man and the machine. Since the machine is not able to behave like a human being, the human being must then behave like a machine. He must adopt many of its characteristics. The most important ones for man-machine purposes are standardization, mass-producibility, and replaceability. These very characteristics constitute the essential elements of depersonalization as well.

The second factor is the worship of speed. Many Americans even want cultural evolution and social progress to advance at technological rates. This can come about only with the broad imposition of an overall collective blueprint for the technological human being. The expression of individual personalities and personal differences would impede the program. Variations among the masses are to be discouraged. Equality is to be identified with uniformity. Deviants are to be suppressed. Technological orthodoxy is to be the doctrine of the day.

Yet depersonalization is rarely reciprocal in social affairs. Herein lies the nagging asymmetry in our depersonalized system of social equity.

A million soldiers personally suffer and die for the French and the German states at Verdun, but "they" at government headquarters respond impersonally by adjusting the casualty lists and shaking "their" heads at the inability to make a breach in the impersonal enemy's lines. The plant manager personally suffers a heart attack resulting from his driving work for the company, but "they" in the executive suite respond impersonally by transferring funds from the "salaries" to the "sick payments" account. Rioters spit at the policeman as an impersonal representative of the "Establishment," but the policeman personally feels the slimy sputum; the policeman clubs the rioters as impersonal breakers of the law, but the rioters personally bleed.

Having gotten into the habit of preaching personal ideals and executing impersonal actions, the persons of power keep repeating the same cycle over and over in ever-increasing intensities. A poetic portrayal of the fateful amalgam of the impersonal and the personal in the compulsive pistons of power was given by Torquato Tasso in his romantic epic *Gerusalemme Liberata*. One day the hero, Tancred, engaged someone in enemy armor in combat and killed him. Tearing off the mask, he saw the face of his beloved Clorinda. After grieving over the tragic mistake and burying Clorinda, he and the crusaders wandered off into a strange magic forest, which struck terror into their hearts. As Tancred slashed wildly at a tall tree, blood gushed from it and the voice of Clorinda, whose soul was imprisoned in it, was heard to cry that Tancred has wounded his beloved yet once again.

78 **Personal options** The world is a vast, ever-changing agglomerate of faceless and nameless "them." "They" are conditioned by a million years of evolutionary progression, engulfing a person as "they" dispassionately roll along. And, as part of this "they," the same person is continually engulfing the individual next to him as "they" dispassionately roll along. At any given point in time then the rest of the world is undergoing power plays which are making a person do something he or she would rather not. In turn, he or she is involved in power plays making somebody else do something that the latter would rather not.

One may wonder about the philosophical options available to an individual being continually engulfed by these successive waves of power. He or she might choose to go along with "them." "Kismet," he would say. She would allow herself to become the statistical result of the power play among "them." After all, what can one little person do against the world?

At least two implications are involved in such a resolution. These are: (1) The rest of the world determined the course of action for a person in those areas in which he or she could have had no decisive influence, and (2) he or she determined the course of action for the world in those areas in which he or she could have had a decisive influence. The world had to go along with the weighted "minority" judgment, instead of the weighted "majority" had he or she thrown his or her weight into the balance.

Although the occasions in the latter category are relatively rare, they are nevertheless not nonexistent. Every person has a certain number of power plays in his life in which his mere living could make a difference for himself and the world. The question arises: How should the average person go about selecting those power plays in which he or she should participate in an active fashion?

An offhand piece of advice would be: Participate in those power plays in which the potential returns outweigh the effort required. But such a selection is easier said than done. It is impossible to predict the total consequences of the long chain of events initiated by even a relatively innocuous act. Who could have predicted that Atilla's wedding to a young bride would have saved Rome from an invasion the following summer, when he burst a blood vessel during the nuptial night and died?

At times the following four-step sequence is considered by the uninitiated gingerly stepping into the arena: (1) At the beginning, he would observe the immediately predictable events and participate in those activities that would provide the essentials of living for him and his family. (2) Next, he would take part in those immediately predictable events that fortify his basic philosophy on social institutions. (3) He would then proceed on a calculated risk on a course of action to develop a base of affluence, without jeopardizing the resources required for the first objective above. (4) Given the attainment of the base of affluence, he would then go as speedily forward as his ambition desires and the opportunities allow.

Unfortunately, world events do not unfold to suit the convenience of any particular individual. Additional rules of thumb are therefore called for as one goes about intuitively fashioning a more practical path to power.

For long-term success, one should not commit all of his resources at any given time. It is prudent to let enticing but uncertain chances pass than drain one's reserve to the bottom in a gamble. A fair part of the resources is to be maintained for promising surges, critical emergencies, and recuperations after the inevitable setbacks along the way. These kinds of unforeseen occasions arise much more frequently in power competitions than in other activities. One should always be prepared.

The degree of human warmth and naturalness with which persons relate to others is a reflection of their self-confidence, which, in turn, is a function of their native capability, relative to the increment of change being pursued. Should the latter lie fully within their own capacity to accomplish, they can deal with the world fraction in question on a relatively more personal basis. Should they be contented with minimum levels of material goods and power, while going around sprinkling sunshine into people's lives as they go along, it is conceivable that practically all their dealings with the world fraction involved can be human and personal.

As persons begin to crave power beyond that which their own natural capacities can sustain, however, life becomes an uncertain adventure. The less confident they are of their unassisted ability to achieve it, the more allies will they be driven to seek. The more outsiders they invite, the less will they know about the true strength and motivation of the members of their team. The less they know about them, the greater the margin of safety will they feel they need to possess. Meanwhile, the words of Mephistopheles to Faust echo in their ear:

> The worst society is some relief,
> Making thee feel thyself a man with men.

They inspire their diverse followers with the rallying cry of some higher purpose. The moral burden is transferred to this effigy and they themselves are caught up in its righteousness. They become incisive in dissecting, tenacious in pursuing, crafty in bargaining, combative in willing. They spread awe and fear in friend and foe alike.

New persons of power have arrived on the scene.

79   **Duty**   The person of power is faced with continuing accommodations to three interacting sets of distinct duties, which overarch every act of his or hers. These are: (1) that which is morally required of oneself as a human being, (2) that which is required of oneself in one's institutional status, and (3) that which is required of oneself as a person of power.

Although the duties of power frequently override the duties of institutional status, which in turn frequently override the duties of the human being, there is a certain variable latitude of overrides delimiting what is generally considered acceptable by the community at large. As a rule, the prudent person of power instinctively stays just within these boundaries. In so doing, he not only grows in power without public opposition but also enjoys the reputation of an effective executive and a good human being at the same time.

Should he, however, overemphasize (1) over (2), he would before long probably be fired as a poor executive, thereby disrupting at least temporarily his career in power without an operational base. Should he overemphasize (2) over (3), he would be well respected as an effective executive, but his acquisition of greater power would be drastically reduced. Should he overemphasize (3) over (1), he would be denounced as a dictator and movements to depose him as a person of power would gain dramatically in strength.

As far as the individual human being is concerned, every social group since antiquity had developed conventionally acknowledged duties. To the Navaho, it is one's duty to speak the truth because it follows common sense. The neighbors will trust you and vice versa. The tribe gets along better that way. Besides, it is against Navaho tradition to do otherwise. The young are trained in the practice as a well-tested custom.

The Stoic philosophers of ancient Greece formalized their concept: it is the duty of a human being to live virtuously, regardless of happiness. Rabbinical legalism and Christian gospels pointed in the same general direction, in their advancement of the law of the supreme God. The Western penchant for the logical derivation of duty reached its heights with thinkers of the eighteenth century. One of the most popular of the notions was the so-called categorical imperative, the supreme law of duty. It is one's duty to obey that law, revealed intuitively by the rational will universally without contradiction, regardless of consequences.

Regardless of personal ethics, the ethics of institutions has one dominating meaning. This is upholding the interests of the institution of which one is a senior member or chief. Rightly or wrongly from other points of view, the chief has already accepted this premise the moment he took the oath of office. If he is a bishop, then the growth of the number of communicants and the superseding of his own church's teachings over all others must be among his essential concerns, regardless of the Stoic's thesis. If he is the chief executive officer of a corporation, then the long-term profit maximization and increasingly stronger competitive standing in the economic world must constitute two of his essential objectives, regardless of the Christian gospels. If he is a prime minister, then national ascendancy must rank highest in his essential priorities, regardless of the categorical imperative.

To be sure, there is a measure of personal duty to which an office holder adheres most of the time, which endows the office with an aura of fairness and kindness in the eyes of the community. There is a general obedience to the laws of the land. There is a high level of honesty in the descriptions of its goods and services. There is a reasonable degree of consideration for the interest of others. There is a reliability in the honoring of commitments and contracts. Such behavior may be considered virtuous even within the rules of personal morality. But they also fall within the ethics of institutions, because they do usually contribute to their long-term health.

If the personal expressions of virtue neither harm nor benefit the institution, then they are basically irrelevant to institutional ethics. Under these conditions, if a member of the institution feels highly inclined towards virtue, the institution will probably condone or even commend them, as part of the morale-building program. However, should the two be in conflict, then by the standards of institutional ethics, the personal preferences must be compromised. If the person feels strongly to the contrary, he or she can always resign. In this case, the institution feels no pain, since the person has rendered himself, virtues and all, irrelevant. There is the ever-available imperson-module to plug in his place.

Another consideration of importance is the proper balance of short-term versus long-term welfare of the institution. One of the forms in which the dilemma is frequently expressed is the challenge by unit chiefs of the decisions of higher echelons. As head of a subsidiary entity, it is one's duty to protect it against the siphoning off of essential resources by the parent organization for purposes of its own. One must ensure that the voice of one's own unit is heard in the higher councils, so that the overall policies that are damaging to one's group will not be promulgated. It is one's duty to fight vigorously against all encroachments. It is one's duty to protect one's people to maintain their effectiveness. At the same time, however, the long-term interest of one's own requires a strong parent body. There is a limit, therefore, as to how far one should go in bucking the higher echelons—not from the standpoint of their interest but from that of one's own.

A certain statesmanship is expected from the wielders of power at any level. Johannes Messner pointed to the differences in statesman-like attitude between the labor leaders of Central Europe and of England following World War II. In the former group, self-restraint was practiced in advocating their own interests, thereby making higher capital investments possible toward the restoration of the economy; an incredibly rapid economic growth resulted. In contrast, the British labor unions kept the national economy under a continuing state of unrest through a succession of authorized and unauthorized strikes for ever-increasing wage demands, thereby decreasing the magnitude of capital investments; the value of the pound sterling dropped and the English economy sputtered.

On a more elegant plane, the well-being of the institution also calls for a certain behavior on the part of the senior members to uplift and maintain its dignity. Institutions, too, have a certain kind of pride. In the words of James Bryce in 1888, individuals in a high position should be inspired by the magnitude of the responsibilities and conduct themselves at an appropriately higher level than they normally would as private individuals. "Their horizon ought to be expanded, their feeling of duty quickened, their dignity of attitude enhanced. Human nature with all its weaknesses does show itself capable of being thus roused on its imaginative side; and in Europe, where the tradition of aristocracy survive, everybody condemns as mean or unworthy acts done or language used by a great official which would pass unnoticed in a private citizen. It is the principle of *noblesse oblige* with the sense of duty and trust substituted for that of mere hereditary ranks."

As far as duty to power is concerned, the following seems to express the practicing consensus among persons of power: It is one's duty to reach ever for greater power but never once for more than can be gotten away with. As long as the institution does not effectively object to an executive of power bleeding off resources for the aggrandizement of one's own personal power, which might incidentally add to the power of the institution itself, and as long as the target population accepts or objects only ineffectually, then one would be operating within the acceptable social norms of power. But should one overstep that bound, a turmoil ensues, leading to the loss of one's bases of power. Such action would constitute a breach of duty to oneself as a person of power, because it has resulted in an injury to one's own status of power.

Aspirants to power without a sense of the proper blend of dignity and duty are nothing more than ruffians. Even if they do get to the top, they do not last long.

80 **Compassion**   Compassion is an essential term in all equations of power. One should be clear, however, regarding the practical distinction between necessary compassion and magnanimous compassion. More often than not, the distinction is a matter of degree. But the master of power always knows the optimal mix for any given move.

Necessary compassion represents that minimum of actual or cere-monial compassion considered acceptable for membership in the human society. In addition, there are special opportunistic occasions to power through undertaking what may appear to be heroic compassion. Rallying the poor and alleviating their wretched lot for the purpose of overthrowing established authorities, campaigning on a strong civil rights plank for the purpose of getting elected, and fighting for under-privileged farm laborers for the purpose of enlarging one's base of power also fall within the category of necessary compassion. Other examples include the provision of minimum welfare, hospitalization benefits, and unemployment compensations for the purpose of preclud-ing violence to one's entrenched domination.

Magnanimous compassion, on the other hand, represents the ex-tension of assistance beyond that required for the maintenance or accretion of power. A big banker joining a movement to raise family assistance allowance to the indigent at home or to feed the hungry abroad may be an example. While this action may be construed as necessary compassion on the part of the President involved in domestic tranquility and foreign alliances, it is much more an act of magnani-mous compassion on the part of the banker, whose power does not re-quire his participation in such endeavors.

The amount of magnanimous compassion a person of power can afford to dispense depends, in large part, on his or her store of reserves and his or her degree of confidence. But reserves or no, confidence or no, he or she cannot do without necessary compassion.

81 **Nobility** Friedrich Nietzsche would define the noble deed as that which provides happiness to the greatest number. Buddha would define it as that which minimizes suffering to human beings.

One may wish to reflect on the difference between the two orienta-tions. The former may be attained at the price of increased suffering to a segment of the population; the latter may be attained at the price of decreased happiness to a segment of the population. The former calls for increased generosity to some and decreased compassion to others. The latter calls for increased compassion to all and decreased generos-ity to some.

It might well have been that in Nietzsche's day the economy of the world might have been such that any attempt at minimizing suffering would have still left most people in pain and only a few in happiness, materially speaking. Any difference between the two managerial philosophies might have been academic. In today's economy of abundance, especially in countries like the United States, the picture is entirely otherwise. Suffering on the part of all can be drastically reduced through more efficient and less Faustian leadership on the part of persons of power in control of the surplus.

Should one wish to consider himself not just a person of power but a noble person of power, then his power plays should not only achieve the purposes of his office and augment his own reservoir of power, but also decrease suffering to man and beast as an ever-present byproduct within the totality of their ramifications. Besides the nobility of the act in the decrease of suffering, there is the nobility of the self in the confidence of largess. In view of the fact that his opponents have not in all probability encumbered themselves with the same burden, such a gesture would also display the graciousness of nobility in the arena of power.

This duplexing might not be feasible during your own scrambling to the top. But it might well be worth thinking about, at least after you are reasonably well established.

Speaking on behalf of those too poor to buy this book, too ignorant to read it, and too pained to care, I would ask for your serious consideration. You might even discover through your noble response that there is a deeper meaning to power than the mundane. It can border on the divine.

SELECTED
BIBLIOGRAPHY

Alinsky, S. D. *Rules for Radicals*. New York: Random House, 1971.

Barnard, C. I. *The Function of the Executive*. Cambridge: Harvard University, 1938.

Beilenson, L. W. *The Treaty Trap*. Washington: Public Affairs, 1969.

Bettinghaus, E. P. *Persuasive Communication*. New York: Holt, Rinehart and Winston, 1968.

Blackstock, P. W. *Agents of Deceit*. Chicago: Quadrangle, 1966.

Boorman, S. A. *The Protracted Game*. New York: Oxford University, 1969.

Bullitt, S. *To Be a Politician*. Garden City: Doubleday, 1959.

Burger, C. *Survival in the Executive Jungle*. New York: Macmillan, 1964.

Burling, R. *The Passage of Power*. New York: Academic, 1974.

Canetti, E. *Crowds and Power*. Translated by C. Stewart. New York: Viking, 1962.

Carter, J. F. *Power and Persuasion*. New York: Duell, 1960.

Cohen, A. *Two-Dimensional Man*. Berkeley: University of California, 1974.

Copeman, G. *The Chief Executive*. London: Leviathan, 1971.

Coser, L. A. *Greedy Institutions*. New York: Free, 1974.

Crossman, R. *The Diaries of a Cabinet Minister*. New York: Holt, Rinehart and Winston, 1976-1977. Volumes I and II.

Dichter, E. *Motivating Human Behavior*. New York: McGraw-Hill, 1971.

Downton, Jr., J. V. *Rebel Leadership*. New York: Free, 1973.

Eisenstadt, S. N., Ed. *Political Sociology*. New York: Basic, 1971.

Ellul, J. *Propaganda*. Translated by K. Keller and J. Learner. New York: Knopf, 1965.

Feinberg, M. R., R. Tanofsky, and J. J. Tarrant. *The New Psychology for Managing People*. Englewood Cliffs: Prentice-Hall, 1975.

Felker, D., Ed. *The Power Game*. New York: Simon and Schuster, 1969.

Francesco, G. de. *The Power of the Charlaton*. Translated by M. Beard. New Haven: Yale University, 1939.

Friedrich, C. J. *The Pathology of Politics*. New York: Harper & Row, 1972.

Gamson, W. A. *Power and Discontent*. Homewood: Dorsey, 1968.

213

Goble, F. *Excellence in Leadership*. New York: American Management Association, 1972.

Gurr, T. R. *Why Men Rebel*. Princeton: Princeton University, 1970.

Guzzardi, Jr., W. *The Young Executive*. New York: New American Library, 1965.

Haley, J. *The Power Tactics of Jesus Christ and Other Essays*. New York: Crossman, 1969. Pp. 19–52.

Hart, B. H. L. *Strategy*. London: Faber and Faber, 1967. Fourth Edition.

Hendel, S., Ed. *The Politics of Confrontation*. New York: Appleton-Century-Crofts, 1971.

Hutchison, J. G., Ed. *Readings in Management Strategy and Tactics*. New York: Holt, Rinehart and Winston, 1971.

Jay, A. *Management and Machiavelli*. New York: Holt, Rinehart and Winston, 1968.

Jennings, E. E. *Routes to the Executive Suite*. New York: McGraw-Hill, 1971.

Klonsky, M. *The Fabulous Ego*. Chicago: Quadrangle, 1974.

Korda, M. *Power!* New York: Random House, 1975.

Krieger, L. and F. Stern, Eds. *The Responsibilities of Power*. London: Macmillan, 1968.

Landis, P. H. *Social Control*. Philadelphia: Lippincott, 1939.

Lea, H. D. *The Inquisition of the Middle Ages*. (1887). Abridged by M. Nicolson. New York: Macmillan, 1961.

Leamer, L. *Playing for Keeps in Washington*. New York: Dial, 1977.

Leas, D. and P. Kittlaus. *Church Fights*. Philadelphia: Westminster, 1973.

Loasby, B. J. *Choice, Complexity and Ignorance*. Cambridge: Cambridge University, 1976.

Lorenz, K. *On Aggression*. Translated by M. K. Wilson. New York: Harcourt, Brace & World, 1966.

Luttwak, E. *Coup d'Etat*. London: Penguin, 1968.

Maccoby, M. *The Gamesman*. New York: Simon and Schuster, 1976.

Macchiavelli, N. *The Prince and The Discourses*. Translated by L. Ricci and C. E. Detmold. New York: Modern Library, 1940.

Matles, J. J. and J. Higgins. *Them and Us*. Englewood Cliffs: Prentice-Hall, 1974.

McGregor, D. *The Human Side of Enterprise*. New York: McGraw-Hill, 1960.

McLuhan, M. *Understanding Media*. New York: McGraw-Hill, 1964.

Meares, A. *How To Be a Boss*. New York: Coward, McCann & Geoghegan, 1970.

Messner, J. *The Executive*. Translated by E. J. Schuster. St. Louis: Herder, 1965.

Milgram, S. *Obedience to Authority*. New York: Harper & Row, 1974.

Mintz, M. and J. S. Cohen. *Power, Inc*. New York: Viking, 1976.

Morgan, R. E. *The Politics of Religious Conflict*. New York: Pegasus, 1968.

Mosca, G. *The Ruling Class*. Translated by H. D. Kahn. New York: McGraw-Hill, 1939.

Nagel, J. H. *The Descriptive Analysis of Power*. New Haven: Yale University, 1975.

Newman, W. H. and E. K. Warren. *The Process of Management*. Englewood Cliffs: Prentice-Hall, 1977.

Nicolaevsky, G. I. *Power and the Soviet Elite*. Edited by J. Zagoria. New York: Praeger, 1965.

Nierenberg, G. I. *Fundamentals of Negotiation*. New York: Hawthorn, 1973.

Nigg, W. *Warriors of God*. Translated by M. Ilford. New York: Knopf, 1959.

Olson, M. E., Ed. *Power in Societies*. New York: Macmillan, 1970.

Reeves, J. *The Rothschilds*. New York: Gordon, 1975.

Rockwell, Jr., W. P. *The Twelve Hats of a Company President*. Englewood Cliffs: Prentice-Hall, 1971.

Russell, B. *Power*. New York: Norton, 1938.

Sampson, A. *The Sovereign State of ITT*. New York: Stein and Day, 1973.

Sanford, M., D. Comstock, and Associates. *Sanctions for Evil*. San Francisco: Jossey-Bass, 1971.

Schelling, T. C. *Strategy of Conflict*. Cambridge: Harvard University, 1964.

Selekman, S. K. and B. M. Selekman. *Power and Morality in a Business Society*. New York: McGraw-Hill, 1956.

Sereno, R. *The Rulers*. New York: Praeger, 1962.

Sharp, G. *The Politics of Nonviolent Action*. Boston: Sargent, 1973.

Siu, R. G. H. *The Man of Many Qualities*. Cambridge: MIT, 1968.

Stogdill, R. M. *Handbook of Leadership*. New York: Free, 1974.

Summer, C. E., J. J. O'Connell, B. Yavitz, N. S. Peery, Jr., and C. S. Summer. *The Managerial Mind*. Homewood: Irwin, 1973. Third Edition.

Swanberg, W. A. *Norman Thomas*. New York: Scribner's, 1976.

Swingle, P., Ed. *The Structure of Conflict*. New York: Academic, 1970.

Vance, C. C. *Boss Psychology*. New York: McGraw-Hill, 1975.

Weidenbaum, M. L. *Business, Government, and the Public*. Englewood Cliffs: Prentice-Hall, 1977.

Westin, A. F. *The Uses of Power*. New York: Harcourt, Brace & World, 1962.

Wilson, B. R. *The Noble Savages*. Berkeley: University of California, 1975.

Zaleznik, A. and M. F. R. Kets de Vries. *Power and the Corporate Mind*. Boston: Houghton Mifflin, 1975.

Zaltman, G., P. Kotler, and I. Kaufman, Eds. *Creating Social Change*. New York: Holt, Rinehart and Winston, 1972.

Ziegler, E. *The Vested Interests*. New York: Macmillan, 1964.

INDEX

217